John C. Rainbolt received his Ph.D. in history from the University of Wisconsin. He was Associate Professor of History at the University of Missouri until his untimely death in October 1973.

From Prescription To Persuasion

Kennikat Press
National University Publications
Series in American Studies

General Editor
James P. Shenton
Professor of History, Columbia University

John C. Rainbolt

From Prescription To Persuasion

*Manipulation of Eighteenth Century
Virginia Economy*

National University Publications
KENNIKAT PRESS • 1974
Port Washington, N.Y. • London

Virginia Historical Society has granted permission to use material from "A New Look at Stuart 'Tyranny' " *Virginia Magazine of History and Biography,* LXXV (1967).

The *Journal of Southern History* has granted permission to use material from "The Absence of Towns in Seventeenth-Century Virginia," JSH, XXXV (August 1969) Copyright 1969 by Southern Historical Association.

William and Mary Quarterly has granted permission to use material from "The Alteration in the Relationship Between Leadership and Constituents in Virginia," WMQ, XXVI (1970).

Library of Congress Catalog Card No.: 73-83268
ISBN: 0-8046-9057-X
Manufactured in the United States of America

Published by
Kennikat Press, Inc.
Port Washington, N.Y./London

To my mother and father

ACKNOWLEDGMENTS

This study's deficiencies are, of course, the author's. Its merits result from the generous assistance and encouragement I have received from mentors, colleagues, and institutions dedicated to scholarly research. Professor James Morton Smith, presently Director of the State Historical Society of Wisconsin, read portions of the dissertation from which this study emerged. For his criticisms, especially in regard to my discussion of the relationship of economic diversification efforts and Bacon's Rebellion, I am grateful. I explored in a paper delivered at the Southern Historical Association in November 1967 some of the themes incorporated in my analysis of the consequences of Bacon's Rebellion. The critique of that paper by Wesley Frank Craven helped me to refine my thoughts in this area, and to him as well I convey my appreciation. Several of the themes in this study relating to the effort to develop ports appeared in a different version in an article in the *Journal of Southern History,* whose editor, Professor S. W. Higginbotham, provided helpful suggestions. A similar word of appreciation I extend to William M. E. Rachal for his editorial supervision of an article on the crown's policy toward Virginia after Bacon's Rebellion which appeared in the *Virginia Magazine of History and Biography* and which is incorporated in an abbreviated and revised version in this study. I discussed in an article appearing in 1970 in the *William and Mary Quarterly* aspects of the alteration in the relationship between the leaders and their constituents. Thad W. Tate applied his considerable editorial skill to that piece. To him also, therefore, I express my appreciation. Summer fellowships from Colonial Williamsburg, Inc. and from the Research Council of the University of Missouri provided invaluable uninterrupted time for research and writing. Edward M. Riley and his staff at the Research Division at Colonial Williamsburg, Inc. graciously complied with an excessive number of requests. I wish to acknowledge also particular gratitude to the staffs of the Wisconsin Historical Society, the Alderman Library at the University of Virginia, the Manuscript Division of the Library of Congress, and the Manuscript Room at the Virginia State Library.

An illness left me unable to attend fully to the final proofreading and indexing. Several of my colleagues, Professors David P. Thelen, Noble E. Cunningham, Jr., Claudia Kren, Charles E. Timberlake, Michael J. Cassity, Charles G. Nauert, Jr., Robert J. Rowland, Jr. and William M. Wiecek, most generously contributed valuable hours of their own research and writing time to help me with these details that I could not accomplish alone. Their assistance is deeply appreciated while they are of course absolved from any responsibilities for the author's errors.

For Professor David S. Lovejoy I have a sense of gratitude which no amount of formal recognition can convey. He provided essential direction in the research and writing of the original dissertation. The origin of my interest in colonial history in general and Virginia in particular lies in the seminars he conducted at the University of Wisconsin, Madison.

In the midst of preparing for her own academic career, my wife, Martha, has overseen and encouraged this study at every stage. Though usually more kindly phrased than the reaction of other critics, her evaluations of the successive drafts have always been rigorous and insightful.

J. C. R.

University of Missouri—Columbia

CONTENTS

From Prescription To Persuasion

INTRODUCTION

The prospect of building new societies in an untouched wilderness was heady wine to Englishmen in the seventeenth century. Assuming that America in contrast with the settled and complex old world would prove malleable to men's intentions, most of the founders of British colonies developed grandiose plans for the construction of ideal societies. The visions varied considerably. Puritan leaders were intoxicated with the hope of erecting godly communities which would serve as a transforming example to England. Some Englishmen planned a restoration in the new world of a dying feudal order. Still others conceived of erecting colonies which would fit an ideal pattern of economic mercantilism.

The provincial leaders in seventeenth-century America met with quite varied results in their efforts to secure from the members of their societies behavior consistent with the ideal patterns. In New England the initial social and economic realities and perhaps even the attitudes and values of the majority of the people accorded roughly with the ideals of articulate Puritan rulers like John Winthrop. Declension set in but remarkably late and slowly. Elsewhere in seventeenth-century America declension is an inadequate concept for interpreting the history of particular colonies for the simple

3

reason that there was never any early success to deteriorate. Notwithstanding extensive advance planning by William Penn for the establishment of a particular social and political structure, disorder marked the early years of Pennsylvania. In their evolution the southern proprietary colonies bore virtually no resemblance to the elaborate, semifeudal societies envisioned by the initial proprietors.

The difficulties involved in preserving or obtaining the ideal colonial communities in the end proved insuperable. Yet most of the initial hopes were remarkably long-lived. Only slowly did the new world realities alter the initial expectations. Leaders succeeding the founders often doggedly adhered to the initial notions of what colonial society ought to be like. If the actual schemes for colonial society broke down or were never established, the conviction that such plans were feasible persisted. From this point of view the colonial experience is essentially an illustration of the imperviousness of basic mental constructs to new realities.

One result of the enduring commitment to early ideas of the ideal colonial societies was that generations of leaders drifted toward new methods of governing. Rather than abandon the original plans, rulers first turned to new techniques for securing the people's obedience to those designs. Initially the expectation of leadership was that in the new world the traditional relationship between rulers and ruled would continue. Ordinary settlers would deferentially pattern their lives to conform with the values and goals of men whom God had ordained to lead. The mode of governance exercised was "prescriptive," not in the extreme sense that governors, councillors, representatives, and others in ruling positions frequently resorted to naked force to compel obedience, but in the sense that men in power believed that the art of government consisted of ordering rather than influencing a passive people. The new method of leadership which emerged when the first failed stressed persuasion. The first technique sought obedience based on deference, the second, without necessarily abandoning the expectation of deference, sought in addition the consent and understanding of the citizens.

The transition in leadership styles was nowhere abrupt or complete during the colonial period. To summarize the essence of the direction of change necessarily entails over-simplification. Seeds of the more persuasive style of leadership appeared from the outset of each colony's development, and later generations of leaders retained elements of the earlier prescriptive mode. The precise expressions of both leadership styles were not identical in all provinces, and the pace of alteration varied from colony to colony as well. At times the process of change was arrested or even reversed. And, of course, evolution of leadership methods, even where most advanced, during the first century of the colonial experience differed markedly from the popular politics of the revolutionary period and the nineteenth century. Yet notwithstanding all of these qualifications the metamorphosis of leadership styles in the early colonial period was significant.

Having turned to government by persuasion, leadership, however, frequently found that the line between a constituency which concurred with plans offered by elites and a populace which expected to shape or even dictate the policies it supported was difficult to protect. In the end the techniques of persuasion were no more successful than the more authoritarian style of leadership in achieving conformity to the initial goals for colonial societies. Indeed the innovation in methods of leadership often proved counterproductive as the newly consulted constituencies at times threw their weight against continued pursuit of the traditional goals.

Adherence to traditional plans while attempting to stimulate movement toward these ends by new methods which proved ultimately self-defeating was a pattern common to leadership in the new world. Especially did this sequence unfold in Virginia from the Interregnum to the early eighteenth century. During these six decades provincial leadership fairly consistently sought to remold the colony along the general lines of the original expectations for England's first plantation. The Virginia rulers did not articulate their ideal conceptions for the province in one convenient document comparable to William Penn's Frame of Government of 1682 or the Carolina proprietors' Fundamental Constitutions, but the pattern of that leadership's public policies and the recurring themes in their scattered tracts and petitions reveal nonetheless that the Virginia elite like other provincial rulers were caught up in a compelling vision of an ideal colonial order. In essence the goal of the Virginia leadership was a colony of compact settlement and a highly varied and expanding economy supporting a social and political structure which, though offering degrees of affluence for all, would be hierarchical, deferential, and orderly. The chief element of this conception of Virginia's proper development was economic diversification of the predominately tobacco economy, and this expectation, in turn, rested on the belief that the land of the province was capable of virtually unlimited development.

Diversification appeared essential not only for economic health and to meet the standards set for the colonies by mercantile theory but also as a prerequisite for the growth of a society carefully stratified into numerous ranks. A colony where most men pursued the same occupation of tobacco planter seemed ill suited to the emergence of a hierarchical social system. A province where most men lived in relative isolation on scattered plantations prevented that constant scrutiny of inferiors by their superiors deemed vital to the order of a society. American history affords not a few examples of a basically conservative leadership seeking to erect a more stable social and political order by advocating very radical alterations in the economic structure. The Virginia rulers of this period offer an early instance of this phenomenon, for to them drastic change in the economic organization of the colony seemed the path to eventual social and political tranquility.

Social and political order through economic diversification was a persistent objective of the provincial leadership, but in another important respect the rationale behind economic diversification shifted radically by the century's end. Initially in the period covered by this study, the ruling class imagined that diversification would increase the economic interdependence of the province and mother country. The public economic policy pursued before Bacon's Rebellion did not question that plantations should serve the mother country and could prosper only by doing so. Before the turn of the century a significant portion of the provincial ruling class came to see in diversification a means of increasing Virginia's economic self-sufficiency. Diversification shifted from a symbol of provincial leadership's acceptance of a subordinate status for the colony to an expression of leadership's growing identity with the distinct interests of Virginia.

Yet whether imagined as a program consistent with or in opposition to colonial mercantilism, diversification and the stability it would hopefully bring remained the constant goal of leadership. The desire of this new elite to transform the colony's economic and social condition between 1650 and the early eighteenth century was a critical factor in most major political decisions and disputes. In no instance was this factor a single cause of public policy, but on few important issues was it altogether lacking as a consideration. The intensity of interest in economic and social transformation rose and fell, often but not invariably in response to trends in the tobacco market, yet the remarkable trait of the expectation was its essential continuity and resiliency.

In the struggle to alter the economic and social structure of Virginia to accord with initial expectations, the provincial leadership gradually came to experiment with new techniques of shaping political and economic behavior. The failure between 1650 and 1676 to secure proper social and economic action from the planters by means of edicts and sanctions was followed not by the abandonment of the goal as unrealistic or by skepticism regarding the efficacy of government intervention into the economy, but by the emergence of persuasive techniques to achieve the same ends. The mode of leadership's intervention in the provincial economy shifted from prescription to appeal.

I

The Persistent Context Of Leadership

The changes in the identities and leadership techniques of Virginia's provincial rulers seeking economic diversification of the colony described in Parts II and III of this study occurred within the context of two persistent conditions. Throughout the later seventeenth and early eighteenth centuries Virginia lacked conditions conducive to the growth of a thoroughly deferential attitude in the mass of common planters. Also during this period the major provincial leaders' expectations of the members of society remained high, defined by an ideal conception of the proper economic and social structure for the colony. The conditions were incongruent. The goals of provincial leadership were ambitious and involved large demands upon the ruled, but the rulers' ability to secure behavior consistent with their aims was severely limited by the absence of obedient habits among the common planters.

1

WEAKENED RULERS AND EXPANSIVE GOALS

Three fairly distinct groups of provincial leaders struggled to rule Virginia between the Interregnum and the early eighteenth century. The first were the most successful of the moderately substantial immigrants arriving in Virginia around mid-century. These new men were members of established English merchant families. Many of the new arrivals who quickly obtained top political status had also supported or sympathized with the cause of Charles I and retained Royalist sentiments. Some actually served the king during the Civil War—Francis Moryson is an example—while others like Henry Corbin and Edward Digges came from families attached to the crown's interest. Frequently the new arrivals married into prominent colonial families of some wealth and constructed a complicated web of marriage ties among themselves. Their wealth and connections enabled a portion of this group to attain political power rapidly. Particularly after the Restoration the most successful formed a close-knit ruling class centered around Sir William Berkeley, who himself personified the career pattern of the new immigrant ruling class.[1]

Following Bacon's Rebellion several of the major figures under Berkeley's regime continued in positions of provincial authority, but the younger lieutenants who under Sir William held more subordinate and obscure roles in provincial affairs, and who lacked the sentimental Royalist attachments, emerged as the dynamic leaders in both the council and assembly. Most conspicuous in this second wave of provincial leaders were Robert Beverley, Philip Ludwell, Nicholas Spencer, and William Byrd I. Forced to react to the home government's effort after 1676 to reduce the autonomy of Virginia, this generation of leadership proved less cohesive. Then immediately before or after the Glorious Revolution the sharers and heirs of Berkeley's power bequeathed top status in provincial politics to their sons or close kin who formed the first generation of native-born leaders.

From the vantage point of royal officials at the beginning of the eighteenth century the influence of these provincial leaders appeared excessive. The more aggressive members of the fledgling colonial bureaucracy perceived the emergence of a powerful Virginia aristocracy unchecked by either the crown or the people. In 1696 as Surveyor General of the Customs in America Edward Randolph urged drastic alterations in the land grant procedures to halt the growth of a landed elite. Six years later in a report promoting a more uniform and centralized colonial system, Robert Quary serving in the same office described Virginia's leadership as a class which had consciously parlayed economic power into an unchecked sway over the mass of common planters.[2] In fact, however, these three generations of provincial political rulers in Virginia dealt from a position of considerable weakness in their relationship with the ordinary planters whose behavior they sought to control. The basic social and economic conditions in the colony conspired against the effective control of the citizenry by the provincial leadership.

A central impediment to effective rule was that the provincial leadership confronted a society of individuals whose personal expectations of life in the new world were largely unfilled. The tracts which sought to spur colonial immigration reported that in Virginia "some from being woolhoppers and of as mean and meaner imployment in England have grown great merchants, and attained to the most eminent advancements the Country afforded." Moreover, the need to recruit labor for the colony caused writers of promotional literature to hedge at times in their promises to prospective immigrants on the seventeenth-century dogma that persistent labor was a prerequisite for wealth. To be sure the tracts warned would-be colonists against indolence. Industry was the path to wealth. Yet at the same time, and contradictorily, these writers hinted that the amount of diligence required for advancement in the colonies was less than in the mother country. Writers alleged that "little or nothing is done in the winter time . . . ," and that the indentured servant was not "required to labor before sun rising nor after sun set. . . ." In the summer the colonists allegedly could "rest, sleep or exercise themselves five hours in the heat of the day" without impairing their chances for gaining wealth.[3]

In England the effort was underway to develop a disciplined labor force with regular and evenly paced work habits. The urban and agrarian working classes which made up the great bulk of ordinary settlers to Virginia in the seventeenth century were encountering greater pressure to abandon the habit of intense but sporadic periods of labor interspersed with periods of total rest and play and adopt the regular work habits needed for efficient production in the emerging market economy. The suggestions in the promotional literature for Virginia that in the colony the accumulation of wealth was not at all incompatible with a pattern of energetic work interrupted by times of total leisure may well have been, therefore, an effective appeal to both the common Englishman's nostalgia for an older, more natural, work style and his acquisitiveness.[4]

The actual personal expectations carried to Virginia and retained by the common people of course cannot be certainly known. Undoubtedly the aspirations varied considerably among individuals. Yet it is not an unreasonable conclusion that the hopes of most reflected the themes of the promotional literature: a dream of significant economic advancement without tedious, unremitting labor.

Neither half of the expectations materialized in Virginia for the bulk of the settlers. The hope of escaping from a strict work routine was not congruent with the requirements of the tobacco culture which occupied all planters. The preparation, planting, care, curing, and packing of the plant involved painstaking and tedious labor over nearly the entire year. Initial work on a crop began in December with the preparation of special seed beds and the seed itself. The actual sowing in the seed beds normally occurred in mid-January. The seedlings subsequently required careful protection against the elements. Constant tending was required as well to guard against insects and disease which could strike the seedlings. The work of readying the fields for transplantation of the seedlings was also laborious. Following transplantation each plant required individual care. Laboriously the planters had to pick the horn worm from each plant and weed the fields constantly. After the tobacco plant produced a certain number of leaves the planter had to break the top from each. Having topped each plant individually, he thereafter took pains to remove all new leaves which sprouted. After cutting the plants the planter carried the tobacco to tobacco houses and there arranged the plants on sticks by a tedious process of inserting a small peg through the stem of each plant. The tobacco was then hung up to cure. The process of curing complete, the planters removed the tobacco from the stalk and stripped the stems from the leaf. Finally the planter packed his tobacco into casks. Tobacco production consumed the greater part of the year and was "never out of hand till in the hogshead."[5]

The exacting labor required in tobacco cultivation, however, did not necessarily lead to the achievement of the other half of the personal expectations of the settlers—rapid individual economic advance. The cost of establishing a viable plantation was great and the rate of return on the investment slow. In the Albemarle region between 1665 and 1672 Peter

Carteret, fourth cousin of the Carolina proprietor, Sir George Carteret, oversaw the establishment of the plantations of the proprietors. Over a six-year period he sank £1,117 into the Albemarle holdings, receiving in that period of time only £241, most of which came not from the plantations themselves but from the sale of whale oil somehow obtained. Nathaniel Bacon the rebel had much the same experience, for in two years he allegedly expended over £1,800 in setting up a plantation in Henrico County, Virginia, without realizing any return. The successful planter had to absorb the loss of the first year given over to the clearing of the land. Moreover, the abundance of cheap building materials was an advantage more than offset by the costs of labor.[6]

Without large scale production it was difficult to earn enough profit to facilitate economic expansion. Expansion depended upon one's ability to transport servants into the colony. The headright system provided the best and thus the most widely used method of securing both land and labor. The cost of transporting an indentured servant from England— £6—remained fairly constant during the seventeenth century.[7] This standard transportation expense, however, represented only one small part of the total cost of procuring a servant. Numerous fringe costs added to the expense. The cost of housing and feeding the servant in England while he waited for a ship to depart increased the expense by £3 for each six weeks delay in sailing. Moreover, clothing, shoes, and blankets for the servant added an additional £3 8s. Tools for the servant cost nearly £2, and ship captains frequently charged up to £5 for transporting the belongings of the servant in addition to the basic £6 for the servant himself. These figures, all drawn from the promotional literature, which was probably conservative, indicate that the total expense involved in securing a servant was nearly £20. At no time in the later seventeenth century could the small planter afford to obtain many servants at this price. For most of the second half of the century, the price of tobacco fluctuated below 2d per pound, dropping on occasion to as low as a halfpenny. At 1½ d per pound a planter producing 1,200 pounds of tobacco a year would have grossed only £7 10s.[8] With the labor of a son and one servant, perhaps £23 or £24 would have been realized, scarcely enough to secure numerous indentured servants after other expenses had been paid. These figures, moreover, do not take into account certain conditions which tended to increase the profits of the large owner and reduce those of the smaller planter attempting to rise. The former acted as middleman collecting the tobacco of the latter for sale to the English merchants who preferred to secure their cargoes in bulk and at a few locations. As middlemen the larger planters also controlled much of the indentured servant market.[9] The result was that the small planter received less for his tobacco and paid more for his servants.

Given these impediments to the successful establishment of a plantation, it is not surprising that the majority of ex-servants or immigrants of small means did not experience the great improvement in economic status promised in the promotional literature. Ex-servants were not usually entitled to grants of land as part of their freedom dues at the end of the period of servitude. At the most the servant received clothing, provisions, and some tools. Denied land for their adventure to Virginia, ex-servants subsequently experienced considerable difficulty in securing even a small plantation. Although in the initial years of tobacco cultivation, when prices paid the planter were high, ex-indentured servants often secured land, in the latter part of the seventeenth century probably less than six per cent became landholders.[10]

Rather than securing "a competent estate" some fell into a class of poor unable to support themselves after they had acquired their freedom, while perhaps the largest number of ex-servants who could not secure land became tenants. The larger planters in Virginia commonly sought tenants to work new plantations, for the renters were expected to construct a home and other buildings, which the landowners then secured at the end of the tenancy. The general conditions and social status of tenancy apparently was not high, for many landless

men fled to submarginal land and became squatters in preference to becoming tenants.[11]

Ex-servants who did secure small amounts of land and
planters of modest means who began their careers with moderate initial land patents did not subsequently enjoy sustained
advance. In Gloucester County in the last half of the seventeenth century fewer than one-fifth of the individuals whose
first land patents were for less than 200 acres later managed
to obtain additional land patents in that county. Only about
one-quarter of the persons who initially patented between
200 and 399 acres secured additional holdings in the county.
In contrast, over 45% of the planters whose first acquisition
exceeded 800 acres went on to secure additional land patents
in Gloucester.[12]

The absence of substantial economic improvement for
the bulk of Virginia planters led to a concentration of wealth
in the hands of the small proportion of planters who did experience advance. This is revealed in the rent rolls of the
planters' landholdings prepared to facilitate quitrent collections in 1704-1705. In only four of the twenty counties included in the rent roll did more than three-fourths of the adult
free males possess land, and in Isle of Wight, Charles City,
Gloucester, York, and Warwick counties over half of the
adult free males were landless. The pattern of the distribution
of the land among those who possessed some real estate differed from county to county and even among parishes within
the same county, yet the variations were all on the same
theme: concentration of wealth in a small proportion of the
population. In Nansemond County the share of the total
landed wealth controlled by the largest 10% of the landholders
was small compared to other counties, yet even here the
wealthiest 10% possessed nearly one-third of the land. In
King and Queen County the wealthiest 10% owned approximately 53% of the land. In every county recorded in the
rent roll the top quarter of the landholders possessed at least
half of all of the land. In five of twenty counties recorded in

the rent rolls—James City, Henrico, Charles City, Middlesex, King and Queen—the top quarter of landholders controlled in excess of 70% of all acreage.[13]

Complex economic conditions produced the sustained depression in the tobacco economy and consequently the lack of economic opportunity for most Virginia planters. The impact of the Navigation Acts, the Dutch wars and later King William and Queen Anne's wars, overproduction resulting from population growth, an increase in per capita production of tobacco, and the rise of other tobacco-producing colonies were the critical causes which drove the price of tobacco down. Historians today still struggle to comprehend the relative weight of the causes of the sustained tobacco depression. To the common planters at the time the economic situation which thwarted the realization of their personal economic expectations must have been largely incomprehensible. The ills of the tobacco economy were not only complex but unique as well from the standpoint of Englishmen in Virginia. Their English experience accustomed them to think of economic difficulties in terms of inadequate production and scarcity. Now in Virginia the baffling combination of abundant production and economic hardship appeared.

When individuals are barred from their goal by a barrier which is ill defined, complex, and multifaceted, and thus not a clear target for frustration, they may focus their animosity on one element of the complex impediment. The stymied individual expectations of the common planters thus created a condition conducive to the emergence of hostility toward the provincial leaders. The barren personal economic experience of the ordinary settlers was not, then, a soil suitable for the growth of a generalized deferential attitude upon which provincial leadership might depend for obedience to its specific commands.

Perhaps strong institutions designed to inculcate proper social and political values could have nurtured deferential attitudes even under these adverse conditions. In Virginia, however, a key institution whose role it was in the seventeenth century to promote respectful habits toward authority was especially underdeveloped and constructed, moreover, in a manner which actually eroded rather than supported the growth of deferential attitudes.

Despite repeated attempts to create a viable church structure in the first half of the seventeenth century, the Anglican Church was an established church in theory only. The weak social significance of the church was not fundamentally a consequence of especially low caliber in the ministers of Virginia. The ministers were basically similar in social and economic background and training to the priests in the rural parishes of England.[14] Essentially the church could not play its traditional role of fostering obedient habits because throughout the last half of the seventeenth century its expansion lagged behind population growth and spreading settlement. In 1680 thirty-five Anglican clergymen were in Virginia. By 1702 thirty-nine held appointments and the number increased to only forty-three in 1714. During the same period of time the population, however, expanded from approximately 43,000 to nearly 80,000. Moreover parishes were frequently vacant. At one point in the last decade of the century fewer than half of the parishes had active ministers.[15]

The paucity of the clergy was not the only cause of the weakness. In addition, the church had little continuity in its leadership at the parish level, for the rate of turnover in ministers was exceedingly rapid. Five ministers served Hampton Parish in Elizabeth City County between the Restoration and the Glorious Revolution. Christ Church in Lancaster averaged nearly two ministers per decade in the last half of the seventeenth century. Until the eighteenth century tenure exceeding ten years in one parish was quite exceptional. The conditions in St. Peter's parish in New Kent County while perhaps not typical nonetheless illustrate the extreme discontinuity which could exist. Between 1682 and 1710 the parish had thirteen ministers.[16]

The system of selecting ministers for parishes allowed this discontinuity in clerical leadership. In the mother country the right to nominate ministers to the bishop for appointment to a parish was a traditional right held by a dominant landowner, lord, or institution such as a college of the great universities. Induction of the nominee was for a life tenure. By law in Virginia, vestries, which after 1662 were self-perpetuating bodies dominated by leading local planters, nominated ministers for permanent induction by the provincial governor. In practice clergy were "to their several vestries in the nature of hired servants, agreed with from year to year, and dismissed if they pleased at the expiration of such agreement. . . ." The vestries simply neglected to submit names to the governor, contracted with ministers for limited terms of service, and retained the right to look for a new divine when the incumbent's term expired.[17]

The larger planters who controlled the vestries were supporters of autonomy in ecclesiastical affairs. They doubtless imagined that the strength and unity of authority was promoted if local social and economic leadership determined the local religious leadership. The vestrymen apparently did not perceive that in the long run the system weakened the foundation of all political authority by discouraging the growth of a cohesive, permanent, and influential body of Anglican clergy who could have been counted on by virtue of the tradition and theology of their church to advocate obedience to rulers.

At the century's end recognition of the impaired capacity of the church to inculcate deferential attitudes came most clearly to the Reverend James Blair owing to the fact that he stood to gain most from a centralization of ecclesiastical authority. Appointed in 1689 commissary—or the Bishop of London's representative in the colony of Virginia—and soon after a councillor, Blair led an effort to improve ministers' salaries and stabilize their tenure in office, and his labor did result in an act fixing the minimum annual salary for parish clergy. Yet his goal of focusing ecclesiastic power in his own hands, the rancor he quickly displayed toward governors Nicholson and Andros when he judged their concern for the church insufficient or their attack on the political position of Virginia councillors excessive, and the dislike of him inspired by his Scottish nationality in many of the clergy combined to factionalize the church leadership. When after 1702 councillors Blair, Philip Ludwell, John Lightfoot, Matthew Page, and Benjamin Harrison, all closely connected by marriage, mounted a campaign to secure the removal of Nicholson, the majority of the ministers backed the governor with petitions attesting to his concern for the church and scoring the commissary's arbitrary designs. The exchange of accusations by both sides degenerated into abusive reflections on the integrity and morals of Blair, Nicholson, and their respective political and church allies.[18] The reputation of neither side among the mass of Virginia planters could have been enhanced by the exaggerated indictments. Ironically, Blair's efforts to reform the church thus only reduced still more the contribution the clergy could make toward the building of a deferential society.

Nor did the dissenting churches in Virginia in the second half of the seventeenth century fill the gap in the socialization process created by a weak and divided Anglican Church. With the exception of the Interregnum period, dissenting clergy faced the same disabilities and persecutions as their counterparts in the mother country. Only following the English Act of Toleration in 1689 were dissenting congregations with regular ministers established, but even after the Glorious Revolution the growth was slow. As late as 1705 only five dissenting congregations existed in the colony.[19]

Educational institutions did not expand to fill the vacuum created by the absence of a strong clergy. "Good Education of Children is almost impossible . . . ," complained William Fitzhugh. He referred to the opportunities for the youth of the more affluent. Even less developed were formal education customs for the children of ordinary planters. In England the parish reader or clerk customarily offered instruction in reading and writing as part of his official duty. In Virginia these lay officers did not assume this responsibility, although some readers were chosen because they happened to be private teachers. Ministers at times served as parish teachers but that practice too was not universal, especially in the seventeenth century. As late as 1724 probably no more than six endowed grammar schools offering free education existed in Virginia. Provincial statutes modeled after English law enjoined masters to teach apprentices to read and write. Similar legislation adopted from England required county and vestry officials to take responsibility for the education of children whose parents were too poor to assume that task. The implementation of these statutes was less than rigorous. Private tutoring existed but its quantity and availability to the mass of planters is a moot point. The lament made in 1722 in York County that "We have not had a schoolmaster in our neighborhood until now in five years" undoubtedly applies with even greater force to earlier Virginia.[20]

The very origins and traits of provincial leadership, as well as the character of the citizenry and the absence of well developed religious and educational institutions, also weakened the elite's ability to command obedience to its demands. Although the gentry who dominated at the provincial level had not risen from low status, the expansion of their initial wealth was rapid and placed them in a new-rich category. Social status and political legitimacy did not adhere well to the recently acquired wealth. The common planters, Governor Francis Nicholson observed at the start of the eighteenth century, could easily recall the origins of the great planters. "The ordinary sort of planters that have land of their own, though not much, look upon themselves to be as good as the best of them, for he knows, at least has heard, from whence these mighty Dons derive their originals . . . and that he or his ancestors were their equals if not superiors."[21]

The provincial leadership, as historians have long stressed, was not a leisured class. Yet the significant characteristic of the elite's work routine which affected its political role was that the great planters' daily habits involved more than a supervisory function. Sharp differentiation of economic roles between the largest planters and their servants and employees did not exist. William Byrd II's diary, the most detailed account of the daily affairs of a member of the provincial elite of this period, reveals that he habitually worked alongside his employees. This sharing by superior and inferior of mundane daily tasks was an impediment to establishing the social distance necessary to evoke a sense of thorough deference. The great planter class which furnished the provincial elite could not hope to induce an attitude of awe because for all the difference in economic status the life style of the upper and all but the lowest ranks overlapped at too many points.[22]

For a variety of reasons then, the position of provincial leadership was fundamentally weak. Rulers like Berkeley and the Beverleys did not have the advantage of attempting to command a citizenry inclined to obedience. Frustrated in their personal economic hopes by a bewildering set of economic circumstances and infrequently subjected to the teaching of church and school, the common planters were not ideal tools with which to construct leadership's version of a British colony. Lacking the prestige of long establishment and the mystique of a leisured ruling class, provincial leadership confronted a society composed of planters who had not internalized attitudes of respect and awe of authority.

Lacking legitimacy in the eyes of the settlers, weakly buttressed by supporting social institutions, and confronted with a citizenry frustrated by unfulfilled hopes, the emerging provincial elite of Virginia in the six decades following 1650 nonetheless struggled to implement a rigid and preconceived notion of the ideal colony. The provincial leadership did not pare its objectives to its circumscribed abilities to govern. Relative weakness was the salient trait of the provincial leadership but expansiveness marked the leadership's goals. The provincial leadership's grandiose aim was a socially and po-

litically stable, yet economically dynamic colony, a province
with a varied economy and expanding productivity which
nonetheless supported a hierarchical and deferential social
structure. The keynote of this vision was a thorough economic
diversification of the tobacco economy.

The historian's perspective reveals that in fact remarkable expansion and growth occurred in Virginia in the decades
following the annulment of the Virginia Company's charter.
On the eve of the Indian massacre in 1623, settlement was
confined to the James River with the exception of a few
small areas on the tip of the Eastern shore. At the end of
the century the planters had settled the entire Tidewater area
and were pushing rapidly into the Piedmont. Similarly the
trade of the colony constantly expanded. The colonists increased their annual production of tobacco from fifty thousand
pounds in 1620 to around thirty million by the century's end.
In the second decade of the eighteenth century the tonnage
of British ships engaged in trade to Virginia far exceeded
that of other mainland colonies. Indeed, Virginia tonnage
comprised about 45% of the total for the mainland and over
one-fifth of the total for all British possessions in the new
world.[23]

At the time, however, most articulate Englishmen in
Virginia rendered a negative judgment on the progress of the
Chesapeake province. They ignored or even deplored achievements. The central motif of thought on Virginia at mid-century was the unfortunate discrepancy between the potential
and actual accomplishments of the settlers. While late seventeenth-century New England Puritans in jeremiads decried
the declination from their fathers' successful creation of a
godly society, Virginia leaders verbally flagellated themselves, their society, and their predecessors for failing to
implement the more temporal vision of the founders. If the
Virginia writing was more concerned with silk than with
souls, its fundamental purpose, like the Puritan sermons, was
nonetheless exhortatory, its basic mood self-reproach, and

its central theme condemnation for the failure of the people to measure up to the initial dreams.

The counterpoising of reality and potential in Virginia appeared faintly even in the earliest reports on the province. By the Restoration the theme was central in the general description of Virginia, and at the century's end the emphasis on Virginia's underdevelopment continued unabated. In their lengthy report to the Board of Trade at the close of the century, Henry Hartwell, James Blair, and Edward Chilton penned perhaps the most direct and succinct statement of the theme which pervaded all the writing on Virginia as they established their main thesis in the opening paragraph:

For the most general true Character of *Virginia* is this, That as to all the Natural Advantages of a Country, it is one of the best, but as to the Improved Ones, one of the worst of all the *English* Plantations in *America*. When one considers the Wholsomeness of its Air, the Fertility of its Soil, the Commodiousness of its navigable Rivers and Creeks, the Openness of its Coast all the Year long, the Conveniency of its Fresh Water Runs and Springs, the Plenty of its Fish, Fowl, and wild Beasts, the Variety of its Simples and Dying Wools, the Abundance of its Timbers, Minerals, wild Vines and Fruits, the Temperature of its Climate, being scituated betwixt the Extremities of both Heat and Cold; in short, if it be look'd upon in all Respects as if it came out of the Hand of God, it is certainly one of the best Countries in the World. But on the other Hand, if we enquire for well built Towns, for convenient Ports and Markets, for Plenty of Ships and Seamen, for well improv'd Trades and Manufactures, for well educated Children, for an industrious and thriving People, or for an happy Government in Church and State, and in short, for all the other Advantages of human improvements, it is certainly for all these Things, one of the poorest, miserablest, and worst Countries in all *America,* that is inhabited by Christians.[24]

Despite the development of the province, then, Virginia's provincial leadership after 1650 considered that the settlers had failed to labor properly. A century of actual colonial experience scarcely altered the ideas regarding the desirable improvement of the province. In 1588 Thomas Harriot listed the products which a plantation might reasonably be expected to produce: silk, flax, hemp, pitch, tar, turpentine, wine, iron, and a variety of other staples. The second half of the seventeenth century witnessed little change in the vision of what Virginia ought to produce. Sir William Berkeley expected a colony with a diversified economy, in which artisans and skilled workers mined iron and lead, felled trees for masts and ships' timber, cultivated silk, hemp, flax, wheat, cotton, and fruits, and produced pitch, tar, and potash. At the end of the seventeenth century Robert Beverley continued to list the traditional products expected of Virginia.[25]

A corollary to the goal of extensive economic diversification was the design to redirect the settlement in Virginia from a dispersed agrarian to an urban pattern. Indeed, the forcing of town growth by government action emerged in the last half of the seventeenth century as the single most important means advocated for achieving the economic and social transformation of Virginia. The earliest authors who wrote to promote colonial expansion of England in the late Elizabethan age assumed that the planters would erect plantations centered around towns, and the failure of towns to develop in early Virginia became a matter of concern to the initial leaders of the colony both in England and America. Edwin Sandys continually urged the settlers to draw themselves into "compact and orderly villages" and buttressed his argument with the claim that all plantations in ancient times as well as the contemporary Spanish settlements succeeded only if the provincial economies revolved around towns. George Sandys lamented after the Indian massacre that the planters' dispersed settlement fostered all the ills of the colony: loose government, inadequate defense, and the absence of staple commodities.[26] These assumptions of the colony's founders became more explicit and elaborately developed in the second half of the century as the promotion of towns became the key aspect of most economic fantasies.[27]

The persistent depression in the price of the colony's staple was, of course, a major force preserving the hope for diversification and town growth. Although the state of the tobacco market varied, at no time in the period after 1650 were conditions really favorable for the planters. Yet persistent economic difficulty was not the only factor which sustained the desire for fundamental economic reform. The commitment to economic diversification derived support also from notions about nature's characteristics in the new world generally and the Chesapeake area particularly. The initial colonizers had not viewed Virginia as a mere wilderness. Rather it seemed that in the new world nature had ordered itself and awaited only the final touch of the Englishman's genius to become a garden. The impressions of George Percy, who accompanied the first voyage of the Virginia Company to Virginia, illustrate the way the first Englishmen strained to find evidence of nature's progress away from wilderness in the new world. "We past into the thickest of the Woods, where we had almost lost our selves," reported Percy on the expedition's stop at Nevis. "We had not gone above halfe a mile amongst the thicke, but we came into a most pleasant Garden, being a hundred paces square on every side, having many Cotton-trees growing in it with abundance of Cotton-wooll, and many Guiacum trees. Wee saw the goodliest tall trees growing so thicke about the Garden, as though they had beene set by Art, which made us marvell very much to see it." Subsequently in Virginia Percy again employed the analogy of the gardens and orchards of England to describe the appearance of the land.[28]

In John Smith's thought the theme of nature's prior preparation for the English artificial designs was even clearer. He found the main rivers as carefully dispersed across the land as the blood vessels of the human body and the groves of mulberry trees similarly prearranged to facilitate efficient silk production. In Virginia, Smith concluded, "heaven and earth never agreed better to frame a place for mans habitation being of our constitutions, were it fully manured and inhabited by industrious people. . . . The mildnesse of the airs, the fertility of the soile, and the situation of the rivers are so propitious to the nature and use of man as no place is more convenient for pleasure, profit, and mans sustenance."[29]

Percy and Smith cited the seeming orderliness of nature in the new world not to show that an opportunity existed for escape from labor but to prove that the fruits of work would be exceptionally abundant. Both offered the absence of wildness in Virginia as an incentive to complete by labor what God had already begun—the transformation of nature into civilization.

Through the second half of the seventeenth century this image of nature in Virginia persisted and undergirded the belief that the fertility of nature beckoned the colonists "to exercise their industry upon everything Genius leads them to."[30] Indeed, it seemed that the colony's potential seemed not dormant so much as abeyant or suppressed. Virginia leaders imagined the colony's flowering would have occurred earlier but for the early blunders of the Virginia Company and the crown. The predisposition of the wilderness to proper development by man before the arrival of the English had been reversed. In *Discourse and View of Virginia,* Berkeley censured the encouragement given tobacco production and scored as well the home government's restrictions on the trade of the colony. Berkeley declared that the proclamations of the early Stuarts confining the tobacco trade to England, and the Navigation Acts of the Interregnum and of 1660, placed the welfare of forty English merchants above that of forty thousand colonists and plunged the planters into a poverty that prevented the accumulation of capital necessary for diversification projects. Allegedly the inclination of nature toward a diversified garden had been thwarted also by the "dismembring" of Virginia by proprietary grants which divided a unified geographic area into rival political units. Government's errors of omission as well as commission seemed responsible for the failure of nature to evolve according to its normal bias toward order and improvement. Lax efforts to formulate and enforce tobacco production controls, and especially the failure of the Virginia Company to prevent the dispersal of the colony's population on isolated plantations, was evidence of early leadership's oversight in meeting nature at least half way.[31]

If men had stymied nature, it followed, however, to Virginia leaders in the second half of the century that men could encourage her to fulfillment as well. Rivaling their pessimism over what colonists and mother country had failed to do was an optimism over what the government acting vigorously might still accomplish. The basic attitudes of these Virginians included high confidence in the efficacy of government action. Steeped in the theories of mercantilism, they assumed that government ought to engage in social and economic engineering. They did not question that government had the duty and the ability to shape the development of a society's economy. In England long before the end of the seventeenth century, Parliament had abandoned efforts to regulate and stimulate the internal economy of the country. Mercantilistic intervention internally ceased even as the institutions and statutes of colonial mercantilism were being created. In the domestic economy of the mother country laissez-faire was a fact though certainly not an accepted philosophy by 1700.[32] Virginia's leaders, however, held to the dying concept that a government ought to establish the economic goals of society. By emphasizing the ability of government to determine the economic and social structure of a society, Virginia's leadership did not ignore the importance of the economic determinants. Critics of Virginia's alleged underdevelopment recognized the difficulties inherent in shifting from a one-crop to a diversified economy, but invariably concluded that action by the home or provincial government could overcome these natural impediments.[33]

The spur of chronic depression, the images of nature in the new world, and an unquestioning faith in the duty of government to govern the economic behavior of the members of society combined to preserve leadership's commitment to the traditional hope of a diversified and town-oriented economy. To these motives and assumptions was added the assumption that a transformed society would also be more orderly. The expectation was that prosperity would follow the rise of port towns and economic diversification, but of no less importance was leadership's assumption that social and political stability would also accompany this drastic economic innovation. Implicit in the vision leadership had for Virginia was the premise that a heterogeneous economic structure was the foundation for a healthy social and political hierarchical arrangement. An economy in which most pursued the same economic goal seemed a weak basis upon which to erect a deferential society where each man occupied a clearly defined and distinct station. The assumption was that social differentiation required economic diversification. The tumults and revolts which punctuated the colony's history after the Restoration were taken as evidence that a homogeneous economy and social order were incompatible.[34]

Especially did the connection between economic diversification and social stability appear in the hopes which articulate Virginians attached to the growth of towns. Towns not only promised the varied economic base necessary for social and political status differentiations, but additionally concentrated the citizenry and made it easier for government "to restrain vitious & overawe rugged & stubborn disposition." Moreover governments might more easily quash "sudden & dementick insurrections" if the population were not dispersed.[35] Most importantly, it was hoped that compact settlement would permit leadership to exercise the day to day influence leading to a deferential society in which rebellion was not a threat. Hopefully, in a diversified economy centered around towns, "*good Discipline and careful tending under* faithful Teachers and Magistrates" would occur.[36] By the late eighteenth century the lack of large towns received praise. The Jeffersonians celebrated the rural society because it allegedly promoted individual autonomy and a jealousy of excessive power for authority. The articulate Virginia leadership in the seventeenth century, which lacked faith in the common planters' inherent virtue, agreed that towns stymied individualism in all ranks of society and promoted compact settlement for that very reason.

The radical transformation sought in the economy and settlement patterns of the province, thus, aimed ultimately at a conservative end. The provincial leadership sought an economic revolution in Virginia in order to establish a traditional social and political order of hierarchical arrangements and deferential attitudes where superiors perpetually supervised inferiors. The dilemma confronting provincial leadership in the pursuit of this goal is obvious. The demands upon the people entailed in the design of economic diversification and town development were substantial. A reasonable effort by the people to comply with the vision was likely only if a strong inclination of the citizenry to obey already existed, or if authority was already capable of coercing the settlers effectively. Provincial rulers were in a vicious circle. They believed that economic change was an essential ingredient in the making of an orderly society in which the ruled automatically obeyed and where occasional deviance was efficiently controlled, but general support of the ambitious program designed to establish this base was possible only if society was already deferentially inclined and well policed. The provincial rulers sought a goal which would have been less urgently needed if that leadership had possessed the ability to attain it.

The realities of the weakened position of provincial leaders clearly required a severe modification of demands placed on the citizenry. Not until the early eighteenth century, however, did the provincial ruling groups abandon the hope of revamping the economy and social order of Virginia. For nearly two-thirds of a century, beginning with the emergence of the new immigrant ruling groups during the Interregnum, Berkeley and the Virginia leadership clung to the conviction that in spite of the weakened springs of their authority they could achieve the almost utopian goals of a diversified and town-oriented economy and a traditional social order in Virginia.

II

Prescription: 1650-1676

The new provincial leaders who dominated the shaping of public economic policy in the third quarter of the seventeenth century believed that diversification would benefit both the economies of Virginia and the mother country while fostering social and political stability in the colony. Initially after the Restoration the crown shared this view, although not as intensely, and the home and provincial governments moved toward establishing a meaningful partnership effort to transform the tobacco economy. The provincial leadership regarded this support from England as an essential reinforcement to their weakened base of authority.

Although their economic policies aimed at benefits for all Virginians as well as themselves and the mother country, the leaders between 1650 and 1676 also assumed that ordinary planters were incapable of perceiving that their true interests and the welfare of the emerging empire were identical. The provincial government, therefore, believed that its function was to compel the settlers to pursue the proper economic activities. The intent of public policy was benevolent. The means were prescriptive. The consequence was rebellion.

THE QUEST FOR REINFORCEMENT

Only after the Restoration did the new immigrant leadership class clearly dominate Virginia politics at the provincial level, but even in the 1650's their rising influence was apparent. Many secured their initial political position in the decade. Nathaniel Bacon, elder cousin of the later rebel, entered the council in 1657 seven years after he came to Virginia. Henry Chicheley, arriving in 1649, soon emerged to play a key role in the House of Burgesses and later became lieutenant governor. Francis Moryson served as speaker of the House of Burgesses in the 1650's although he did not settle in the colony until 1649. In the last session of the assembly prior to the Restoration over 40% of the burgesses were immigrants who had arrived in the colony during the period of Civil War and Interregnum in England.[1]

The initial rise to power of these new immigrants coincided with an increase in economic intervention by the provincial government. Even though during most of the Interregnum Virginia experienced its first period of neglect by the empire's central government, the tempo of the provincial government's intervention into the economy picked up. Indeed the pace of government action increased even though the spur of a badly depressed tobacco market was absent. The political turmoil in England disrupted trade in the home market and caused a drop in the price of tobacco sold at London and the outports, but direct trade to the continent in Dutch ships in violation of the new Navigation Act supported prices received by the planters at levels slightly above those of the latter years of the previous decade.[2]

Only the details of the acts passed during the initial decade of the rise of the new immigrants were innovations. The assembly endorsed somewhat novel methods to achieve traditional goals. In the 1650's for example, a change in the method of forcing diversification by regulations on the quantity and quality of tobacco production occurred. In earlier years the government sought to reduce the quantity by restricting the number of plants each planter could tend and specifying even the maximum number of leaves on each plant.[3] During the 1650's a new method appeared to supplement the old—the stint. "Stint" was an old feudal term which referred to a pasture on a manor where tenants and sometimes even the lord could graze only a fixed number of cattle. Frequently the use of the pasture was also restricted to a certain season of the year. At the end of the reign of Elizabeth and again in the 1620's and 1630's, cattle became too numerous for the available grazing land in some parts of England and the custom of the stinted pasture which had virtually died out briefly came into vogue again. Virginians adopted the term in legislation during the Interregnum. Normally the planters began to transplant the tobacco seedlings from the hot beds to the fields in late March and April and continued setting out the plants during most of July. The tobacco stint statute aimed at curtailing production by fixing an arbitrary date after which no new plants could be transplanted. In theory a stint would promote diversification both by facilitating capital accumulation through high tobacco prices and by giving planters more time to apply to the growth of other staples.[4]

The Interregnum witnessed also new attempts to foster diversification by the establishment of ports and markets throughout the province. Frequent attempts had been made in the past to center trade at Jamestown. In 1655 the Interregnum assembly passed a more ambitious law designed to create ports throughout the colony. The measure required the justice of the peace of each county to designate a maximum of two locations as the sole points for landing and sale of imports. Only after goods had remained unsold at the entrepôts for eight months did the law permit traders to retail merchandise up and down the rivers and creeks in the usual manner.[5]

These novel methods in legislation, however, did not signify a basic new approach to the manner in which the provincial representative authority exercised its power to stimulate innovation and foster the common good. The new departures were essentially minor variations on an old theme which stressed the necessity of restraints rather than positive encouragements for the common planters. The Virginia Company had largely relied on this method, and the assumptions of mid-century leadership about the proper relationship between authority and the members of society did not differ enough from the founders of Virginia to permit any fundamental shift in the method of leadership. To be sure, the assembly authorized bounty payments to larger planters who greatly surpassed the minimal requirements for the cultivation of silk, wine, and other products. Government did not coerce men of wealth and standing, but gently encouraged them to excel in promoting society's welfare by offering special rewards. For the ordinary colonists, however, the stick rather than the carrot seemed appropriate.[6]

Both the vast cost involved in these economic plans and the weak position of provincial authority required that the colony's leaders seek the home government's support of their effort to prescribe the proper economic behavior for the Virginia planters, and the bid for energetic assistance from the home government began in 1657 with the dispatch to London of Edward Digges as the colony's agent. Digges was a leading representative of the new immigration. He came from a Royalist background. His father, Sir Dudley Digges, was master of the rolls to Charles I. The elder Digges had acquired holdings in Virginia, and in 1650 Edward arrived in the province to develop this property. In 1654 he entered the council and the following year became governor. Digges' plantation produced a superior brand of tobacco known as "E-Dees" tobacco, but he did not limit himself to tobacco production. Following his arrival in Virginia, Digges became the leading exponent of efforts to stimulate silk production. After his replacement as governor by Samuel Mathews, Jr. in 1657 Digges accepted the position as the colony's agent, taking with him a sample of silk for Charles II.[7]

The official purpose of his trip was to persuade the English merchants to increase the price of tobacco. The assembly instructed Digges to inform the traders of the various laws passed in the province to increase the quality and decrease the quantity of tobacco, and to urge them to reciprocate by paying the planter a better price. Once in London Digges did not adopt a belligerent attitude toward the merchants. He discovered that influential spokesmen of the English merchants interested in the plantation trade were pressuring Cromwell's government to establish an effective system for dealing with colonial matters. English merchants, like the Virginia planters, desired to exploit and develop the possibilities of the new world and expected the consent and support of government in their ventures. Martin Noell and particularly Thomas Povey, a close friend of Digges, served as spokesmen and leaders for the merchant group which was instrumental in the formulation of the Navigation Acts and commercial policy of England at mid-century. In 1660 they welcomed the Restoration with its promise of stability. In the middle 1650's Povey, on behalf of the merchants, urged the Protector to establish a separate council to handle colonial affairs, which too often were neglected by the Council of State in favor of more important problems. When constituted, Povey hoped the council would have the power to reduce all the provinces which were now virtually autonomous to a uniform system of government.[8]

Digges recognized that the goals of the merchants and the planters whom he represented were basically similar. Both wanted an end to government drift and confusion in England in order that schemes for colonial development, whether emanating from the mother country or in the province, might proceed. Conscious, too, of the influence over colonial appointments wielded by Povey and the merchants, Digges joined his efforts with theirs. The result was a report to Cromwell from the Council of State's Committee for His Highnesses Affaires in America, which had been created in accordance with Povey's suggestion. Undoubtedly written in large measure by Digges, the report urged Cromwell to reestablish the control of the central government over Virginia, where the assembly in the absence of any firm direction from England had been electing its own governor and council, by appointing Digges governor, and to grant him specific instructions for the regulation of the provincial government and the improvement of the colony's economy.[9] Despite Digges' efforts the recommendation, however, came to nothing, for more pressing matters of state diverted Cromwell's attention from colonial matters until his death. The bid for support from the central government thus failed owing to the confusion in affairs during the waning days of the Interregnum in England.

Another and more ambitious appeal for reinforcement by the home government followed quickly after the Restoration and ended in greater success. Conditions in England in the early 1660's favored the Virginia leaders' bid for support and encouragement more than at any other time during the last half of the seventeenth century. The Restoration promised stability and encouraged a confident spirit conducive to experimentation. The plantations in general and Virginia in particular occupied a conspicuous place in the torrent of ideas and hopes unleashed by the promise of political stability and domestic tranquility. Symbolizing the Restoration spirit was the Royal Society of London, formed in 1660 and officially chartered by the king in 1662. With a membership which included the leading Englishmen of intellect and affairs at mid-century, the Society served as a semiofficial brain trust. Poets, scientists, prominent merchants, courtiers, and even the king himself on occasion met to hear and discuss ways in which Englishmen might improve upon nature.[10] Virginia was one of the first subjects of inquiry by the members of the Royal Society. In March 1660 Thomas Povey on behalf of the organization wrote to an unknown friend—perhaps Edward Digges—in Virginia to convey the king's satisfaction with the gift of silk from the province and his hopes of further progress in the colony. Povey inclosed a list of specific inquiries regarding the potential of Virginia. Some of the questions reflected merely an idle curiosity. Were Indians born white? Were the natives in the northern part of the province "still of such a Gigantish stature as hath been reported?" Were others "of a Dwarfish nature?" Most queries, however, showed the concern of the Royal Society for knowledge that might lead to profitable economic experiments in Virginia.[11]

The interest in developing and improving the plantations was not, of course, limited to academic discussion at Royal Society meetings. Many of the leading society members would soon occupy prominent places too in the important Restoration ventures in trade and colonization, such as the Royal African Company, chartered in 1662, the Carolina proprietary grant in 1663, and the Hudson's Bay Company, which began operations in 1670. In the administration of these enterprises the men of the Restoration period kept a sharp eye out for profit, but at least in the early 1660's, they also attempted to pursue self-interest in a manner which also served the larger interests of the mother country and promoted the welfare of all parts of the empire. The proprietors of South Carolina hoped that settlers in Carolina would produce staples not grown in other plantations but which England secured at a great cost from foreign nations. Particularly did they want to discourage the production of tobacco and sugar, for they feared the "overthrow [of] . . . other plantations which may very well happen, if there be a very great increase of sugar works and more tobacco . . . than the world will vent. . . ." The proprietors thus viewed their holdings in relationship to the emerging British Empire as a whole.[12]

The most important indication of a broad concept of empire which existed immediately after the Restoration came when members of the Royal Society and new-chartered companies functioned in a third role: ministers of state. The colonial mercantile ideas of the government found expression first in the Navigation Acts. The Navigation Acts of 1660 and 1663 reaffirmed and advanced beyond the Navigation Acts of the Interregnum, which in turn drew upon various precedents stretching back as far as the fourteenth century. The act of 1660 forbade foreign ships to trade with the colonies and created a list of enumerated articles, including tobacco and sugar, which could be shipped from the plantations only to England or to another British colony. The Staple Act of 1663 required that most European goods sent to the plantations be channeled first through the ports of England.

The second major step of government in giving substance to its view of empire was the appointment of boards to supervise plantation and commercial business. Less than three months after Charles II landed at Dover, his chancellor, Clarendon, announced the king's intention to establish councils to promote the growth of trade and the plantations staffed by persons who were sensitive to the general interest of the empire rather than the advantage of any particular trade or interest. By the end of the year, two select councils consisting of courtiers and influential merchants existed, the Council of Trade commissioned on November 7, 1660, and the Council for Foreign Plantations on December 1.[13]

The instructions issued to the select councils reveal that the crown's rationale for the creation of this rudimentary system of colonial supervision stressed the welfare and development of the empire as a whole. The Council of Trade's business encompassed all aspects of England's commerce. The plantation trade, however, was to be an important concern of the Council of Trade. The king charged the body to study the colonial situation and make specific recommendations on how the plantations could be strengthened by placing restraints and impositions upon foreign imports of goods grown in the plantations. The Council for Foreign Plantations had special responsibility for colonial commerce. The Council of Trade in formulating policies for the whole trade of the kingdom would draw upon the advice and recommendations of the Council for Foreign Plantations. The first task of this last body was to secure information about the colonies in order "that the true condition of each part of the whole may be thoroughly understood; whereby a more steady judgement and balance may be made for the better ordering and disposing of trade & of the proceede and improvements of the Plantacons; that soe each place within it self, and all of them being collected into one view and management here, may be regulated and ordered upon common and equall ground & principles." The method was centralization but the intent was paternalistic in theory. A "balance" of the various parts of the empire was the key idea of the 1660 instructions to the select councils. In theory, at least, the interests of the mother country and her dependent colonies were similar.[14]

To be sure, the great interest in stimulating and controlling colonial trade rested upon more prosaic motives than a statesmanlike concept of empire. "What matters this or that reason," the Duke of Albemarle remarked in 1664 as England went to war with the Dutch over the issue of colonial trade. "What we want is more of the trade the Dutch now have." Clarendon in particular saw in an expanding colonial trade a partial solution to the government's fiscal problems. The arrears of the Interregnum army, the debts of Charles I before his death and of Charles II while in exile, and the normal expense of government combined represented a debt which even a loyal and relatively compliant Cavalier Parliament could not face squarely. The Commons at the time of the Restoration voted Charles grants estimated to yield £1,200,000 each year. This sum was to cover all past and present obligations of the crown. This amount itself was inadequate and the actual receipts more so. An expansion of trade was necessary to close the gap between the actual and estimated revenues of the king, for customs duties represented the largest single source of income to the government.[15]

The official rationale formulated to justify the passage of the Navigation Acts and the creation of the councils, however, cannot be ignored entirely. Their ideas were not formulated in the detailed coherence of a colonial policy, but their attitude was clear. Many of the Restoration courtiers, merchants, and theorists who expressed their concern with empire by their interest in the Royal Society, their participation in new trade and colonial ventures, and their decisions in government believed what they said in the optimistic atmosphere immediately following 1660. They sincerely thought the colonies' economic and political well-being was "mingled . . . with the rest of his Majesty's Dominion" and they imagined that it was possible to make the plantations "usefull to England *and* England helpfull to them."[16]

Early in 1661 the Council for Foreign Plantations began to apply to specific cases the principles implied in its instructions. To Virginia the Council wrote pledging that any progress in economic diversification would "stir up his Majesty to give you his most perticular favours and Indulgencie as often as your affairs shall have Occasion thereof" and urging the province in the meantime "to represent and agitate such things as may tend to the advantage of his Majesty and his Collonie of Virginia."[17] Colonists seldom needed urging to press for their interests. Even before receipt of this letter, the assembly had asked Governor Berkeley to undertake a special mission to England. The assembly, upon authorization from the king, elected Francis Moryson governor during Berkeley's absence, and in late April or early May 1661 Sir William sailed for England. Upon his arrival in August the Council for Foreign Plantations requested him to prepare a written report on his province based on the questions sent out the previous February. Berkeley's tract, *Discourse and View of Virginia,* may have been his response to the Council's request. Not until late spring and summer of 1662, however, did the government, the governor, and various merchant groups engage in serious discussions about a program for the development of Virginia. A petition dated May 26 to the king from the planters, presented by Berkeley and Virginia merchants, initiated the talks.[18] Crown, colonial leadership, and traders soon discovered that the common interest of the empire was a difficult thing to discover when one got down to specific cases.

The May petition noted that the price of tobacco owing to overproduction had dropped so low that it scarcely enabled the planters and merchants to pay the customs and, more importantly, prevented the accumulation of investment capital necessary for developing more useful and profitable staples, especially naval stores. The solution was a tobacco stint. More concerned with economic progress than with assembly prerogatives, the petitioners urged the crown to bypass the legislatures and by a royal proclamation prohibit the planting of tobacco in the Chesapeake colonies after June 10 annually until the price of tobacco rose.

The Council for Foreign Plantations initially rejected the petition out of hand with the additional declaration that "they would nott henceforth receive any Peticon of that Nature," but ten days later the board reversed itself, asserted it had not intended to discourage anyone petitioning to promote the welfare of the colonies, and ordered the whole matter reopened and debated.[19] The reasons for the government's original position and sudden about-face are obscure. The crown had an ambivalent attitude toward tobacco at this time. The early seventeenth century reservation about basing a colony's economy on the production of a frivolous luxury persisted, but a clear recognition of the revenue possibilities of the tobacco trade existed as well. In explaining the reversal of the Council, one might reasonably surmise that the merchants involved brought considerable pressure to bear upon members of the Council who had opposed the scheme for a stint. Perhaps too, a fuller council meeting on the thirteenth accounted for the reversal. The Council for Foreign Plantations included many who could be expected to support the stint proposal and its objectives. William Berkeley himself sat on the board, having been added to it after his arrival in England. John, Lord Berkeley, his brother, was also a member, as was the individual most prominent in matters of colonial policy and administration during the Interregnum and Restoration period, Thomas Povey. He vigorously supported the idea of producing "solid comodities" in Virginia and praised Governor Berkeley as "a Person of most eminent Ingenuite and one that hath made verie many Tryalls and Experiments." Others, like Anthony Ashley Cooper, later the first Earl of Shaftesbury and the leading Carolina proprietor, were also eager to foster the development of colonial staples other than tobacco.[20]

Whatever the reason for the reversal, the petitioners again submitted their proposal for a stint in Maryland and Virginia, which this time found a more cordial reception. Although unwilling to impose a stint upon the Chesapeake plantations by royal decree, the crown upon the council's recommendation did instruct Berkeley to initiate negotiations between his government and Baltimore's and gave its approval in advance to any stint plan which the two colonies could agree upon.[21]

A second proposal advocated by Berkeley in the summer of 1662 was a prohibition upon the departure from Virginia of ships carrying tobacco until after the first of June each year. This suggestion precipitated more disagreement than any other proposal. The argument for an embargo on sailing until June stressed the protection from pirates and enemy ships which a convoy system would afford. The scheme was also viewed by the Virginia planter elite as a method to generate more capital for diversification by altering the market relationship and the division of tobacco profits between merchants and planters in favor of the latter. Under prevailing conditions, which the petitioners deplored, tobacco ships left England individually at various times in the fall, arriving in Virginia in the winter months. Uncertain of the number of ships which would arrive in any given year, the planters often were tempted to sell their tobacco immediately at a low price in return for assurance of freight space. The settlers also competed in getting their tobacco to England first, hoping thereby to command a high price. Should the ships remain in Virginia until a specified date the planters in general would enjoy a more favorable bargaining position. The idea, however, also found favor with the more substantial merchants whose trade patterns were more orderly. Led at this time by John Jefferies, they desired a stable trade and resented the wildcat operations of the smaller traders, who were willing to risk marauding pirates and privateers and to avoid customs collectors in order to secure the early English tobacco market and sell at lower prices.

Opposition came from John Bland, spokesman for the smaller, rising tobacco merchants. Although he allied himself with Governor Berkeley in opposition to the Navigation Act of 1660, which he viewed as advantageous to the few large engrossers of the tobacco trade, Bland and Sir William took opposite positions on the embargo issue. Bland's group argued that if ships could not depart from the province until June first, merchants would not dispatch their vessels until the hazardous winter sailing months, when few immigrants would risk the trip. The petitioners predicted that England's burden of unemployed would increase sharply since the emigration to Virginia would drop by a third. Bland's memorial also argued that, owing to the late arrival of the ships, Virginians could not secure English-made clothing and other items necessary for the winter months until January or February and would turn to the Dutch for supplies. Disadvantages there were for the king, too, which Bland's memorial noted. The government could not expect the "Early Customes from Virginia." Some tobacco ships normally arrived back in England as early as February, but an embargo on sailing would delay the first customs payments until the early summer.

The petitioners revealed their status in the English commercial world when they noted that an embargo by destroying freedom of trade would undermine the small, rising merchants. The smaller merchants, lacking large amounts of capital with which to finance their trading activity, operated on a month-to-month basis, using the profits from the sale of tobacco brought in by their first ships to pay the freight and customs of the tobacco imported in a second and then a third group of ships arriving later. Moreover, if an embargo were imposed all ships would arrive at about the same time, there would be a glut of the commodity in the English ports, and prices would fall and drive out of the market all small traders who could not withstand a narrowing of the profit margin on each tobacco hogshead.

Confronted with this sharp disagreement on what was the common interest of the empire, the crown again chose to avoid a decision and accepted a suggestion at the end of Bland's petition. As he had done in the case of the stint proposal, the king ordered Berkeley along with his council and the assembly and the Maryland government to consider the proposal and formulate a suitable plan.[22]

A third proposal for the advancement and development of Virginia related to the problem of planter debts to the merchants. By the mid-seventeenth century many planters were deeply in debt to the tobacco traders. Estimates placed the annual indebtedness of Virginia at £50,000. In a manner characteristic of agricultural producers, the Virginia planter, hoping to liquidate his debts in the good times just around the corner, sought credit in the poor years from the merchants. In the relatively good years the planter overextended his credit and could not meet his obligations when the price of tobacco dropped.

Berkeley and others reasoned that the debt cycle prevented the colonists from turning to the production of other staples. Once in debt, the planter committed himself to produce tobacco year after year to satisfy his obligations. Planters could not reduce their production of tobacco and still honor

their commitments. Sir William thus proposed to the Council
for Foreign Plantations that the crown allow Virginia to enact
a law "deviating from the Lawes of England" to solve the
problem. A statute was needed, he argued, to prohibit any
planter from contracting a debt in tobacco which might not
also be satisfied by payment in other products such as corn,
cattle, silk, flax, and hemp.

The decision of the crown on this matter does not appear in the extant documents, but possibly Berkeley received
tacit permission to submit such a bill to the Virginia assembly.
In any case, the provincial legislature subsequently did attempt, without success, to substitute other staples as tender for
the payment of tobacco debts.[23]

Prohibition of tobacco production in England was another part of the general plan to increase the price of tobacco
and thus, indirectly, facilitate diversification. This demand
simply called for the more vigorous enforcement of a long-
standing policy, for the early Stuarts had issued proclamations
against tobacco production in the mother country and the
Interregnum government had prohibited the practice by law in
1651. Despite numerous petitions urging the strict enforcement of the measure and efforts by Cromwell to comply with
the requests, the act accomplished little. The quantity of
tobacco produced in England actually increased during the
1650's.[24]

Areas in England capable of tobacco production resented
the ban on tobacco planting in England, and John Worlidge,
author of *Systema Agriculturae,* voiced this opposition.
He saw no inconsistency in arguing both that Virginia would
sooner be forced to turn to the production of silk, wine, and
other staples if tobacco were grown at home, and that the
plantation tobacco trade would not notice the domestic competition. There was, however, no strong tobacco interest in
England. The part of Gloucestershire where much of the
planting occurred was "a miserable poor-place." The ban did
not alienate the large landed interest in England, but it did

square with the interest of both planter and merchant and promised to increase the king's revenue. Few proposals connected with Virginia's trade rested upon such a consensus. Of all the Virginians' requests it thus won strongest backing from the crown. The government issued numerous proclamations calling for enforcement of the law and dispatched troops to destroy the tobacco plants. These measures all but eliminated tobacco production in England by the fourth quarter of the century.[25]

A fifth aspect of the appeal for support of the crown for diversification was the demand for the promotion of port towns. The demand came from several sources. On this issue John Bland and Sir William again concurred. Bland urged the crown to require all ships to unload goods and load tobacco at a few "particular places as an encouragement for handicraft men or ingenious artists to settle, or reside there." It was possibly at this time and in support of Bland and Berkeley that the crown received the anonymous "proposals concerning building of Towns in Virginia." The memorial succinctly summed up the argument for towns: Virginia, though the oldest plantation and the best endowed by nature, improved slowly owing to the scattered mode of settlement and lack of ports. The New England colonies and Barbadoes, though possessing fewer natural advantages, had developed faster owing to the growth of towns in those provinces. With equal pointedness the author asserted that towns would appear quickly if the king would simply grant substantial privileges to persons who built and lived in ports and if the crown also would restrict all commerce to designated points.[26]

To these arguments was added the case for town promotion from the point of view of the colonial clergyman Roger Green. In a tract carefully contrived to supplement the economic rationale presented by Bland, Berkeley, and the anonymous tract, Green insisted that only a colonial society built around towns could prosper in religion, education, and culture. Owing to the dispersed settlement on individual plantations,

Green contended, the colonists were unable to attend church and thereby deprived God of the public adoration He demands. Green asserted, indeed, that the failure of the Virginians to erect a strong religious community around towns had brought the curse of God upon the province. The scattered mode of settlement destroyed the proper relation of man to man as well as that of man and his God. Identifying towns with civilization, the author suggested that the planters were returning to a state of barbarism. As a consequence of the relatively isolated plantations, Virginians could not practice Christian charity. They sorely needed daily scrutiny and "brotherly admonistions" as well as pious examples of superior Christians and the frequent and regular services of trained ministers. Lacking the "Benefit of Christian and Civil Conference," the settlers were turning from brotherhood and charity to licentious living.[27]

Charles II's predecessors had often urged the settlers to build Jamestown into a more respectable town, largely for purposes of defense. Apparently persuaded by the barrage of arguments for the wholesale creation of towns, the king and his Restoration colonial advisers now urged Berkeley to construct a town on each of the major rivers, beginning with the expansion of Jamestown on the York.[28]

One proposal to aid Virginia found no favor among Restoration courtiers and government officials. Berkeley and John Bland both leveled sharp criticism against the Navigation Act of 1660, especially the enumeration clause. Bland denied that the act would increase British commerce, predicting that without some direct trade with the Dutch, the province would languish. In a short time no trade would exist for anyone, English or Dutch. Bland proposed to guarantee Virginia's economic expansion as well as the long-range interests of the English merchants by allowing Dutch trade with Virginia with a duty large enough to give English merchants an advantage, yet not so excessive as to discourage the Hollanders completely. Berkeley too viewed the Navigation Act of 1660 as an impediment to diversification. Despite some strong language criticizing the merchants who backed the act, his position was not as extreme as Bland's. The governor urged exemption of Virginia-built ships from the act's prohibition on direct trade to the continent in enumerated goods. Hopefully the privilege would help increase the price of tobacco by expanding the market and spark a flourishing ship-building industry in Virginia as well. The government, however, clearly instructed Berkeley to enforce the Act of 1660 and render a strict account of his proceedings to the home government.[29]

The final proposal concerned the problem of capital needed for diversification. To Berkeley capital formation was a crucial problem. His opinion was seconded by a colonial entrepreneur, Anthony Langston, who undoubtedly hoped to have a share in the management and profit from any subsidies the home government might advance. A resident of about fourteen years before he composed his petition shortly after the Restoration, Langston maintained that town growth was "the onely defect wee have to make us the most flourishing and profitable Plantation his Majesty hath," that the rise of towns depended on the establishment of a colonial iron industry, and finally that relatively small crown subsidies were essential to solve the problem of the lack of investment capital in this area.

The Virginia assembly's proposal for solving the problem of capital formation was that the English Parliament add a penny per pound to the customs in England on imported tobacco and grant the proceeds to Virginia. By providing the capital necessary to construct iron works and saw mills and funds for adequate wages, the additional duty would enable the province to secure artisans skilled in the production of silk, hemp, flax, iron, and other products. Berkeley also believed it desirable to discourage production of tobacco by excessive taxation. He later urged Lord Clarendon to persuade Charles and Parliament to impose "more custome and greater on this vile weed." If the crown were unwilling to increase the customs, Berkeley urged an increase in the provincial tax of two shillings per hogshead on exported tobacco to three or four shillings. This alternative might still enable the province to pay the expenses of government and have enough remaining to begin the work of diversification.[30]

These various proposals regarding the problem of capital received consideration by the council in July and August. Since the suggestion touched upon matters affecting crown revenues, the council made a special effort to discuss it with all persons and interests which might be affected. The action taken in mid-August was a disappointment to Berkeley. The suggestion to add a penny to the customs on tobacco did not receive serious consideration, and the government decided that it was in no financial position to provide directly any funds for the development of Virginia. The government, however, did not object to an increase in the provincial tax and sanctioned the use of any surplus after the cost of the provincial government had been paid for advancement of new economic enterprises.[31]

Compared to John Winthrop's mission to England on behalf of Connecticut during these same years, recent scholarship has judged Berkeley's efforts a failure.[32] Winthrop sought and obtained a royal charter which provided a large measure of autonomy for the Puritan province. His task, however, was far simpler than Berkeley's, for the New England Puritan asked for nothing requiring a direct financial sacrifice by the crown. However much the Virginia proposals promised ultimately to increase England's trade and crown revenues, they threatened to reduce the income derived from the tobacco trade temporarily. Yet despite disappointments Berkeley did not return to Virginia with no victories. Indeed he left England with more concessions and compromises on his various proposals than might have been expected.

Translating the vague and lofty concept of an empire united in mutual interest into a specific program for the oldest colony had necessitated compromise. Virginia received no satisfaction on its suggestion that the Navigation Acts be revoked or modified. The statutes defined the basic principles of the empire and were not subject to negotiation. The crown's finances did not permit Charles to grant funds for diversification, but he did promise to invest directly in provincial iron works if the prospects looked good after detailed study. The king also sanctioned use of surplus provincial revenues for diversification schemes. The proposal of an embargo on shipping until a fixed date stirred up great antagonism between diverse interest groups, and the government, reluctant to make a decision, referred the problem to the provincial government for consideration. Similarly the crown charged the governor, council, and burgesses of Virginia to come up with a workable plan for a tobacco stint. This was an important concession, for a stint necessarily would result in a decrease in royal revenues derived from the tobacco trade. The crown also assigned responsibility to the provincial government for creating towns. Indeed, in much of the discussions which took place during Berkeley's agency, the crown exhibited a willingness to permit the colonists, through their provincial government, to participate in the business of formulating an economic policy for Virginia. Sir Edwin Sandys had created a representative assembly in part to expedite the Virginia Company's diversification program four decades earlier. The Restoration government now recognized the assembly as an integral part of the effort to reshape the Virginia economy. The crown apparently took seriously its idealistic profession of an empire of "mingled" interests and sought the counsel of all concerned—governor, planters, and merchants—in defining and implementing a policy designed to serve that interest. To be sure, the crown did not approve the proposals, such as exemption of Virginia-built ships from the Navigation Acts and direct and substantial investment in diversification schemes, which undoubtedly would have had the greatest effect on Virginia's economy. Nor was the government as forceful in pushing schemes, like the establishment of towns, as it was in demanding obedience to the Navigation Acts. The actual policy fell far short of the ideal of a balanced empire. Still, the crown in 1660 made some effort to achieve the theoretical goal. Considering the financial difficulties already threatening the restored monarchy, even modest concessions were significant and symbolized an intense concern with experimentation and long-range development of Virginia and the empire as a whole even if the capability was absent. The crown believed with the colony's leadership that the interests of the crown, England, and the province were the same—the promotion of economic diversification in Virginia.

The provincial leadership's quest for reinforcement from the central government had fallen short of the full expectations, and certainly the crown's limited support did not begin to fill the gap between the excessive goals and the weakened position of authority of that elite; yet Berkeley departed from England believing that the crown and his colony had established a partnership to reshape the economy and, ultimately, the society of Virginia. The crown's minor concessions appeared to be both important tokens of that agreement and a promise of greater assistance in the future if the home government's finances improved and if Virginians themselves gave greater evidence of the development of their land's imagined potential.

3

TOBACCO CONTROLS

During and following Berkeley's mission to England, Virginia's leadership struggled to achieve the modicum of success judged necessary to transform the crown's interest into significant direct support of diversification. As in the 1650's, the mode of leadership practiced on the colonists to secure their support of diversification remained essentially prescriptive and occurred along three lines. The assembly legislated directly to promote introduction of new forms of economic activity. Indirectly the colony's government worked to annul proprietary grants within Virginia and preserve the colony's direct political relationship to the crown, a condition regarded as a prerequisite for economic progress. Thirdly, the provincial government worked for implementation of tobacco production controls. The last efforts, the focus of this chapter, occurred principally between 1662 and 1667 and aimed specifically at a comprehensive plan for limitation of tobacco cultivation in Virginia, Maryland, and Albemarle. The crown's willingness to permit the local assemblies to formulate and implement a stint seemed a chance for the colonials to work out their own economic salvation. Virginia's provincial leadership resolved not to forfeit the opportunity.

The severe drop in the price of tobacco after the Restoration increased the hopes for diversification. From a level of about twopence per pound in 1660, the price of tobacco sank to one halfpenny per pound in 1667 before turning up again slightly in 1668. The Navigation Acts, by severing direct trade with the continent, were an important cause for the plummeting price the planters received for their crop, but overproduction was the major factor. The years immediately following the Restoration witnessed the climax of the tenfold increase in tobacco imports into England from 1637 to 1668. The greater crops in Virginia resulted in part from a rapid increase in population after 1640. Population more than tripled in three decades. But this was not the entire story, for tobacco production expanded at a much faster rate than population. In the half century between 1640 and 1690, per capita exports of tobacco rose from about 115 to over 335 pounds. A sharp rise in the average size of land grants after 1640 suggests that the increased per capita production was a consequence of individuals, notably the more affluent new immigrants, securing larger acreage and expanding the scope of their operations.[1] Ironically, the private economic behavior of the great planters exacerbated the economic condition their public policy sought to resolve.

The impediments to crop limitations programs were considerable and stemmed largely from the division of the economic region into distinct political units. Maryland's dependence upon a one-crop economy was as great as Virginia's in the last half of the seventeenth century, but the younger province's interest in production controls was less acute. Compared to Virginians, the Maryland planters grew more Orinoco than sweet-scented tobacco. The major market for the lower grade, harsh-flavored Orinoco was the continent, while sweet-scented tended to sell in England. By producing a higher quality tobacco, Virginians were more vulnerable to the glut of the English domestic market.[2] Maryland was not only less anxious about production controls, but the bitter factionalism between proprietary and antiproprietary interests also frequently hamstrung its government. Marylanders could scarcely agree among themselves, let alone establish a consensus with Virginia. The establishment of settlements in Albemarle under the Carolina proprietary grant further complicated the task of devising production controls by creating a third political division of a single economic unit.

Opposition to tobacco controls also came from some traders. While leading merchants like Jefferies endorsed the idea of a stint, Berkeley doubted their sincerity and suspected them of working to undermine the project. Some traders did in fact seek to build opposition to a stint by offering at times slightly higher prices for tobacco and spreading false rumors that the glut in the market would soon end owing to a "new vent" in Russia.[3] Through a dogged persistence over a five-year period and by a willingness to compromise on the form of control, the Virginia government overcame these impediments only to have their victory annulled by the last minute intervention of Lord Baltimore and by a change in the crown's attitude toward curbs on tobacco exports.

Even before Berkeley obtained the crown's approval for tobacco limitation in the colonies, Virginians after the Restoration attempted to implement tobacco stints. Drawing upon the precedent of the stint legislation of 1658, the assembly in 1661 forbade the planting of tobacco after July 10 under any circumstances and after June 10 if Maryland would agree to the harsher restriction. When the proprietary province refused to cooperate, the Virginia government vigorously enforced its own deadline and urged the crown to impose the stronger plan by royal fiat.[4] In the spring of 1663, following Charles II's injunction to the two provinces to negotiate a stint plan, commissioners from both colonies met at the home of Isaac Allerton in Northumberland County, Virginia, just across the river from Maryland.

Maryland's delegation consisted of individuals attached to the proprietary interest, Philip Calvert, Henry Sewall,

Edward Koyder, and Henry Coursey. The Virginia contingent illustrates the source of leadership for the diversification efforts. Included among the commissioners was Richard Lee, a first-generation colonist who came to Virginia in 1640 and held numerous offices, beginning with the position of clerk of the council in 1641 and followed by the attorney generalship in 1643 and the council after 1648. Lee, according to legend, made several trips to the exiled Charles during the Interregnum. John Carter also was a first-generation settler. He established himself in Upper Norfolk County in 1643 and during the 1650's sat as a burgess from Nansemond and Lancaster counties until in 1658 he entered the council. He was a leader in the Interregnum assemblies and was noted for his Royalist sentiments. A third commissioner, Robert Smith, did not appear in Virginia until after the Restoration but moved quickly into the council and thereafter became a prominent leader in provincial affairs. He frequently represented Virginia as an agent. He was on a later commission which negotiated with Maryland regarding a tobacco cessation. In the middle 1670's he served with Francis Moryson and Thomas Ludwell in England in the effort to secure a colonial charter from the crown which would guarantee the rights of Virginia. Henry Corbin, who also served on the 1663 commission, came to Virginia in 1654. As in the case of Richard Lee, Cavalier legends have surrounded Corbin. Allegedly he helped Charles II escape from the field after the battle of Worcester, then in order to avoid arrest by the Cromwell regime fled to Virginia and settled in Lancaster County. After serving in 1659 and 1660 in the assembly as a burgess of that county, he became a customs collector and a member of the council following the Restoration. Thomas Ludwell served as secretary of the Virginia delegation. He came to Virginia as a young man with Berkeley in 1642. During the Civil War he returned to England to serve in the Royalist army, attaining the rank of lieutenant. After the Restoration he became one of the prominent political figures in Virginia, having received a commission as secretary of state from Charles II, presumably in return for his services during the Interregnum.[5] The commissioners, then, without exception were first-generation colonists, and many of them were conspicuous in their loyalty to the Stuarts during the Interregnum. They were representatives par excellence of the new immigrants.

Conflict appeared at the outset of the talks, but the delegations managed in the end to devise a compromise plan to submit to the respective assemblies. The Marylanders believed that a stint date applied uniformly to the Chesapeake Bay area would discriminate against their province owing to its northern location and later planting season. They thus proposed in lieu of a stint a total cessation of planting in 1664 and every three years thereafter. Berkeley's commission objected that a cessation would cause excessive fluctuations in the provincial economies and in the long run cause the price of a smaller quantity of tobacco to remain low by driving merchants out of the trade. On this central issue the proprietary delegates surrendered to the logic of the Virginians and agreed to a stint. The Virginians bought this agreement, however, by concessions on virtually all other aspects of the basic plan. The Virginia delegation wanted to impose a stint after June 10, but Maryland successfully held out for June 20. Enforcement of the agreement was left to each province acting autonomously. Especially did the Virginians object to the Maryland commissioners' insistence that the plan receive approval of the respective provincial assemblies prior to its implementation each year, but on this point too they yielded.[6]

As feared by the Virginia delegation, the demand of the Maryland delegation to submit the plan to the assemblies proved the undoing of the scheme in 1664. The Virginia legislature readily approved and added to its endorsement the threat that if Maryland failed to follow suit Virginia would no longer enforce its milder stint laws while Maryland planters were unrestrained. Despite the warning the Maryland assembly withheld approval. In contrast to the amicable relations of governor, council, and burgesses in Virginia after 1660, the governor and council controlled by the proprietary

interest were frequently at odds with the lower house dominated by men who were envious of the political power and
social position of the proprietary clique. The representatives
vetoed the proposal, objecting that the agreement favored
Virginia and that no restraints would be effective in increasing
the price unless imposed upon all English colonies in the
West Indies as well as on the mainland.[7]

Virginia reacted quickly and angrily to Maryland's action. The assembly which convened in the fall of 1664 reiter-
ated its abolition of all restraints on the planting of tobacco
in Virginia and declared that Marylanders would be responsible for the economic hardships which must follow the un-
restricted production of tobacco in both provinces. At the
same time, the Virginia assembly sanctioned a mission by
Lieuenant Governor Sir Henry Chicheley to England to secure
the crown's support in forcing Maryland's compliance with a
program of tobacco limitation.[8]

In England the lieutenant governor followed the patterns
established by Edward Digges in 1658 and Berkeley after the
Restoration. Sir Henry sought out and cooperated with the
Virginia merchants and with prominent planters who were in
London to bring pressure to bear on the crown. Digges himself was on hand in 1664, and Francis Moryson, who served
as governor during Berkeley's absence, had returned to England where he acted until 1677 as permanent agent for the
province. Both joined with Chicheley to press Virginia's case
in London. A third and most valuable ally to Chicheley was
John Jefferies, a London alderman and the tobacco merchant
who had worked with Berkeley two years earlier.[9]

On August 10, 1664, Chicheley presented the General
Assembly's petition against Maryland's actions to the Privy
Council, which, after considerable delay, ordered the Virgin-
ians and Lord Baltimore to confer and resolve their difference.
Apparently even at this time the crown was willing to go along
with a plan upon which the two colonies could agree. The
Virginia agents and merchants and the lord proprietor, how-
ever, reached no meeting of the minds. Baltimore renewed the

original Maryland proposal, but Chicheley and the others would have nothing to do with a total cessation every three years. Baltimore, in turn, would not agree to any stint unless Maryland received at least twenty additional planting days to compensate for its northern location and shorter growing season.[10]

Separating the proprietor from the Virginians was more than a difference in opinion over the weather of the two colonies. Baltimore doubted the ability of the provincial government to enforce a stint and feared the consequences of an attempt. The governments lacked an adequate bureaucracy for inspection to insure that planting ceased after a fixed date. Baltimore recognized that enforcement would depend upon informers and believed the program would ultimately undermine all deference to authority by encouraging "servants to inform against their Masters, or next Neighbours one against another. . . ." Chicheley maintained that economic depression, which only a stint could arrest, would cause discontent and revolts. Baltimore on the other hand was apprehensive that upheavals would occur if the crown ignored the assemblies' autonomy and sanctioned drastic economic experimentation.[11] The conflicting views on tobacco controls thus rested ultimately on different assumptions about the likelihood of economic diversification producing orderly colonial societies.

Unable to reach a compromise, both parties in November carried their cases to the Privy Council. In a petition which also renewed Berkeley's earlier pleas for crown subsidies for diversification and for controls on the departure of tobacco ships from the provinces, Chicheley and his colleagues again urged the crown to impose a stint upon both colonies.[12] Unfortunately from the Virginians' standpoint, the crown's financial condition had worsened rather than improved since Berkeley's agency. By late 1664 the inadequacy of the Restoration financial settlement was painfully obvious. The king tried without success to solve the problems of the Exchequer by selling crown lands, and he even contributed the dowry of his wife to the treasury. Approaching war with the Dutch heightened concern for the revenue of the crown. At the same time that Chicheley and the others presented their petition, the Royal Commissioners of 1664, backed by four English frigates, sailed into Gravesend Bay off New Amsterdam and demanded the capitulation of that Dutch colony. Earlier Sir Robert Holmes, on behalf of the English Royal African Company, had seized the Dutch ports of Gorce, near the Gambia River, and Cape Coast Castle on the Gulf of Guinea. In October 1664 James, Duke of York, as Lord High Admiral began fitting out the navy for full-scale war. Although the official declaration of the Second Dutch War did not come until April 1665, that conflict, which placed a severe strain upon the royal treasury, had begun in fact when Chicheley, Digges, Jefferies, and Moryson appeared before the Lords.[13] Financially pressed to a greater degree than in the immediate post-Restoration period, the crown repudiated the support given to the stint proposal in 1662.

The decision of the crown came on November 25, 1664, when the Privy Council approved a recommendation of the Lords' Committee for Plantations. Significantly, the committee consulted the farmers of the king's customs in coming to a decision—a procedure absent from the negotiations in 1662 but one which occurred regularly thereafter—then recommended rejection of all proposals for reducing the quantity of tobacco as incompatible with the crown's growing need of the revenues derived from the customs duties on tobacco. The decisions literally forced upon the crown by the inability of Baltimore and Chicheley to agree were a repudiation of the compromise worked out with Berkeley just two years before. Yet the crown did not entirely reject the concept of economic diversification. The Committee for Plantations suggested, and the Privy Council approved, instead as a gradual and less painful transition to a diversified economy in the Chesapeake Bay area the abolition for five years of all duties on hemp, pitch, and tar produced in Virginia and Maryland. At this time the crown also gave Governor Berkeley the right to export to England duty free 300 shipping tons of tobacco for each 300-ton ship sent home with a cargo of silk, hemp, flax, and other "solid commodities."[14]

Virginia provincial leaders were reluctant to accept the crown's new stance. They imagined that progress toward diversification had been considerable even without a tobacco stint and that success would be certain if only the two provinces concurred on a workable plan to control tobacco production. The persistent depression in the tobacco market continued to reinforce the Virginia leaders' desire to secure the cooperation of Maryland in a program to curtail tobacco production despite the king's commands. Thomas Ludwell noted in February 1667 that two years' crops still remained in the province, while Berkeley feared that more tobacco was on hand "then in humane probability will be Carried home in three yeares ensueing. . . ."[15]

Spurred by a combination of hope and fear, the provincial leadership thus ignored the crown's ban on schemes for control over tobacco production. Through the fall and early winter, Sir William wrote frequently to the Maryland authorities, but they refused to commit themselves and returned only "ineffectuall" answers. Finally in the mid-winter of 1665-1666, the governor and a few councillors sailed up the icy waters of the Chesapeake Bay to Maryland, where they personally prevailed upon Baltimore's chief executive to make another try at tobacco regulation. At length, Governor Calvert and his advisers agreed to use their interest with the assembly in order to secure tobacco restriction. To procure this pledge, the Virginians had to abandon their insistence upon a stint and agree to cooperate in a cessation, but they made clear to the Maryland government that they regarded the cessation merely as an experiment. The Virginians would not concede the Marylanders' contention that a cessation was the only equitable way of controlling production in both colonies, but their eagerness for some restriction overrode their better judgment as they agreed to a total curb on planting for a year.[16]

The Maryland burgesses who met in April 1666 initially showed no more inclination to support a cessation than they had a stint in 1663, but after an extensive debate between lower house and council on the merits of regulation and, most significantly, after important proprietary concessions to the representatives, the proposal did win endorsement. The alterations included bringing the Albemarle government into any cessations. The lower house also demanded as part of any agreement an arrangement for the modification or staying of debt payments during cessation years. Further, the legislators obtained their own representatives on the delegation appointed to negotiate the final arrangements for a cessation.[17]

The Virginia assembly met in June, "readily & Cheerfully" accepted Maryland's modifications, and authorized negotiations between the three colonies. Conscious that their actions ignored the commands of the crown, the burgesses, councillors, and governor rationalized that a cessation would not reduce the king's customs since the tobacco already on hand was equivalent to the quantity normally exported. Unlike the Maryland government, which viewed the cessation largely as a temporary expedient to increase the price of tobacco, Virginia's leaders stressed the relationship of the restriction to long-range diversification efforts. They hoped that in the "vacant years time wilbe given to the planter to settle himself upon the finding out and improvement of some other staple, as wee have already begun in silke, fflax, and potash."[18]

In June delegates from the three provinces met at Jamestown. The agreement quickly drawn up at the conference confirmed the acts passed by the legislatures of Maryland and Virginia and outlined procedures for enforcement of the cessation. The agreement required all public officials in the provinces from the governors to the lowest clerk to enforce the restrictions on plantings. The treaty authorized any individual of one colony to travel freely into another province to observe whether the laws were obeyed. If he discovered violation of the cessation, he could then make complaint directly to the governor, who was required to destroy the offender's tobacco.

The legislatures of Virginia and Maryland had already agreed to abide by any cessation agreement drawn up by the commissioners, but the Albemarle assembly had not. The treaty thus contained a proviso which annulled the whole scheme if Governor William Drummond's North Carolina assembly failed to pass a similar cessation act and transmit it to the other governments before the last day of September. Drummond assured the conference that he would not fail to secure his assembly's approval.[19] Shortly after, the Albemarle representatives met and agreed to cooperate. Drummond failed, however, to certify the decision to Maryland and Virginia until five days after the deadline specified in the June agreement. Confusion resulting from Indian attacks was the excuse the Carolina governor gave for his negligence. Perhaps, too, Drummond purposely dallied in getting word to the other provinces in order to spite Governor Berkeley, with whom he had quarreled. Drummond had come to Virginia in 1648 and won the friendship of Sir William, who, after the Restoration, appointed him governor of Albemarle. But Drummond soon clashed with Berkeley over the title to land in Virginia. At the very time Drummond participated in the cessation negotiations, he was prosecuting his case against Berkeley. Drummond was also at odds with Berkeley over the administration of Albemarle. He resented Sir William's opposition to the engrossment of large areas of land by individuals who did not pay the proprietary quitrents or fulfill the obligation to seat and develop their patents. Drummond believed that, in general, the inhabitants were "weary of Sir William's Government . . . ," and his personal and policy disagreements with Berkeley may have caused the Albemarle governor to delay ratification of the cessation agreement purposely in order to thwart a pet project of his adversary. Berkeley subsequently removed Drummond as governor of North Carolina. He returned to Virginia, quarrelled intermittently with the provincial leaders, and ended up in 1676 on the gallows, executed as a leader of Bacon's Rebellion.[20]

Whatever the cause of the tardy action of the Albemarle government, Maryland, always skeptical about tobacco controls, hesitated to proceed with the agreement, which technically had been broken. The Virginia assembly convened in late October with Maryland's position still uncertain. The day after the session opened Berkeley wrote to Governor Calvert and his council pleading with them to signify their continued cooperation. Numerous planters had already arranged their affairs assuming a cessation would take place. Everyone agreed, he argued, "that a cessation will make some few merchants venture their goods to us in these dangerous times which otherwise they will keep by them." The commerce of the entire province "is at a stand still," he noted, waiting for word from Maryland. Two days later Calvert replied to Berkeley's plea. He asserted that the previous treaty was now invalid and that another agreement must be negotiated. The Virginia leaders thought Baltimore's colonists overly "tender and scrupulous" but agreed to humor the legalistic decision of their neighbors. The assembly passed an act declaring the cessation law of June in force and sent the old delegates to St. Mary's to renew the agreement. To prevent subsequent sabotage of the scheme by a mere technicality, the law also authorized the governor and commissioners to resolve any difficulties which arose in the future. In mid-December the Virginia and Maryland delegates met again, agreed that the cessation should not "be stifled in its Birth," and confirmed the June treaty. Curiously, North Carolina, which had occasioned all the difficulty, was not represented at the conference, and its willingness to cooperate was taken for granted.[21]

The Virginia commissioners returned to their province "well satisfied." The agreement, Berkeley and his council later recalled, "did in an instant as it were by miraculous effect cause us to despise & forgett our former misseries & filled us with the contemplasion of future happiness & prosperities. . . ." In anticipation of the cessation, some Virginians had made extensive plans for diversification. Berkeley and others invested extensively from their own funds in diversification plans in anticipation of the cessation year, and through the summer of 1666 Sir William exchanged optimistic letters with Richard Nicholls, proprietary governor of newly conquered New York, discussing the prospects of growing flax, hemp, and other products in their two colonies.[22]

In early February 1667, after Virginia and Maryland again ratified the cessation agreement, Thomas Ludwell informed the home government that, since the king had sent no orders against the scheme, the cessation was under way. The Maryland and Virginia governments issued proclamations putting the cessation into effect. Officials in the various counties took the oath to enforce the agreement. Ludwell was confident that the planters would now "most certainly" turn to the production of silk, hemp, and flax.[23]

Preoccupied with war, plague, the London fire, and the imminent downfall of Lord Clarendon, the English government took no notice of the colonial insubordination. Colonial matters as a whole, which had occupied a relatively important place in affairs of state immediately after the Restoration, now received small consideration from the government. The select councils were dormant. The Council for Foreign Plantations met for the last time in the spring of 1665, while the Council of Trade does not appear to have convened after July 1664. Lord Baltimore, on the other hand, moved decisively to annul the colonies' plans even though he had earlier seemed to sanction a cessation in preference to a stint. In late November 1666 he vetoed the Maryland act, and news of his action reached the provinces in mid-February. Governor Calvert had no choice but to issue a proclamation on February 16 terminating the cessation.[24]

Baltimore's action in the end proved irrelevant, for in the spring and summer of 1667 a series of disasters accomplished what the colonists had been unable to achieve by agreement and legislation. In April a storm of hail destroyed a large part of the tobacco seedlings. Then, through the middle of the summer excessive rain destroyed more tobacco, and in August high winds accompanied by floods destroyed much which managed to survive the previous disasters. Ten to fifteen thousand houses and much tobacco stored in warehouses perished in two hours. The Dutch added to the destruction of nature. In June four Dutch men-of-war destroyed five tobacco ships in the James River and captured thirteen after easily overcoming an English ship of forty-six guns, the *Elizabeth,* which had been sent to the Bay to prevent such a disaster.[25] The effect of these misfortunes was to wipe out the surplus of tobacco, though, of course, not in a way which benefitted the planter or aided diversification. Indeed, the few feeble economic innovations boasted of by Ludwell and Berkeley were annulled by the violent rains and storms.

Despite the drastic reduction of the quantity of tobacco in storage and in the fields in 1667, Virginia's leaders concluded that Baltimore's disallowance had robbed them of prosperity when it was nearly in their grasp. The lord's action confirmed and strengthened their conviction that the province could not progress so long as they were "enforced to steere by another compass whose needle is too often touch'd with particular interest. . . ." The governor and council claimed that the province had expended over three thousand pounds of tobacco in making preparations to diversify during the year of cessation. Ignoring the fact that the crown itself had opposed tobacco restrictions in 1664, Virginia's planter elite branded Baltimore's autonomous authority as "an impetuous winde [which] doth blow from us all those seasonable showers" of Charles II's "cares & favours . . . ," and resolved to solicit again the king's support. In October the home government, for the third and last time in the 1660's, listened to a debate over the merits and dangers of tobacco restrictions. Francis Moryson, still in England serving as Virginia's agent, and Lord Baltimore rehearsed the now stale arguments. Doubtless the hearings were mere formalties, for the crown did not hesitate at the end of October to confirm its earlier decision.[26]

In abandoning their earlier support for some form of tobacco restriction, both Baltimore and the crown rationalized that their actions accorded with the interests of the majority of the common planters. Baltimore argued, and the crown accepted the thesis, that the production control schemes were basically designs of the rich planters and merchants to exploit the poorer planters. Lacking ready cash and supplies to tide them over during periods of limitations on planting, the lesser sort, according to Baltimore, would purchase scarce goods at premium prices. The proprietor charged that the larger planters wanted only the opportunity "of getting great estates at an Instant" and that these machinations would cause discontent and ultimately rebellion.[27]

This opinion of the motives behind production controls was erroneous, for the governments of Maryland and, especially, Virginia tried to protect debtors and poor planters against unfair practices of creditors during the year of the cessation. A Maryland assembly passed a measure providing that during the cessation debtors need not satisfy obligations which deprived them of a minimum of one hogshead of tobacco for each poll on their plantation, an amount considered essential to purchase necessities each year. Governor Calvert also agreed to a law which permitted the planter to satisfy an annual tax of twenty-five pounds of tobacco per poll with payments in grain and cattle at the prevailing market rates.[28]

The Virginia legislature's assault upon the debt problem was even more thorough. Merchants usually demanded payment of debts when the price of tobacco was relatively high. When tobacco was more plentiful and cheap, creditors were not eager to collect tobacco debts. Earlier provincial laws provided that debtors could dispose of their tobacco freely if their creditors did not demand payment by January first of each year. Creditors, however, could still sue and require their debtors to give security for payment later, usually by

their next crop. In the session of 1666 the assembly moved to
redress the advantage which this situation gave the creditors.
If a creditor failed to demand payment by January 1, a law
authorized the debtor to satisfy his obligation by applying for
the assistance of two Justices of the Peace before February
20. The measure required the Justices to appoint agents to
inspect the debtor's tobacco. If the tobacco were good, the
agents would then issue certificates of payment to the debtor.
Thereafter the tobacco belonged to the merchant and the
debtor was free of his obligations.

Another measure passed on the eve of the anticipated
cessation stayed payment of half of a private debt until
November 10, 1668, provided the planter satisfied the first
half in kind. In addition the act allowed the planters to pay
their taxes in products other than tobacco. Since the price of
tobacco was expected to rise rapidly, the law also deprived
government officers of a windfall and made fees and fines
payable in commodities other than tobacco.[29] Clearly Berkeley
and the elite which surrounded him expected to benefit from
cessation and diversification, as their investments show, but
this legislation suggests that their policies were not schemes
of the larger planters to exploit the smaller.

The safeguards against exploitation of the common
planters erected by both provincial governments impressed
neither the crown nor Baltimore. The crown's financial position had become too critical and the revenue derived from
the tobacco trade too important to jeopardize. The idea that
restraints of tobacco production were a plot by the prosperous
few against the majority of planters provided a convenient
justification for the government's actions. The reasoning
allowed the crown in its own mind to remain consistent to the
Restoration ideal of mingling the interests of colonists,
sovereign, and mother country while rejecting measures
which threatened the royal revenues.[30]

If the crown came to misjudge the impetus behind the
movement for tobacco restriction, its opposition nonetheless
did shield the tobacco planters from the ill conceived, naive

schemes for tobacco regulation. The stint proposals, as Baltimore sensed, were undoubtedly unworkable given the rudimentary government organization of the colonies. The stint, moreover, rested upon the naive assumption that an arbitrary date each year would control production effectively regardless of the weather, and this approach to crop limitation ignored also the probability that planters would simply strive to plant a normal crop in a smaller amount of time. As Virginia leaders themselves argued before reluctantly acquiescing in the scheme, a cessation could not have failed to dislocate severely the economy of the provinces. In the final analysis, the particular crop-limitation plans seemed practical to Virginia's leaders only because they did not doubt the possibility that the planters could shift overnight to other economic activities, and this belief rested in turn upon an exaggerated faith in the natural potential of the land and in an excessive confidence in their ability to command the behavior of the ordinary planters.

Berkeley and the planter elite thought that the political fracturing of the Chesapeake economic region was a major impediment to effective tobacco production curbs and thus to the prosperity of their society. In fact, the unforeseen consequences of James I's patent to Cecilius Calvert in 1632 was the creation of checks against precipitous economic experimentation which, however benevolently motivated, would have disrupted and harmed the economy of the area. In the later colonial period the "unnatural" division of the Chesapeake may have retarded the effective implementation of more practical, less extreme approaches to tobacco production control, especially the inspection system permanently established in Virginia in 1730. In the seventeenth century, however, the division was not a liability but an asset restraining the vigorous but naive efforts of Virginia's leadership. After 1664 the crown's and Baltimore's positions toward tobacco restriction reinforced the braking influence of the divided Chesapeake area on ill conceived designs for crop limitation. In a sense the crown and proprietor adopted the correct policy for the wrong reasons. Their increasingly narrow concern with protecting revenues from tobacco, and their false apprehensions regarding the motives of the supporters of crop-control legislation, caused them to quash the stint and cessation schemes which would undoubtedly have exacerbated the depression in the tobacco colonies.

4

THE CONSEQUENCES OF BENEVOLENCE

A few critics of the Virginia Company under Sandys' leadership scored "the settinge soe manie staple & rich Comodities on foote at one instant. . . ," and recognized that the failure to establish priorities was "a worke of an ill Consequence for thereby nothinge is done in anie one of them. . . ."[1] The caution did not register on the minds of most of Sandys' contemporaries, and after the Restoration the faith in the unlimited potential of the colony continued to obscure the need for concentrating the limited resources of the government for stimulating economic innovation. The severely qualified success of Berkeley's effort in 1662 to obtain significant assistance from the home government in promoting diversification did not induce the Virginia assembly to pare its activities to accord with its abilities. On the contrary, during and after the struggle to impose tobacco restrictions on the planters Berkeley's regime expended its energies in numerous efforts to evoke novel enterprise. In some areas such as silk no amount of government assistance would have produced significant success. In other instances at least modest potential existed but overzealous activity spent the opportunity in an excessive number of projects. The planters who dominated Virginia provincial politics between 1660 and

1676 repeated the error of Edwin Sandys, who a half century earlier labored as an armchair colonial planner to transform the province, and even as Sandys' actions led to the collapse of the Virginia Company, the comparable campaign between 1660 and 1676 contributed to the overthrow of Berkeley's government. Yet it was not only the economic policies of the provincial leaders per se which led to the discontent which surfaced in 1676, but the prescriptive style of leadership over the ordinary planters adopted in the pursuit of those economic designs.

Berkeley provided the impetus behind the rash of legislation just as he spurred the drive for tobacco production controls, but the governor had enthusiastic and willing followers. Between 1660 and 1675 he did not suffer a single major defeat at the hands of the assembly though his demands were considerable. Indeed, despite severe economic depression, two wars, natural disaster, and considerable social discontent, the governor, council, and burgesses did not clash seriously during the sixteen years of Berkeley's second administration. The lower house approved taxes for extraordinary occasions with a docility few colonial governors experienced. At the beginning of his second administration Berkeley and his council even secured the power to levy small poll taxes for emergencies when the assembly was not in session.

His success did not rest fundamentally upon his domination of the assembly and his councillors. To be sure, Berkeley did not hesitate to use patronage power. Individuals who backed the diversification program secured the choice appointments. Doubtless the rebel, Nathaniel Bacon, had some basis for his charges that burgesses who spoke against the governor's policies were branded with "badges of disfavor" and that Berkeley's councillors serving as the chairmen of the assembly's committees held "great sway" over the burgesses. But Sir William was no tyrant and his success in his relationship with the colony's leadership class cannot be explained by his patronage power or his alleged intimidation of the burgesses. When the governor considered laying down the burdens of his office in 1667, the representatives urged him to remain and praised him for his lenient rule which allegedly made Virginians, despite economic hardship and disaster of war and nature, the happiest of any English colonists in America. This and other testimonials did not emanate from an assembly wholly subservient to the arbitrary will of the governor. Berkeley's failure to dissolve the assembly and hold elections from 1660 to 1676 is evidence of the amicable relations between the burgesses and the governor, not of his desire to dominate them. Colonial governors, like English kings, dissolved assemblies only when an impasse was reached. Berkeley by compromise and concession avoided deadlocks and still secured approval of his policies.[2]

Concession was the method Berkeley preferred to follow in dealing with the assembly. In 1663 he solicited the lower house to appoint a committee of its own members to serve in an advisory capacity between sessions. In 1666 the assembly secured the right to specify the details of expenditures rather than simply make a grant of taxes. When the burgesses in the same year protested expenditures made without the prior approval of the assembly, Berkeley and his council readily agreed to the lower house's demand as "a Rule to walk by for the future." The concession prompted the observation that owing to Berkeley's conciliatory approach to the burgesses "the strings of government are always kept in tune."[3]

The burgesses were not the only beneficiaries of Berkeley's "indulging Government." The council during his administration gained control over the land grant procedure in the province. Berkeley's two administrations and the Interregnum which separated them also witnessed the development of autonomous county government in Virginia. The local gentry with little or no opposition from the provincial government consolidated their control over the courts and offices of the justice of the peace and sheriff.[4]

The power over taxation conceded to the lower house,

the surrender of control over land policy to the council, and the emergence of independent units of local government went to the heart of political power in the colony. These matters later became areas of severe conflict when the crown tried to tighten up colonial administration. The concessions received from Berkeley provided precedents which enabled the colony to frustrate the governors who came to Virginia to implement a more aggressive colonial policy in the last two decades of the century.

Basically, however, it was not Berkeley's political sagacity and power or his willingness to compromise which won him the support of the council and assembly, but his obvious attachment to the welfare of Virginia. Patronage and concessions, as indicated by the dealings of other Virginia governors with their councillors and burgesses, could gain but a few votes. The leaders of the gentry expected rewards for faithfully backing a governor's policy, but they also expected the policy to square with the colony's interest as defined by the principal planters. On the whole, Virginia's colonial governors in the seventeenth and early eighteenth century succeeded only when their policies and attitudes accorded with the welfare of the province as imagined by the leading planters who sat in the assembly and the council. Berkeley could persuade the gentry to support his policies because he was one of them. The leading gentry, and particularly the new immigrants, shared Sir William's belief that Virginia would prosper by benefiting the crown and the mother country.[5] The accord between governor, burgesses, and councillors permitted frequent and vigorous action to spur Virginians toward the traditional economic vision for the colony. Unchecked by internal division, the provincial government expended its energies widely.

Sericulture was the most unrealistic interest which diluted the government's energies after the Restoration. Silk had played that role since the colony's establishment. Crown officials and provincial leaders were aware of the success with silk in Spain's colonial empire, knowing that at one time in the sixteenth century silk raising in Mexico produced nearly as much wealth as the Spanish gold mines. Englishmen saw no reason why Virginia could not succeed as well. The tendency to assume that all countries in the same general latitude were capable of producing identical staples, and the fact that mulberry trees—though the wrong species for silkworms— were indigenous to the province perpetuated the hope. The presence in the colony since the later years of the Interregnum of an experienced Armenian silk grower seemed to remove all impediments to the growth of Virginia sericulture and inspired perhaps the most energetic efforts to produce silk in the colony's history.[6]

Less chimerical than the interest in silk was the post-Restoration fascination with western exploration, although here too realistic justifications for trans-Appalachian expeditions strangely blended with wild imagination as motives for action. Interest in exploration beyond the headwaters existed during Sir William's first administration, and in 1669 under his sponsorship explorations began again. The hope of finding fabulous mines and a short route to the Pacific were two major motives for the expeditions. At this time two dominant views existed regarding the extent of the North American continent. One held that the continent was extremely narrow. Other persons, aware of the implications of Sir Francis Drake's voyage and other explorations of North America's western coast, recognized that a large mass of land separated the two oceans. The latter school, however, still maintained "that the Indian ocean does stretch an arm or bay from California into the continent as far as the Appalachtaen mountains, answerable to the Gulfs of Florida and Mexico on this side." Few doubted that a short route to the Pacific existed.[7]

Another motive for the explorations proved more realistic—the fur trade. The desire to develop the North American fur trade was especially strong after the Restoration as the British merchants gathered in the profits of the Albany fur trade following the capture of New Netherlands in 1664. The chartering of the Hudson Bay Company six years later was a symbol of the rising excitement in England over the furs of the new world.[8]

Englishmen in Virginia caught the enthusiasm. Berkeley in the spring of 1669 planned to lead an expedition of 200 men to find the "East India Sea." Along the way he anticipated discovering silver mines. Heavy rains forced postponement, and Berkeley decided to get permission from Charles before proceeding, since the expedition would undoubtedly impinge upon Spanish claims in the new world. The crown ignored Berkeley's request for a commission, but the following year with Berkeley's blessing John Lederer led three expeditions in an attempt to cross the mountains. Finally, in 1671 a party led by Thomas Bath, Abraham Wood, and Robert Fallam first crossed the Appalachian Mountains. The explorers received a commission to discover "the ebbing and flowing" of the rivers on the western slopes of the mountains and subsequently found a river which was "much like the James River"—actually the New River. Berkeley was elated over the success of the expedition and decided to make the journey himself, and although he was unable to carry out his resolve a final expedition occurred during this period of intense interest in westward exploration in which James Needham and Gabriel Arthur in 1673 reached eastern Tennessee. Modern historians have concluded that Berkeley's promotion of these western explorations ranks him with the governor of New France who sponsored similar activities out of Quebec at this time.[9]

Less fruitful were the exertions of Berkeley's regime intended to translate into legislation and then concrete results the assumption that the promotion of port towns was "Virginia's Cure." In their first session following Sir William's return from England, the burgesses eagerly endorsed the governor's instructions to foster a thriving commercial center at Jamestown as the initial step to promoting numerous towns in the province. Jamestown at the time of the Restoration offered only meager foundations from which to construct a significant urban enclave for the agrarian society. The precise size of the village in 1662 is uncertain. At the end of the period of the Virginia Company's control of the province less than 200 lived there in twenty-two buildings. The town apparently declined thereafter, for at the time of Bacon's Rebellion—after a decade and a half of strenuous effort to improve the site—only a dozen families lived in sixteen or eighteen houses. Anticipating on a smaller and cruder scale the role of Williamsburg in the eighteenth century, Jamestown functioned principally as a gathering place for the government. But the unpromising status of Jamestown did not discourage or deter the assembly. Its legislation in 1662 required each of the seventeen counties to finance and supervise the construction of one house at Jamestown. On the justices of the peace of the respective counties rested the responsibility for securing workers and materials for their county building. Failure to proceed promptly made each justice liable to a fine of one thousand pounds of tobacco. Counties which completed their construction rapidly received the promise of a subsidy of ten thousand pounds of tobacco from revenues collected from a special poll tax levied at the same time. The key section of the legislation made Jamestown the entrepôt for the trade of James City, Charles City, and Surry counties. Confident that the necessary houses and stores would be built within a year, the legislators required the planters in the three counties to bring all tobacco to Jamestown for storage and lading and enjoined all ships receiving tobacco or selling imports to anchor and conduct all transactions at the port.

The assembly anticipated that Jamestown's rapid growth would serve as a pattern for similar town building on the other major rivers. Indeed, the provincial government believed a one-year levy of thirty pounds per poll would suffice for the development of Jamestown and specified that in subsequent years the tax and other measures of the act would apply toward the construction of a central commercial center for the York, Rappahannock, and Potomac rivers in that order.[10]

The opposition of the provincial leadership to new and revived proprietary grants within Virginia was also in some measure part of the larger effort to obtain a diversified economy and an orderly society. After the Restoration Charles II made two grants in Virginia. The first, the Northern Neck grant, encompassed all the territory between the Rappahannock and Potomac rivers and was actually a confirmation of a patent issued in 1649 to seven Royalists. The grant conveyed control over the distribution of land, collection of quitrents, and a variety of semifeudal and political privileges to the proprietors. In 1673 Thomas Lord Culpeper, heir of one of the original Northern Neck proprietors and a future governor of Virginia, along with Lord Arlington, a leading minister in the home government, secured a second grant of land in the Old Dominion. Frequently called the Southern grant, this patent from the king gave Culpeper and Arlington dispensation over all unpatented land in the colony south of the Northern Neck grant. For thirty-one years the two lords were also to receive the quitrents and other dues from all the land south of the Rappahannock River. The Culpeper-Arlington grant included many of the political powers contained in the Northern Neck grant.[11]

The objections to proprietary grants sprang from several considerations. The principal officers in the Jamestown government resented any diminution in their control over public offices and fees for approving, surveying, and recording land grants. All aggressive planters saw in the proprietaries a threat to their land engrossment. The rights conferred upon the courtiers threatened an end to the accumulation of vast acreage by the headright system, for proprietors might prefer to sell land for specie and at hard bargains. Moreover, in contrast to the notoriously lax crown, proprietors could be expected to demand strict payment of quitrents and other semifeudal dues. The proprietary grant of the Northern Neck especially struck at the immediate personal interests of the leading planters. During the Interregnum and the decade following the Restoration, the land between the Potomac and

Rappahannock rivers became the primary area of land speculation.[12]

Opposition to the grants, however, rested on a broader foundation than the immediate and personal economic and political interests of the planters. Berkeley and the other colonial leaders believed that the grants by diminishing the power of the provincial government laid the basis for disobedience, disorder, corruption, and oppression. Debtors and runaway servants frequently fled to Maryland, and it was feared that the Northern Neck grant especially would also serve as a sanctuary for these lawless elements. It was feared as well that the proprietors' political privileges to appoint some officials and to hold special courts would erode still more the precarious authority of the provincial rulers and in the end "put the country in some disorder."[13]

The leaders of Virginia also condemned proprietary grants as a major impediment to economic progress. This was a standard charge leveled at Lord Baltimore's colony, and Maryland did nothing to disprove the belief by its actions regarding the stint and cessation proposals. Leading Virginians had no doubt that the modified proprietary grants within their colony would have the same effect. Planters in Virginia fled to Maryland to avoid restrictions involved in the diversification program. The governor and council believed that the grants "much nearer to us, must (for the same reasons) be much more destructive to the prosperity of this colony." There were apprehensions that the Northern Neck grant would also deprive the provincial government of a large part of the tax of two shillings per hogshead of tobacco exported. Without the proceeds of the tax from that area, remaining receipts would never provide a fund for diversification. These multiple considerations induced the provincial government in 1674 to levy heavy poll taxes for revenue to facilitate negotiations aimed at the sale to the colony of all proprietary interests and the acquisition of a royal charter insuring against a recurrence of the problem.[14]

In addition to its measures promoting silk, towns, and western exploration and opposing the proprietary grants, the government acted also to encourage a wide variety of other staples and enterprises, including flax, hemp, iron, wool cloth, ship building, leather goods, potash, and naval stores. In all of these areas the assembly ignored few methods of stimulating economic innovation. Tax incentives were a part of the provincial government's actions. To discourage artisans from neglecting their trades and turning to planting "merely for the payment of levyes" which consisted of tobacco remittances, for example, the legislature exempted handicraft men and their servants who cultivated no tobacco from all public assessments except for the church. While technically avoiding protective tariffs against goods from England, the legislators sought to accomplish the same end in the case of wine by requiring the sale of Virginia vintages at lower rates than imports. Diversification advocates also erected impediments to the export of raw materials needed for the growth of domestic artisan enterprises. Wool, iron, and leather bore restrictions. In the latter instance, legislators went so far as to embargo the export of hides, placing a large fine of one thousand pounds of tobacco for each hide exported contrary to the law. Berkeley's regime resorted to public enterprise as well by requiring each county to erect a tanning house for the processing of hides and the manufacture of shoes, or suffer an assessment of five thousand pounds of tobacco to be employed, apparently, to help finance the project in cooperating counties. The provincial government also assumed the role of a merchant and attempted to serve as distributor of flax seed. A measure passed immediately after the Restoration required the provincial government to secure a large quantity of flax seed from England and sell it throughout the province by means of designated agents. In 1673 the assembly assigned a similar task to the counties, requiring them at their own expense to procure and distribute one quart of flax and one quart of hemp seed to all tithables.[15]

The reliance upon bounties continued and, despite some

meager increase in the number of rewards for the middling sort, stressed the importance of encouraging men of substantial means whose conspicuous success the smaller planter might then emulate on a smaller scale. A new codification of the province's laws after the Restoration included a statute which provided a large bounty for construction of seagoing vessels. The town legislation similarly included provision for subsidies which only the elite could hope to command. The governor and council received authority to grant ten thousand pounds of tobacco and land to private undertakers who gave promise of establishing themselves as merchants in Jamestown or other paper ports. Indeed, upon the assumption that only the indolence of the common planter prevented him from foregoing tobacco growing and that the effective cure for sloth was chastisement, the assembly passed legislation aimed at furnishing capital and rewards for planters who successfully engaged in large projects out of a fund created by fines on lesser planters who failed to measure up to the minimal diversification efforts required of all.[16]

Regardless of the method employed, the assembly tried to control the smallest details of their schemes' implementation. The law promoting towns prescribed the exact dimensions of the buildings, including even the pitch of the roofs, that the counties were enjoined to build. The legislators also painstakingly spelled out the proper wages of the workmen. Similarly the law creating public-owned tanneries in each county specified the legal price of different types of shoes sold by these enterprises. Other laws laid down the precise distance between the mulberry trees each planter set out. Their attention to minute particulars betrays both the legislators' apprehension that the planters would avoid strict compliance with the spirit of the legislation in the absence of meticulous control and their confidence that exacting regulation by the provincial government was possible.[17]

Ample evidence has survived to show that Virginians did more than pass legislation. The laws succeeded in sparking concrete exertions. Several settlers strove to win the special bounty for silk production. By 1665 Major Thomas Walker of Gloucester County had set out over seventy thousand mulberry trees. The Reverend Mr. Alexander Moray wrote enthusiastically of his progress toward silk production to Sir Robert Moray, a founder of the Royal Society. He reported planting ten thousand mulberry trees. In other areas besides silk production actual essays occurred. The governor and council secured flax seed from Virginia's sometime merchant ally, John Bland, and in accord with the provincial statutes distributed it to the various counties. Several counties complied with the assembly's order to construct tanneries and with the requirements for the construction of facilities at Jamestown.[18]

The governor himself surpassed all others who responded to the provincial diversification legislation. In his private endeavors Berkeley mirrored his government's tendency to engage in a multitude of schemes. Berkeley exaggerated little when he boasted that he "spent his whole tyme and estate in perfecting . . . great and beneficiall Comodityes. . . ." He invested in vineyards and by 1663 announced his intention of sending home a hogshead of wine "as good . . . as ever came out of Italy." He spent personally each year over £500 on wages to skilled workmen whom he had imported. He had no doubts that the efforts would be a great personal advantage to him. The artisans had already assured the governor that in two years he would be able to send to England a shipload of flax, hemp and other products. Berkeley in the mid-1660's sent to England several tons of potash and laid plans for sending two hundred more tons if he received a good price for the initial cargo. Convinced that the province wanted only a few skilled artisans to instruct native Virginians in the production of silk, hemp, and flax, Sir William prepared in the late 1660's to journey to England, France, and Italy to secure artisans. He felt he already knew enough to learn by observation the details and full techniques necessary for successful production of silk and other products. Subsequently Berkeley decided to remain in Virginia, but he urged the crown to recruit workmen from Sicily and Naples and pledged that he or the province would pay the costs.[19]

Some who began eagerly were soon discouraged and abandoned their trials with new commodities. After winds destroyed much of his silk works, leaving him twenty thousand pounds of tobacco in debt, the Reverend Mr. Moray returned to England convinced that Carolina rather than the Old Dominion was the "hopefullest place in the world" for his experiments. But others persisted and imagined that the colony was at last making "a visible entrance" upon its promise. Berkeley thought the progress in potash alone might prove the economic salvation for Virginia, and he calculated that in England 100,000 poor would soon be employed producing soap and glass from Virginia potash. Believing that if the king were only informed of the progress made since the Restoration he would willingly provide large subsidies to spur further development, Virginia's leadership urged Charles II to send commissioners to the colony to verify the achievements.[20]

While a tendency to scatter its strength was the provincial authority's main trait, the government at the same time failed to act vigorously in an area where the colony's potential was greatest. A measure of diversification was achieved in the later colonial period, when planters turned increasingly to the production for export of wheat, corn, shingles, staves, beef, pork, and various other provisions.[21] The markets which largely encouraged this diversification were emerging by the third quarter of the century. The sugar revolution in the West Indies generally and the Barbadoes in particular offered Virginia an opportunity for agricultural reform. Abandoning tobacco in the 1630's owing to competition from the mainland planters, Barbadians experimented with indigo and cotton before turning to sugar after 1640. By the Restoration sugar had supplanted virtually all other crops in all of the English island possessions.[22] The ramifications of this economic venture were felt by islanders and mainland colonists alike. The more efficient production of sugar on larger plantations worked by black slaves squeezed smaller operators and ultimately produced a migration that was a critical aspect of the settlement of early Carolina. The need of the sugar plantations for horses, fish, and lumber, which the islands could not supply, offered to New Englanders a solution to the economic stagnation following the end of the Great Migration. While these consequences are well known, it has been little emphasized that the trends of the West Indies economy created potential markets for Virginia as well. Virginia's ability to produce grains for export had appeared earlier when the initial settlements in Maryland and New England in the 1630's created a market absent during the first two decades of England's first colony's development. The opportunity was fleeting. Marylanders and New Englanders quickly became self-sufficient in these products. The island sugar revolution after mid-century again offered Virginians a market for provisions, horses, cattle, and forest products which proved permanent and expanding. Doubtless the ability of the Chesapeake planters to respond to the demands of the sugar plantations was less than in the 1630's. In the intervening years the strength of the economic commitment to tobacco culture had increased. Virginia and Maryland indebtedness to English merchants grew to an estimated level of £50,000 annually by 1664, riveting the planters to continued tobacco production in order to make remittances.[23]

The problem Virginians faced, however, was not a shift to new economic activity but rather an expansion of domestic production to a signficant surplus for export. In 1650 the colony produced grains and other provisions adequate to its own consumption. The yield per acre of wheat was upwards of twelve quarters, which compared favorably with England. Thus despite the difficulty posed by tobacco indebtedness, Virginians possessed the capacity to respond effectively to the opportunity created by the sugar revolution. By the 1680's the first William Byrd had developed extensive trade connections with the Barbadoes. He exchanged corn, wheat, and pipe staves, and some flour for sugar, rum, and molasses, and was also expanding the wheat trade to southern Europe. But Byrd was not a key figure politically until after Bacon's Rebellion. He belonged not so much to the generation of leaders headed by Berkeley but to the group which attained substantial influence with the decline or death of the new immigrants with strong Royalist identities who surrounded Berkeley.[24]

Berkeley's regime was not ignorant of the sugar revolution, but it failed to grasp fully the significance of the developments for Virginia. That Barbadians were "forced to expend one fifth part of their Merchandise, to provide Victualls for themselves and Servants" seemed evidence of that colony's basic weakness rather than a boon to Virginia. In the third quarter of the century the assembly gave scant encouragement to the promising beginnings of this intercolonial trade. Perhaps the provincial leadership's adherence to traditional colonial mercantile doctrine explains this curious passivity of a government which otherwise lavished designs for economic development upon the province. Both Berkeley and his chief supporters took for granted that a colony's prosperity depended upon its being "instrumentall to the Wealth, and Glory" of the mother country generally and the crown particularly. The provincial councillors could boast that the governor spent "most of his time and thoughts in the contemplation of your Majesty's Interests and in Contriving which way (of all offered) he may be most Servicable," because they had no doubt that Virginia's well-being lay in becoming a greater "Advantage" to England.[25] Conventional colonial mercantile doctrine taught, and the Royalist attachments of the elite dominated by the new immigrants reinforced, this view of the true interest of colonies. If somewhat vaguely, articulate Virginians described the emerging empire as one "nation" in which all parts thrived by serving the common good. A colony in the empire, like an individual in a society and an appendage of a physical organism, prospers by providing sustenance to the central body. Their concern riveted upon serving England *directly,* the provincial government under Berkeley was not fully sensitive to possibilities of benefiting its colony and the mother

country indirectly by fostering commerce with the other con-
stituent members of the empire.

The government intervention into the provincial economy
of Berkeley's regime, then, was paradoxically both too extensive and too limited. Unwittingly the government sought to
force the planters into economic endeavors with little or no
potential but offered little incentives where progress was
possible.

Its spasmodic nature magnified still more the disruptive
impact of the provincial government's involvement in the
economy. The governor, council, and burgesses continuously
tinkered but rarely pursued any specific scheme without interruption. The assembly passed, then five years later repealed,
tax exemptions for potential artisans. When still later the legislature reinstituted the original tax incentive, its effect was
doubtless weakened by the earlier inconsistency of the government.[26] Just prior to the abortive tobacco cessation design in
1667, the assembly repealed virtually all direct diversification
legislation only to reintroduce the statutes in the following
years. The conventional justification for repeal was that a
statute was no longer necessary after its immediate effective-
ness in stimulating a few successful experiments and demon-
strating the lucrativeness of a new staple. The planter would
pursue the larger interest of the colony if in doing so he knew
he would profit individually. The assembly decided that a
legislative scheme had shown the compatibility between the
public and private welfare only to conclude subsequently that
another brief demonstration was needed. The need for indefi-
nite government support of new economic enterprise was a
prospect which the provincial government was loath to recog-
nize. Given the meager revenue available to the provincial
government, admission of the necessity of continuous subsidy
would have been tantamount to conceding the assembly's inability to lead in the realization of the traditional economic
vision.

Berkeley's regime was not entirely reponsible for its sporadic behavior, for circumstances over which it had little con-

trol created extraordinary demands for taxation. The costly struggle to annul the crown's proprietary grants within Virginia was a major factor depleting the provincial government's resources. Even before this drain upon the revenue resources, the Dutch Wars compelled the provincial government to divert taxes to defense. The Second Dutch War led to heavy levies to build a major fortification, and royal commands needlessly increased the cost of defense works by requiring the colony to abandon well-advanced construction at Jamestown and to locate a fort at Point Comfort. Tragically, the expense in the end went for nothing, for as both Berkeley and Thomas Ludwell predicted, the Point Comfort site lacked an adequate foundation for fortifications and could not command the entrance to the Bay without a larger ordnance than the colony possessed. The temporary repeal of many diversification statutes in 1666 was partly a consequence of the heavy poll tax imposed the previous year to finance erection of this fort and other defense needs.[27]

In the Third Dutch War as in the Second, the Dutch inflicted damaging blows on the Chesapeake tobacco ships. Exaggerated fears that the Dutch would go beyond commerce raids and retaliate against England's earlier conquest of New Netherlands by capturing Virginia induced Berkeley's government to raise "20 Regiments of foote and as many troops of horse," even though the government could arm only every tenth man.[28]

Obviously, the problems of war and proprietors created obstacles to steady support by government of the more promising economic potentials. Yet in addition to these uncontrolled depletions of the provincial revenues, a fundamental cause for the assembly's disinclination to support specific new endeavors over a long period of time without interruption was the economic mind which the legislators brought to the task of stimulating economic innovation. The actions of the provincial government rested upon a pyramid of assumptions. The tendency to encourage only briefly a multitude of enterprises grew out of the belief that the example of even minor success would cause wholesale and voluntary pursuit of a new economic endeavor. This conviction rested upon the assumption that a lack of will or "industry" rather than basic economic forces was the greatest obstacle which the colony's leadership had to overcome, an opinion, finally, which was a logical conclusion from the basic premise of the extraordinary fecundity of the land and its proclivity to yield its fertility to the art of the industrious.

The failure of Berkeley's provincial government to formulate a true economic plan which evaluated resources objectively, delineated stages of development, fixed interim goals, and set priorities was also an inevitable consequence of the nature of seventeenth-century colonial government establishments and the legacy of the Elizabethan approach to economic regulation. There did not exist even the most rudimentary government bureaucracy. England itself scarcely possessed one. Political leadership in the colony was a distinctly part-time affair. The governor himself was essentially a planter and only secondarily a public official in terms of the amount of time expended on various activities. Moreover, no example of government economic planning existed for the colonials to copy. Domestic economic regulation in England no longer occurred on a significant scale. The heritage of the Elizabethan approach to economic management of the state was one of ad hoc responses to immediate problems rather than the formulation of coherent policies.[29]

Even had Berkeley's regime possessed the capacity to evaluate the potentials of the colony more accurately and to apply economic regulation more efficiently, it is doubtful that the provincial government could have drastically modified the one-crop tobacco economy. The forces discouraging economic innovation—scarcity of skilled labor, planter indebtedness, a dearth of investment capital, the effects of war and natural disasters, the drain on government revenue of the campaign against proprietary grants—were formidable obstacles indeed. Yet modest alterations in the pattern of Virginia's economy might have occurred under more realistic leadership. During

Berkeley's regime exaggerated confidence in the potential of the colony and the abilities of government caused actions which in fact disrupted rather than spurred the economy.

The decade and a half of government's immoderate, frequently misdirected, and sporadic economic intervention ended with the Indian War in 1675 and Bacon's Rebellion in the following year. The rebellion seemed tragically incongruous at the time. In June 1676 William Sherwood marveled that the planters could condemn a governor who for thirty-four years sought the welfare of the province. From the vantage point of three decades after the event, Robert Beverley, the historian, concluded that it was no easy task to discover why the people overthrew a government led by a man who dedicated "his whole life and Estate" to the welfare of Virginia.[30] Until recently, most modern historians solved the paradox by denying the validity of Berkeley's image presented by his peers and arguing that in fact Sir William's regime exploited the colony. The most recent and thorough scholar of Bacon's Rebellion has returned to the premise of Beverley and Sherwood. Like them, Wilcomb E. Washburn holds that the problem is to explain the upheaval in the absence of significant grievances against Sir William. Aware that political discontent and violence do not invariably erupt in direct proportion to the amount of actual oppression, and skeptical of earlier historians' assumption that movements of the "people" are always justified, Washburn advances to the conclusion that the rebellion resulted largely from a dispute over the method of handling the Indian War, which in turn rested on conflicting attitudes toward the Indians and their right to the land desired by the English. Despite efforts of Berkeley to limit and control expansion, the "rebellious frontiersmen" pushed into land belonging to the Indians. The pressure of English expansion in Virginia and Maryland provoked Indian raids. The frontiersmen, motivated by both fear and contempt of the Indians and covetous of their land, made no distinction between Indians who were hostile and those at peace with

Virginia and could not comprehend Berkeley's policy, which rested on discrimination between the two classes of Indians. Nor were the settlers concerned, as was Berkeley, with justice for the Indians. When the governor decided to erect forts along the frontier for defensive purposes only, neglected to conduct offensive action, and, fearing attacks on Indian allies, forbade voluntary marches against the natives, the frontiersmen eagerly accepted the false charges of malcontents that Berkeley and his clique would sacrifice the settlers to preserve the profits allegedly garnered from the Indian trade.[31]

Few will dispute Wilcomb Washburn's thesis that the dispute over Indian war policy was the essential spark of rebellion in 1676. The issue, however, was inadequate to draw large numbers of the settlers into revolt or to sustain the rebellion. The de-emphasis of social and political grievances—the powder keg for the spark to ignite—distorts the causes of the rebellion. The colonists rebelled against Berkeley's Indian policy because they were already disenchanted with his government. The dispute over Indian policy was the last straw.[32]

The irony of the rebellion is that many of the grievances which provided the essential background for the revolt sprang from the provincial government's overly strenuous attempt to benefit the province. Had Berkeley and his clique been motivated by petty concerns for personal profit, as Bacon charged, it is unlikely that the rebellion would have taken place. Governors who came after Berkeley on occasions engaged in corrupt practices and oppression for personal profit and tried to implement a policy which did not, like Berkeley's, appear to integrate the interests of crown and colony. As a result, these governors found their efforts checked by the burgesses. Berkeley's benevolent program won the support of the political elite, and thus was implemented. The exploitative plans of later governors angered assemblies but seldom went into effect, and rarely touched the people directly. Berkeley's administration could be oppressive precisely because his intent was benevolent. In this sense Beverley was wrong in his assumption that the upheaval occurred in spite of Berkeley's paternal government. The conflict was in part a consequence of an almost fanatic campaign of the provincial government to benefit the province.

Outside of the assembly and provincial leadership, opposition to Berkeley's ambitious designs existed throughout his second administration as governor. Francis Moryson informed Lord Clarendon in 1665 that the levy to promote the growth of Jamestown and other ports drove large numbers of settlers from the colony. The western explorations also produced discontent. Lederer returned from his expeditions in 1670 to receive "Affronts and Reproaches" from the people rather than the expected praise. Earlier, when food ran short and further exploration seemed fruitless, most of his party deserted him and returned to the tidewater. Lederer pushed on. To cover their own lack of perseverance, those who deserted him allegedly spread rumors to discredit the explorer and found that the people were easily persuaded that "the Publick Levy of that year, went all to the expence of his Vagaries." The resentment caused Lederer to flee to Maryland.[33]

Although initially Bacon ignored all issues but the governor's Indian policy, the rebel soon found it useful to tap the latent political and social discontents of the common planters. When Berkeley revoked Bacon's carte blanche commission to lead forces against all Indians, granted under duress during the June assembly, and proceeded to recruit a force of his own to restore government's authority, Bacon responded by elevating to a central position the social and political grievances of the country. Bacon's Declaration of the People and his Manifesto expressed the rebel's calculated assessment of the charges which would provoke a response in his favor among the people.

Heading the list of grievances exploited by Bacon were the government's projects to develop the province's economy. Significantly, Bacon did not censure Berkeley for pursuing the traditional vision but for having been diverted by corruption from obtaining it. In his Manifesto Bacon urged all to "consider wither any Public work for our safety and defence or for the Advancement & progress of Trade, Liberall Arts or Sciences is here extant in any way adequate to our vast charge." It should be obvious to all, the rebel argued, "what spounges have suckt up the Publique Treasure and . . . [how] it hath bin privately contrived away by unworthy Favourites and Juggling Parasites whose tottering Fortunes have bin repaired & supported at the Publique charge. . . ." The first two charges in the Declaration of the People against Berkeley and his "wicked and pernitious Councillors" condemned them "for having upon specious pretences of Publick works raised unjust Taxes upon the Commonalty for the advancement of private Favorites and other Sinnister ends but noe visible effects in any measure adequate." Secondly, the Declaration asserted that, during his long administration, Berkeley had not "in any measure advanced this hopeful Colony either by Fortifications, Townes, or Trade."[34]

To the extent then that Bacon correctly judged the discontents of the planters, his Declaration and Manifesto suggest that the resentment against the provincial government's schemes for economic improvement did not emanate from opposition to government economic intervention per se or from skepticism regarding the vision Berkeley had pursued, but arose out of the conviction that the projects were screens for defrauding the public.

The county grievances submitted in 1677 upon the invitation of the royal commissioners dispatched to determine the causes of the rebellion carry the same implication. Isle of Wight County condemned "The great Quantityes of Tobacco levyed for Building Houses of publick use and reception at James Town, which were not habitable, but fell downe before the Finishing them." Surry County similarly resented "That great quantityes of tobacco were levied upon the poore inhabitants of this Collony for the building of houses att James City, which were not habitable by reason they were not finished." Rappahannock, Lancaster, and York counties each expressed resentment at the effort to establish the capital of the province at Jamestown rather than at a location more convenient to them. In other instances the county grievances reveal that the planters had little or no knowledge of the purposes of the extraordinary levies. Rappahannock County maintained that the people were "in the dark and still ignorant what advantage occures to them" by the heavy taxes.[35]

The people of Charles City County focused their complaints on Edward Hill, Jr., who with his father had been instrumental in diversification efforts. During the rebellion a staunch adherent of the governor's party, Hill became the "most hated person of all the County where hee lives, and that now without Cause too." Among the charges leveled at Hill, and which apparently accounted for the enmity of the people, was the allegation that he had failed to carry out projects for which he received substantial sums of tax money. The grievances condemned him for receiving large amounts of tobacco to construct forts which were never finished. The grievances also alleged that Hill embezzled "great quantities of tobacco . . . raised on us his majesty's poore subjects . . . [for] worke houses, store houses, & other houses for the propogating & encouragement of handycraft, and manufacture which were by our Burgesses (to our great charge and burden by their longe & frequent sitting) invested & proposed. . . ." Notwithstanding the high taxes, the grievance continued, the projects were soon abandoned. The only result of the levies was the "particular profit of the undertakers who as is usual in such cases were large rewarded for thus defrauding us."[36]

The charges of corruption and negligence were for the most part unfounded. But the planters' bewilderment over the purposes of taxation, and their misconception that a dishonest elite had siphoned into its own pockets the proceeds of the tax revenues for diversification, could grow unchecked because the provincial leadership between the Restoration and the rebellion made no attempt to explain and justify their policies to the ordinary planters who were to be the partial beneficiaries. In contrast, as we shall see, to their successors, Berkeley's government established no familiar relationship with the bulk of the planters. As leaders they expected automatic obedience and viewed as a species of insubordination bordering upon treason any "itching desire . . . to pry into the secretts of the grand Assembly of the Country, and to take uppon them to Caluminate and Censure the same. . . ." Matching its concern for improving the colonial society and economy was the leadership's conviction that they acted as trustees responsible for the welfare of society but not accountable to the people. Leadership's actions betrayed its assumption that the task of authority was to command rather than persuade most members of society to serve the common good. Governor, council and burgesses could imagine no reason to seek approval of their actions since they had "this Axiom firmly fix't in them, that never any Community of people had good done to them, but against their Wills."[37]

Among the numerous circumstances which resulted in Bacon's Rebellion not the least important, then, was this conception of the provincial leadership surrounding Berkeley regarding the proper roles of people and rulers. The assumption that the people were incapable of comprehending the general good or even their own particular best interests inhibited the Berkeley regime from developing a style of leadership suitable to the central political reality of Virginia: the citizenry lacked the deferential inclinations essential for the success of rule by a prescriptive style. The failure of provincial leadership between 1650 and the rebellion to cultivate the consent of the colonists allowed distrust of leadership to emerge among a people unconditioned to assume that rulers were invariably wise. The absence of a more persuasive style by the provincial authorities was a situation ready-made for the skills of a demagogue like Bacon who had no compunction about going to the people with petitions and emotional rhetoric. The weakened position of the provincial ruling class in conjunction with the unfilled expectations of the common planters contributed to the emergence of this situation suitable for exploitation by Bacon.

Because most planters were stymied in their own personal

expectations for economic advance and a more traditional, less rigorous work routine, they were undoubtedly particularly susceptible to Bacon's simplistic explanations for the causes of their frustration. Ignoring the complex circumstances which created the tobacco depression and reduced upward economic mobility, Bacon singled out a few individuals as the single cause of the planters' difficulties. He drew backing by substituting for a mystifying complex of economic circumstances clear and vulnerable targets for planter frustrations. Initially the Indians alone served as the receptacle for the diverted hostility of the planters, but in the course of the rebellion Bacon skillfully exhibited the leading members of Berkeley's regime as the chief impediments to the checked ambitions of the settlers. This displacement of aggression onto the provincial leadership was possible, for that group did not possess a fully developed status of legitimacy. The absence of deferential attitudes among the common planters freed them when spurred by Bacon to challenge the provincial rulers without experiencing strong sentiments of guilt.

In summary, by increasing tax burdens and by disrupting the already depressed economy, the provincial government's aggressive economic intervention had contributed to the discontent which sustained, if it did not cause, Bacon's Rebellion. But contributing even more to the escalation of conflict into widespread rebellion was the provincial leaders' incapacity, produced by their basic assumptions about the nature of the art of ruling, to improvise a style of leadership appropriate to the peculiar weaknesses of authority and the undisciplined and frustrated citizenry of Virginia. The arbitrariness in the presentation more than the impracticality of the provincial government's economic schemes alienated a class of common planters already predisposed to hostility toward authority owing to their unfulfilled expectations of personal worldly success and content in the new world. The style as well as the intensity of the government's economic benevolence contributed to its downfall.

In the aftermath of the rebellion the planters signified

that discontent with the method of Berkeley's rule was central to the outbreak of the rebellion. Among the complaints submitted to the royal commissioners were statements which imply that the ordinary planters desired not so much a change in rulers but a different style of leadership. Though incapable of elevating their notions of how governments should relate to the people to an abstract level of political theory, the planters' specific laments amounted to a rejection of the concept that the ruled should unquestionably obey the will of the authority. The larger meaning of the ill-phrased and concrete grievances was that rulers gained legitimacy when their measures met the interests of the people and that leadership had an obligation to demonstrate clearly to their constituencies the utility and wisdom of public policies. The planters did not want in the future to remain "in the dark and . . . ignorant [of] what advantage occures to them by [the] great assessments. . . ." They desired "free libertie to hier and see evrie particular for what it is raised," and they asserted that their willingness to comply with the demands of government would come only after the benefits "plainly appear."[38]

These complaints lacked abstract rhetoric. They nonetheless approached the concept which more articulate Virginians a century later would label actual representation, for the grievances stipulated that the ruled must consent not only to their rulers but also to the policies formed by leaders. The grievances stopped short of endorsing the extreme version of actual representation in which the role of the people is to initiate policies which rulers then execute as mere servants. Yet the demand that leaders justify their measures to the people and obtain their tacit consent was a clear repudiation of the view of Berkeley and his supporters that the art of government consisted in doing good to the members of society "against their Wills."[39] In the years following the rebellion, at least the rudimentary beginnings of this new style of leadership appeared, and the continued effort to achieve diversification was a central impetus to the change.

III

Persuasion: 1676-1710

Contributing to the animosity toward provincial leadership which erupted in 1676 had been a style of leadership which sought to prescribe the economic behavior of ordinary planters, who were assumed lacking in ability to judge the interests of the colony. The ruling class at the provincial level had been largely united behind Governor Berkeley in this economic program. Following the rebellion, the provincial elite divided on economic policy between those who urged continued radical experimentation and rapid innovation in the face of the crown's deepening hostility and those who searched for more modest economic schemes which would be somehow compatible with diversification of the tobacco economy and the crown's interest in expanding tobacco revenue.

The fractured ruling class lost little of Sir William's interest in tobacco controls and diversification, yet a new tone of leadership developed. Especially the advocates of drastic economic change sought to stimulate public support for their schemes. Without design, provincial leadership moved toward a style of leadership which involved a somewhat greater participation and consent of the governed. Simultaneously, the faction of the elite most involved in the new techniques of leadership to stimulate proper socioeconomic behavior by the people altered as well a central aspect of the rationale for diversification. Increasingly, economic innovation was now offered as the route toward provincial autonomy rather than an expression of the integrated interests of crown and colony.

5

THE CONSEQUENCES OF PERSUASION

Bacon's Rebellion had opposite influences on the attitudes of provincial leadership and the crown toward the Virginia economy. The upheaval sustained the Virginians' interest, but accelerated the home government's disinterest, in energetic public schemes aimed at altering the colony's economic structure. A fundamental cause for the conflict between the Stuart government and the Virginia assembly prior to the Glorious Revolution was the growing divergence in views regarding the desirability of altering the colony's economy.

Possibly no colonial event before the Stamp Act riots had a greater impact upon the British court than Bacon's Rebellion. Wild rumors circulated in England through the summer and fall of 1676. In October a newsletter proclaimed that Bacon "plays the absolute master" and that Berkeley had fled to Nevis. Reports told of Bacon carrying the revolt into the neighboring provinces. Some feared the conflagration might spread as far as New England.[1] Combined with the disruption in trade produced throughout English North America by the Indian wars, the revolt caused a sharp decline in the crown's customs revenue. Apparently the loss of colonial revenues was the last straw which compelled Charles to convene a Parliament against his will.[2]

In addition to the loss of customs revenue, the crown spent a large sum on the troops sent to rescue Berkeley's government. The estimates for the cost of the expedition to Virginia for one year exceeded £35,000, and the actual cost far surpassed the estimates. In the Parliament session which met in February 1677, Sir John Ernley asserted that the revolt had already cost the crown over £100,000, a sum equal to the amount Louis XIV gave Charles in early 1676 in return for proroguing Parliament. Charles himself claimed a loss of over £200,000 owing to the uprising in the Old Dominion.[3]

Above all else, the crown wished to prevent a similar upheaval in the future and fashioned its actions toward Virginia to that end. Between 1676 and 1689 the home government sought to eliminate the conditions which it imagined had caused the overthrow of royal authority in Virginia, the disruption of the tobacco trade, and the decrease in revenue from that commerce.

The crown did not doubt that it understood the origins of the violence. The rebellion from the perspective of London was a protest against the excessively vigorous and expensive government of Sir William's General Assembly. This interpretation of the revolt appeared early and remained unshaken until and after the Glorious Revolution. The descriptions of Bacon's movement, whether sympathetic or hostile, contained much to encourage this conclusion. Berkeley's enemies consistently, and even his supporters occasionally, observed that the provincial authority lacked popular support. There was even agreement among the antagonists in 1676 that social and economic grievances produced the widespread hostility, though to the governor's adherents the complaints were imaginary contrivances of a few malcontents rather than legitimate causes for discontent. Provincial loyalist and rebel also concurred that the activist assembly was the prime target of the people's wrath. Though he denied just grievances existed, Berkeley himself confessed that the rebellion was "not against any particular Person but the whole Assembly. . . ." Bacon pictured the assembly as a tool in the hands of a corrupt clique which used their power "to play a Booty game. . . ."[4]

Especially influential in shaping the crown's conclusions regarding the rebellion were the letters of Giles Bland, a provincial customs collector who clashed with Berkeley over the enforcement of the Navigation Acts and died at the end of a rope in 1676 for his support of Bacon. Bland's connections in the home government, most notably, his father-in-law, Thomas Povey, offered him a channel of communications to the English court which he did not hesitate to exploit. Underscoring the connection between the upheaval and revenue of which the crown was painfully aware in 1676, Bland argued that a major cause of discontent was the high poll taxes occasioned by the energetic assembly meeting in frequent and lengthy sessions. Arguing explicitly for a reduction in the number of assembly sessions and burgesses' salaries, Bland's reports implied that political stability, normal conditions in the tobacco trade, and an increase in customs revenue would accompany an end to a decade and a half of activist provincial government which all too often exercised its power to the benefit of a favored clique.[5]

Diagnosis of the rebellion and prescriptions for the future health of Virginia stressed other factors. Bland, for example, also suggested that a meaningful guarantee from the crown that the colonists enjoyed all rights of Englishmen would promote political stability. Others pointed to the Navigation Acts as a contributing cause of the rebellion, but the indictment of assertive legislatures captured the attention of Charles II and his advisers. At this same time, the obstreperous behavior of Parliament at home and the pretensions of little parliaments throughout the empire plagued the crown. The opposition to James was building toward the exclusion crisis of the early 1680's. The General Court of Massachusetts refused to cooperate with the home government's inquiries into the state of affairs in New England, and the assembly of Jamaica at this time "flew high & were in a fair way of treading . . . in the steps of New England."[6] Quite naturally, the crown was easily persuaded that the root of the trouble in Virginia was identical to the source of the crown's difficulties elsewhere—an excess of representative government.

Believing that its actions would appease the planters' resentment against overactive government as well as protect royal prerogative in the colony, the crown between 1676 and 1689 struggled to curtail the energy and influence of the Virginia assembly and particularly the House of Burgesses. The crown sought to replace the vigorous government of Berkeley's era with a regime in which assemblies met infrequently while the governor and council presided over a passive government, enforced the acts of trade, and left the planters free to produce tobacco. While the Stuarts' Lords of Trade and governors in the decade and a half before the Glorious Revolution desired more vigorous government in Virginia in one area—customs collection—on the whole they aimed at reducing the level of public energy. An increase in the power of the prerogative was designed to decrease the range of the provincial government's actions.

The crown's actions in Virginia were representative of its entire colonial attitude in the latter reign of Charles II and after the succession of James II. For roughly fifteen years before the coming of William and Mary, the crown attempted to reduce local autonomy, achieve more centralized direction, and reduce the role of representative government in the empire. Not until George III's ministers tightened the reins of empire during and after the French and Indian War did colonial assemblies experience a comparable threat. The plantation duty of 1673 and the collectors appointed to enforce it were the first major efforts of Charles to crack down on the loose colonial administration. The creation of the Lords of Trade in 1675 provided a committee which vigorously set to work to improve the enforcement of the Navigation Acts. In 1676 Edward Randolph began his infamous career of harassment in the colonies, with particular, but by no means exclusive, emphasis on New England. Four years later William Blathwayt became the first Surveyor and Auditor General of

Plantation Revenues. William Dyer in 1683 took up his duties as the first Surveyor General of the Customs. Since proprietary and chartered colonies were allegedly the worst offenders against the Navigation Acts, the crown initiated or seriously considered quo warranto proceedings against all of them. The Dominion of New England was the final achievement of the militant colonial policy initiated under Charles and completed by James.[7]

The crown's colonial administration was vigorous in those years. The government's goal, however, was narrower than either the designs for the empire formulated immediately after the Restoration or the plans of the Board of Trade after 1696. The policy makers both in the early 1660's and at the turn of the century believed in colonial experimentation and long-range development. The diversification schemes for Virginia worked out in London in 1662 illustrate the home government's colonial outlook after the return of Charles II to the throne. The naval stores program of the Board of Trade is the prime example of the same general attitude after 1696. If the hopes were chimerical, they nonetheless symbolized the broad concept of empire entertained in both periods. But the Lords of Trade had no similar program. Their interest was administrative reform which would improve the operation of the Navigation Acts and consequently increase the customs revenue. The Lords wanted wider implementation of a more circumscribed concept of empire and lacked interest in promoting innovation in the economic development of the plantations.

The crown embarked on its new colonial policy hesitantly, however, at least as far as Virginia was concerned. The mother country's effort to quiet the energy of the Virginia assembly began modestly and increased only when the burgesses resisted even minor reductions in their privileges and refused to cooperate with the crown's effort to redress other grievances of the planters immediately after Bacon's Rebellion. Pending an extensive inquiry into the causes of the rebellion by the special commission dispatched with troops to aid Berkeley, Charles II resolved that the burgesses should immediately agree to a reduction in their per diem salaries, a limitation of fourteen days on assembly sessions, the abolition of the custom of annual meetings which prevailed during much of Berkeley's second administration in favor of sessions every other year, and new elections for each assembly.[8]

Commissioners Sir John Berry, Francis Moryson, and Herbert Jeffreys, who arrived in 1677 with instructions to obtain these changes from the assembly, found the representatives unwilling to yield on any but the question of salary. Even here the burgesses acted only under pressure and did not cut their income as much as the commission desired. This assembly sitting at Green Springs also refused to endorse the crown's appeasement of Bacon's followers. The home government in 1676 imagined that pardon of all but Bacon himself was a necessary tactic to end the rebellion, and the commissioners, arriving after the collapse of the revolt, insisted upon the need of a universal pardon to prevent another outbreak of violence. Berkeley's concern that he and his supporters during the time of troubles receive just compensation for damages at the hands of the rebels and his belief that "too much lenity would incline the rabble to a new rebellion," caused him to issue along with the king's pardon a proclamation exempting leading rebels and sanctioning suits against individuals who had plundered or destroyed loyalist property. The burgesses in 1677 backed Berkeley and enacted legislation which facilitated damage suits, placed fines on rebels, and confiscated for treason the estates of Bacon's principal followers. Far from fulfilling the hope that the representatives would be a "healing Assembly," in the view of the commission they "made a Statute of Remembrance, to last and intayle trouble from one Generation to another."[9] Nor did the Green Springs assembly enhance the Stuarts' opinion of representative bodies by its reaction to the commission's attempt to collect and redress the grievances behind the revolt. The lower house made short shrift of the county petitions of grievances presented after the revolt and in at least one instance placed a heavy fine on the petitioners for their impertinence. The commissioners on the basis of their own canvass for grievances in the several counties recommended a reform in the tax structure of the province, including the substitution of taxes computed on either the value or quantity of land for the levies by the poll. This grievance the burgesses also spurned.[10]

To Berry, Moryson, and Jeffreys the assembly appeared bent on keeping the colony in turmoil by obstructing their pacifying mission in every way possible. The Green Springs session ended in early April without submitting a report on confiscations and the general proceedings to the royal agents. Berry and Moryson later demanded the lower house records from the clerk, Robert Beverley. The two commissioners showed Beverley the portion of their royal order which authorized them to examine the assembly's records and, when he refused to surrender the documents, took the papers by force. When the assembly met again in October 1677, the lower house promptly condemned the two commissioners, who along with Governor Berkeley had since left for England. Jeffreys, now serving as lieutenant governor, was embarrassed when he discovered that his companions had neglected to leave a copy of their instructions. He could not prove that the commission had the authority to demand copies of the assembly's journals. The burgesses in turn asserted that they doubted the king could grant such power to his agents.[11]

However justified the burgesses' demand for compensation of sufferers at the hands of Bacon, or accurate their contention that no legitimate grievances existed, their posture toward the commission in 1677 only confirmed the crown in its opinion that the assembly had been responsible for the rebellion in the first place and persuaded Charles' ministry that a more thorough retrenchment of the assembly's role in provincial politics was needed. In the fall of 1678 the Privy Council referred the lower house's protest regarding the seizure of its records to the Lords of Trade and instructed them to consider the steps necessary to bring the Virginia assembly under proper control by the crown.[12]

By the end of 1679 a "scheme" for the regulation of Virginia appeared in the crown's instructions to the new Virginia governor, Thomas, Lord Culpeper. The immediate concern of the crown was to settle the disputes which had arisen in the wake of Bacon's Rebellion. The crown formulated an "Act of Oblivion" and required Culpeper to secure the assembly's approval of the measure. The bill recognized the equity and necessity of some of Berkeley's actions by exempting from royal pardon many of the leading rebels named in Berkeley's supplementary proclamation and in the laws of the Green Springs assembly; but on the crucial point of the right of loyalists to sue for recovery of goods plundered by the rebels, the crown abandoned the governor and his supporters. The law brought to Virginia by Culpeper forbade further prosecutions relating to destruction or seizure of property by rebels. The measure did permit loyalists to sue for recovery of specific goods in the actual possession of other persons, but this salvo was small comfort to the loyalists. The provision was similar to the commission's initial position against which Governor Berkeley fought so bitterly. If the crown's solution lacked justice for the leading supporters of the governor, it represented in the crown's view the only practical answer to a vexing problem.[13]

Hoping that the measure would restore harmony in the tobacco colony, the Lords of Trade then formulated instructions for Culpeper to ward off future discontent. The crown ordered that except on extraordinary occasions the General Assembly convene only with the home government's consent to consider only legislation previously reviewed and approved by the crown. In effect, these instructions extended the principle of Poyning's Law for Ireland to Virginia.[14]

Probably the crown did not fully expect to implement these severe restrictions, which aimed at fusing the interests of prerogative and people by paring the scope of the assembly's actions. Charles II ordered Culpeper to withhold official announcement of the instruction for six months after arriving in the province and before this deadline withdrew the policy. In the interval Culpeper was to obtain the assembly's approval of a permanent revenue measure drafted in England. The statute included three impositions: two shillings per hogshead exported from Virginia, six pence for every person transported to the colony, and a duty of three pounds of shot or one shilling and threepence per ton on all incoming vessels. The taxes were not innovations, nor strictly speaking was the permanent nature of the act a novelty, for earlier laws imposing the two-shilling tax contained no limitations clause. A striking difference about the measure drawn up in England was that the revenues collected went *"to the kings most excellent majestie,* his heires and successors forever, to and for the better support of the government of . . . Virginia." Early revenue laws kept the power of expenditure of the revenue in the hands of the assembly. The earlier taxes were perpetual, but frequent assembly sessions were necessary to appropriate the revenue collected. The crown hoped that the new revenue proposal would, in general, diminish the power of the assembly and, in particular reduce both the number of legislative sessions and the opportunity for agitation for economic diversification. The harsher limitations on the assembly in Culpeper's instructions undoubtedly were meant to serve the purpose which they in fact did—a threat to quicken passage of the more realistic reform.[15]

Culpeper in June 1680 convened his first assembly for the purpose of securing approval of the measures formulated in England. By a combination of threats, including the extension of Poyning's Law to Virginia, and concessions, he secured approval of the statute of pardon and the permanent revenue bill.[16] The first measure had the effect desired by the crown, for most animosities engendered by the rebellion soon evaporated. Disputes arising out of the revolt were infrequent in the 1680's, a situation in sharp contrast to Leisler's Rebellion in New York in 1689, which precipitated a generation of conflict and hatred between the rebel faction and the anti-Leislerians.[17]

The passage of the revenue act was a major achievement, for at no other time before the American Revolution did the crown persuade a colonial assembly on the mainland to grant a permanent and independent revenue. Unlike the act of oblivion, however, the revenue statute's success was qualified. The two-shilling tax on exported tobacco barely covered the normal expense of the provincial government. Any problem which required extra expenditures necessitated the calling of the assembly. Yet the crown did cut down on the number of sessions after 1680. During Berkeley's administration the legislature usually met at least once a year. From the passage of the permanent revenue bill in the summer of 1680 until the Glorious Revolution, only six sessions were held.[18]

Especially did the crown seek to reduce the frequency of sessions and circumscribe the role of the assembly in these various ways in order to avoid new ventures at economic meddling. The opposition to tobacco production curbs deepened after 1676, and the passive support of other diversification designs which prevailed from the middle 1660's to the Rebellion turned to hostility. The elimination in 1685 of the traditional instructions to Virginia governors to promote the growth of new staple commodities was the formal confirmation of the position which the crown and its governors embraced after Berkeley's administration. The home government did not determine that the economic transformation was impossible. It no longer seemed desirable either for the interests of the royal revenues or the common planters, who the crown assumed had in Bacon's Rebellion repudiated Berkeley's activist government.

The crown's attempts to constrict the function of the assembly began, however, at a time when the need for forceful and creative economic intervention by the government seemed obvious to the political heirs of Berkeley's regime. Drought combined with the turmoil of Bacon's Rebellion led to short crops and a slender increase in price, but the modest improvement only encouraged overproduction in subsequent years. By 1679 the crop was perhaps triple the normal yield, and the planters found no buyers for ten thousand hogsheads of their tobacco.[19] Demands for decisive government action accompanied the depression. The call for a revival of the dynamic government of Berkeley's era emanated as well from a deepening concern for the political and social decay of the colony's society. The Rebellion merely strengthened in some minds the opinion that the economic structure of Virginia was ill suited for the preservation of deferential habits toward legitimate authority.[20]

Spearheading the effort to sustain Berkeley's activist tradition was Robert Beverley, a transitional figure between the new immigrants of mid-century and their sons who inherited power fully in the late 1680's and 1690's. Though he headed after 1676 the faction which identified most closely with Berkeley's policies, he had not been a conspicuous member of Sir William's clique before the Rebellion. Beverley arrived in Virginia in 1663 after most of the new immigrants. He came from a social background which differed from the origins of the educated and relatively cultured sons of England's merchant families and does not appear to have been attached to the Royalist cause. His political enemies regarded him as a man of "mean Parts" whose wealth had tainted origins. The Rebellion created conditions suitable for the rise of Beverley. He supported Berkeley zealously and was conspicuously successful in leading parties against the rebels in the latter stages of the conflict. His capture of Bacon's lieutenant, Thomas Hansford, helped break the back of the uprising. If his critics' view is credible, Beverley, in contrast to most of Berkeley's adherents, profited largely from the revolt as he plundered "without distinction of honest men's estates from others. . . ." Allegedly he complained that "the Rebellion ended too soone for his purpose." His military achievements and the increment in his wealth during the revolt moved him from a marginal to a prominent position in provincial politics. As clerk of the House of Burgesses elected after the Rebellion, Beverley refused in 1677 to surrender records to the commissioners voluntarily, and his adamant stand in favor of the lower house's privileges confirmed his position of leadership of the representatives even though he did not himself possess a seat.[21]

Beverley's rise to an influential position occurred partly owing to a vacuum in political leadership in the lower house. The generation of new immigrants around Berkeley came to an end in the late 1670's. Berkeley died shortly after his return to England following the Rebellion. Henry Corbin and Edward Digges had died on the eve of Bacon's uprising; Thomas Ludwell was dead by 1678. Having served as colonial agent during the charter negotiations and then on the royal commission of 1676 and 1677, Francis Moryson wanted to escape the turmoil of Viriginia affairs. He died soon after his return to England in 1677. Sir Henry Chicheley lived until 1682, serving occasionally as acting governor, but he provided little leadership in his closing years. Colonel Nathaniel Bacon continued to exercise considerable influence in the council until after the Glorious Revolution, but he was the exception which proves the rule.[22]

With the exception of Philip Ludwell and Henry Whiting, the councillors in the 1680's made no attempt to assume Berkeley's mantle but either supported with varying degrees of enthusiasm the crown's new posture or sought to moderate it. Even Ludwell until the later part of the decade was quite circumspect in challenging governors. The burgesses between 1660 and 1675 had acquiesced in the leadership of Berkeley and his councillors because basic goals and interests matched. The hostility of governors after the Rebellion to an activist role by the assembly and the reluctance of most councillors to head an opposition faction were circumstances which literally forced the burgesses to generate their own leadership. Beverley filled the need.

In Culpeper's first assembly, which met in June and July 1680, Beverley led the burgesses in drafting a comprehensive design for altering Viriginia's economy, comparable in scope to the plans of Berkeley's era. Beverley's proposals included a bill "for Cohabitation and encouragement of Trade and manufacture," which, following the pattern of earlier town acts, provided for the restriction of commerce to specific sites on the major rivers. Specifically the measure limited tobacco exports after January 1 and imports of merchandise after September 29, 1681, to twenty locations, and to improve the bargaining position of the planters over the merchants, prohibited the sale of tobacco at the sites before March 20 each year.

Crucial parts of the overall design appeared in a petition to the king drawn up to supplement the town act. The petition requested Charles II to remit the plantation duty on tobacco exported by inhabitants of the ports and asked similar exemption for seven years of the halfpenny duty on tobacco reexported from the mother country to the continent. The burgesses obviously believed that partial reduction of the duties imposed under the Navigation Acts was a sure inducement for settling the towns. The capstone of the program was a cessation of tobacco planting in 1681, which the burgesses hoped would both increase the price of tobacco and induce the colonists to move to the "towns" and "divert part of their labors in Carrying on some other Manufacture, & not solely depend upon that uncertayne comodity tobacco. . . ."[23]

While the assembly obviously drew upon the precedents of Berkeley's earlier schemes, the departures were perhaps as significant as the similarities. Beverley's design struck more of a balance between tactics of prescription and "encouragements" to induce town settlement and diversification. The proposals called for a striking increase in the number of ports, twenty compared to the single entrepôt on each major river envisioned by Berkeley. The enlargement reflected the origins of the bill in the lower house and the desire of each burgess to obtain the imagined advantages of a port for his own locale. The new provisions of Beverley's design represented, as well, a greater inclination for provincial leaders to render their schemes attractive to constituencies. Under Beverley's leadership, the burgesses began to depart from the older axiom that innovations must be thrust upon an unwilling people and to embrace a new style of authority which cultivated the endorsement of the community at large.

Beverley's design differed from the diversification efforts prior to Bacon's Rebellion also in lacking supplementary proposals to the cessation scheme which protected debtors against a sudden rise in the value of tobacco, authorized payment of debts in other commodities, or prevented the engrossment of tobacco for speculative purposes. In short, Beverley's plan invited profiteering. This aspect of the diversification scheme of the early 1680's accorded too with a style of leadership which sought general support "out-of-doors" by exhibiting policies as compatible with both the immediate and narrow self-interests of planters and the long-range general good of the colony.

Absent, too, from the 1680 proposals was a rhetoric explaining the benefits of diversification to England and professing the colonists' eagerness to develop their province to serve the "mingled" interests of crown and colony. The omission was a significant one, for it betrayed the erosion of a rationale for economic experimentation which had been central since the founding of Virginia.

The design was a vivid expression of the idea of an energetic assembly, yet ironically the burgesses' fascination with the proposal induced them to approve Governor Culpeper's permanent revenue bill, which embodied the contrary concept of an inactive legislature with infrequent sessions. Initially the lower house approved a committee recommendation against the revenue measure drawn up in England and subsequently confirmed the action by voting twenty-one to seventeen not to resume debate on the bill. Recognizing that his reputation as a crown servant depended upon passage of the bill, Culpeper applied all of the pressure available to him to reverse that resolution. In addition to references to the extension of the principle of Poyning's Law to Virginia, the governor menaced the burgesses with the suggestion that the arrears in quitrents due to the crown before 1669 and to himself and Arlington as proprietors of the southern grant since then would be demanded if the revenue bill did not pass. Culpeper also intimated that without the permanent duties the provincial government could not pay its debts to individuals and county governments which had assumed the cost of quartering and victualing the troops sent from England to quell Bacon's Rebellion, a threat that struck at Beverley, a principal creditor, and at least four major counties—James, York, Isle of Wight, and Nansemond. Supplementing these warnings was Culpeper's hint that positive action on the revenue bill would win "the King's favour in everything you may aske to a cessacon or otherwise in this low ebb of tobacco. . . ."[24]

The combination of intimidation and promises won for Culpeper only a shift of four votes, but this was enough to reopen debate on the revenue bill, and after Culpeper reluctantly consented to an amendment exempting Virginia-owned ships from the duty the measure passed. Immediately following his triumph Culpeper paid his political debt by surrendering the southern grant proprietors' claims to quitrent arrears, approving the cohabitation act, and supporting the petition to the king concerning the cessation and special privileges for residents of the planned ports.[25]

In August the governor sailed from Virginia boasting that he had "successfully performed all the King commanded and expected and that alsoe to the entire satisfaction of the country (a thing very rare now a dayes). . . ." Unfortunately the "good order" in Virginia for which Culpeper took credit rested upon expectations which the governor could not fulfill. He had purchased approval of the crown's policy with commitments which threatened to annul that victory, for he pledged the home government's sanction of a grand economic design in order to obtain an act which aimed ultimately at producing a dormant government in the area of economic experimentation. The Exclusion crisis, then at its climax, precluded even serious consideration by the crown of any action tending to diminish the revenues. Nicholas Spencer had accurately foreseen that the plans involved "such a diminution to his Majesty's customes . . . that [it] may bee feared itt carryes with itt its own deniall. . . ."[26] In October 1680 Charles approved the permanent revenue bill but disallowed the assembly's proviso regarding Virginia ships. The proposal for a cessation received an adverse report from the Commissioners of the Customs in January 1681. Echoing the old arguments Maryland used against tobacco controls in the 1660's, the customs board called attention to the possibility that a cessation would only stimulate more production in the Spanish, Dutch, and French colonies, which would then capture the European tobacco market where Virginia now enjoyed a prominent position. The commissioners also asserted that the cessation proposal was only "Calculated for the advantage of the Wealthier sort in Virginia and might be of Advantage chiefly to the Merchants who are Engrossers here and have great quantityes in their hands," but the crucial objection was the fact that a cessation allegedly would cost the crown £100,000 in customs revenue.[27]

The government did not consider the town act and the petition requesting suspension of duties imposed by the Navigation Acts until the end of 1681, but in December the Commissioners of the Customs finally reported on the act. They indicated they could endorse the establishment of official "Wharfes and keys" in Virginia to facilitate regulation of trade and the more efficient collection of duties, but not ports and towns designed to abet diversification. Principally the customs spokesmen feared that the Virginians' scheme by requiring ships to trade at fixed points before adequate facilities existed would undo the tobacco trade. Trade, they argued, must be "Courted" not "forced." The Lords of Trade and in turn the Privy Council endorsed the report of the Commissioners of the Customs. Thus by the end of 1681 the crown had discarded every part of Virginia's design. Culpeper informed the colonists that "Charles has suspended the execution of anything prejudicial to the Customs."[28]

News of the crown's decisions was a severe blow to Virginia planters, and especially to those who had engrossed large quantities of tobacco in anticipation of a cessation. When the tobacco ships arrived in the Chesapeake Bay in the winter and spring of 1682, Robert Beverley and others tried to stop the captains from collecting tobacco except at the places designated in the town act, for official word of the king's veto had not yet arrived in the province. When the captains refused to obey the impractical law, prosecutions were brought against them and county courts controlled by supporters of the cohabitation act attempted to confiscate the cargo of ships which loaded tobacco in violation of the act.[29]

The uncertainty surrounding the status of the entire economic design in the winter of 1681-1682 occasioned a critical transformation in the political techniques of some leading planters. With authority split over enforcement of the port act and the inauguration of a cessation without the explicit consent of the crown, the faction favoring the economic design resorted to extralegal tactics in an effort to mobilize the common planters behind the program and tip the balance of power in its favor. Beverley had opposed Bacon's movement, but he had also learned from the rebel the utility of a more familiar political style and the possibility of increasing the power of one's position by backing it with popular demands. Beverley's cohorts went thus "out-of-doors" to the planters seeking signatures on petitions which demanded an assembly session for the purpose of enacting a cessation. As early as December the Middlesex County Court received such a memorial, and when the justices convened, the people thronged about the courthouse demanding that they endorse the petition. In effect Beverley had arranged pressure on himself, for he sat on the court which ordered that the petition be put to a voice vote of the assembled planters. The mob "unanimously . . . consented . . . ," enabling Beverley to plead the voice of the people in his campaign to commit the provincial government to action.[30]

The elderly and indecisive lieutenant governor was apparently susceptible to the popular clamor organized by Beverley's faction, and doubtless Chicheley was inclined to support the design which resembled the undertakings of Governor Berkeley whom he had served so long. In March Beverley persuaded Chicheley to order the provincial secretary of state, Nicholas Spencer, to issue writs for an assembly election. Possibly Beverley even pilfered the writs and distributed them when Spencer hesitated to act. Whatever machinations Beverley used, he succeeded, for in mid-April the burgesses met, five days after Chicheley received orders from Charles not to convene a session until Culpeper arrived.[31]

Adding to the tension and confusion was the crown's decision at this time to end support of the two foot companies which stayed in Virginia after the rest of the troops sent to quell Bacon's Rebellion departed. As pressure for a cessation mounted, the Privy Council in November 1681 decided to cut off support of the troops after Christmas. Fearing its action might provoke a mutiny, the crown subsequently altered its decision and consented to provide partial support until the first of April but reduced the pay of the soldiers twopence per day and cut off the officers' salaries altogether. The home government instructed Chicheley to disband the companies unless the assembly was willing to maintain them after the end of March. Apparently the king also refused to provide passage home to England for the discharged troops. Understandably the men were disgruntled.[32]

Since the king's order not to hold an assembly arrived too late to cancel the election, and because the problem of the troops demanded an immediate solution, the council and Chicheley decided not to prorogue the burgesses immediately but to persuade them to provide support or, at least, to rectify the short pay until the soldiers were disbanded. The councillors resolved to prohibit any discussion of a cessation during the session, but many of the burgesses who gathered at Jamestown on April 19 had other ideas. They refused to consider any measure for the troops until after the enactment of a cessation plan. Under the council's domination once again, Chicheley refused to compromise and on the twenty-fifth prorogued the assembly. Before adjourning, the burgesses resolved to return to their respective counties and there read publicly the sessions' journals to their constituents.[33]

A week later mobs began destroying newly planted tobacco in Gloucester County. Before the end of May the tumults had spread to Middlesex and New Kent counties, which bordered upon Gloucester. Chicheley reported that "the Burgesses big with the thoughts of a Cessation, and being unexpectedly yet necessarily Prorogued per your Majesty's command have blown this Cole which hath inflamed the People. . . ." Rebellion threatened the province for several weeks. A mutiny broke out among the troops who were now being disbanded, and the soldiers and plant cutters "both gave hopes and vigor to each other." The foot companies "emboldened up by the madnesse of the Rabbles" occupied the main powder magazine at Green Springs and made certain demands, including the restoration of the pay reduction. Only a capitulation to the soldiers' demands ended the mutiny and left the lieutenant governor and council free to deal decisively with the plant cutters. On May 3 the council ordered Mathew Kempe, head of the Gloucester militia, to suppress the insurgents. Kempe organized a mounted party, broke up several mobs of cutters, and arrested the ringleaders.[34]

Nicholas Spencer and most of the councillors had no doubt that Beverley directly instigated the tobacco destruction for reasons of personal profit. Beverley, Spencer informed the Lords of Trade, "to advance those great quantities of Tobacco now on his hands . . . hath instilled into the multitude (as is vehemently suspected) to justifye the Right of makeing a Cessation by cuting up plants." Circumstantial evidence tends to support Spencer's charges. Beverley's family physician and political associate, Henry Whiting, lost his seat on the council "for using words of dangerous consequences, 'if care be not taken for cessation, we must all go plundering with others. . . .' " Beverley himself was a victualer of the troops and undoubtedly had accumulated a considerable quantity of tobacco in payment for his services. His close political ally, William Fitzhugh, secured at least thirty-two thousand pounds of tobacco for maintaining soldiers; and during the riots he joyously informed the London merchant John Cooper that "the market will rise upon the news of the great destruction by cutters and Pluckers who at the writing hereof have not yet desisted. . . ." Indeed, Fitzhugh and Beverley were not only political allies but business partners and had apparently worked out a scheme for selling tobacco in the year of the cessation.[35]

Whatever Beverley's motive and role, his arrest upon orders by the council did not end the tobacco riot. Though Spencer claimed that Beverley's confinement robbed the cutters of leadership, the destruction continued throughout much of the summer. When the council organized mounted patrols in each county, the cutters operated at night. By the end of May the rioters had destroyed nearly all the tobacco in three-fourths of Gloucester, half of New Kent, and parts of Middlesex, Rappahannock, and York counties.

Chicheley issued a general pardon in June, which persuaded many cutters to desist, but sporadic cutting continued until August and then threatened to flare up again. The tumultuous proceedings had convinced Nicholas Spencer that Bacon's Rebellion "has left an itching behind it," while another critical observer concluded that Virginia was "sick . . . , from the sole of the foot even unto the head there is no soundness in it."[36] The consequences of manipulation had proven scarcely less disastrous than the prescriptive style of Berkeley.

The first reports of the tobacco riots reached the Lords of Trade in mid-June. Heeding Lord Baltimore's opinion that the turmoil in Virginia was the prelude to another rebellion like Bacon's, the crown acted with a dispatch remarkable for the bureaucracy and courtiers of seventeenth-century England. On the same day that news of the riots arrived, the Lords summoned Culpeper to appear and before the day was out formulated a plan for dealing with the crisis. The committee ordered Culpeper to leave immediately for Virginia. There he should remove Beverley from all public offices and bring him to trial. Once Beverley was punished, the governor had permission to discuss with the assembly a way "to temper the planting of tobacco and so raise its price" if such negotiations were absolutely essential to avert continued rioting. Three days later the Privy Council approved the plan of action.[37] The crown thought it necessary to consider limited production controls in order to stave off more riots and a complete disruption of the tobacco trade.

Culpeper arrived in Virginia with his new instructions in December 1682 and found the assembly in session. The governor quickly gave his consent to a number of laws already passed, among them another scheme to diversify the economy by providing bounties for the production of hemp and the manufacture of hats and iron. Culpeper was confident the crown would veto the laws, but believed his temporary approval necessary to pacify the continued agitation for remedial measures to solve the ills of the tobacco economy.[38]

Astutely, Culpeper also delayed any proceedings against the leaders of the tobacco riots until after the dissolution of the assembly, but shortly after the New Year he turned to deal with Beverley. Culpeper exempted Beverley from the king's proclamation of pardon and removed him from all public offices, but lacking concrete evidence, he did not bring the troublesome colonist to trial. He remained under technical arrest, confined to Middlesex and Gloucester counties until 1684. Culpeper's successor, Lord Howard of Effingham, and the council finally tried Beverley in May of that year and found him guilty of "high crimes and misdemeanours." But owning his guilt "on his bended knees, in a most submissive manner," he received a pardon and reentered the political life of the colony, only to be displaced again from all offices after clashing with the new governor.[39]

With Beverley isolated and a small upturn in the tobacco market giving the planters hope of better times, politics in Virginia from 1683 to 1684 were relatively calm. Some of Beverley's earlier supporters now drifted toward the governor and council. As a large landholder in the Northern Neck, William Fitzhugh decided to win the favor of Culpeper, who was seeking recognition of his rights in the area over which he now was sole proprietor. Philip Ludwell, who had remained conspicuously quiet during the tobacco riots and the proceedings against Beverley, trimmed and joined with Culpeper in an unsuccessful attempt to win for the council and the governor the right to levy small taxes. Culpeper found that conditions allowed him to suppress his June instruction from the crown empowering him to discuss tobacco restrictions if absolutely necessary. "Finding that I could keep Peace and Quiet without it," Culpeper reported, "I took advantage thereof, and never Discovered it to any one. . . ." Indeed according to his own account, the governor encouraged greater production by offering himself an inflated price for tobacco.[40]

Beverley's temporary exile, the slight upturn in tobacco prices, and Culpeper's Machiavellian tactics temporarily allayed the strident demands for cessation, cohabitation, and diversification, but the political quiet was superficial. The calming of the tobacco riots did not compose the underlying differences separating the crown and Beverley's faction that had now come to fruition as a country or popular party. The disagreement over the responsibility of the provincial government to respond energetically and creatively to the economic deficiencies of the province remained, undergirding the political conflict over the rights of the burgesses.

The revival under the auspices of Beverley of assembly efforts to prod society toward fulfillment of the colony's potential ensured conflict with the crown, which had concluded that the tranquility of Virginia demanded a sharp decrease in the activity of the provincial assembly. Beverley's variations from

Berkeley's style of leadership only hardened the home government's hostility toward diversification designs. Led by Beverley, the burgesses in the early 1680's did not echo in justification of their scheme the elaborate claims of Berkeley's era that the ultimate purpose of diversification was the larger welfare of England. In the hands of Beverley the purpose of diversification altered. To a much larger extent than before 1676, Beverley's design aimed at the immediate benefit of specific individuals who had large quantities of tobacco on hand and particular locales chosen for port sites. Beverley lacked the commitment to England's welfare which was a hallmark of the elite of Berkeley's era. Beverley wanted also a sense of identity with Virginia which second generation colonists like his own son came to develop. Missing a deep sense of commitment to either crown or colony Beverley sought the main chance. His design signaled a growing awareness of the importance of broad support for energetic government. Curiously, however, though Beverley reinforced his demands with popular endorsements, his design was probably less disinterested and less calculated for the general good of the community than Berkeley's. Nonetheless Beverley's design severed the tie between diversification designs and the welfare of the mother country and initiated a drift toward a new rationale for the traditional vision which developed fully by the end of the century and which emphasized the welfare of Virginia distinct from the needs of the mother country. Berkeley's assemblies strained to make Virginia comply with the colonial mercantilism first articulated by Elizabethan empire promoters. Beverley's actions mark the small origins of a provincial mercantilism.

Equally divergent from the style of Berkeley's regime was Beverley's willingness to incite popular support for diversification schemes. His techniques involved the injection of popular politics into the disputes between provincial leadership increasingly divided between loyalty to new governors with a new colonial policy for Virginia and the old designs for economic transformation.[41] Undoubtedly the changes in political identities and political style were related. The weakening of loyalty to the crown following the emergence of hostility by the home government to economic experimentation in Virginia freed Beverley to adopt political tactics Berkeley had never contemplated. Lacking all hope of reinforcement from the crown, a segment of the provincial leadership thus turned to tactics of popular political manipulation.

6

STALEMATE IN GOVERNMENT

During the brief reign of James II, the crown's evolving hostility toward economic innovation in Virginia reached its final stage. The brief Restoration flirtation with the ideal of a colonial policy encompassing experimentation and long-range development had given way rapidly to an attitude of indifference and, then, after Bacon's Rebellion, to opposition. Through the closing years of Charles II's reign the hostility remained largely passive. The crown simply rejected plans which threatened the status quo in the tobacco trade. After 1685 James's ministers initiated measures to improve the receipts from the colony's staple and abandoned all pretense of favoring diversification. The crown's animosity to the orthodox Virginia vision became explicit and aggressive.

The final escalation of antipathy toward the economic dreams of Virginia's leaders followed Parliament's generosity in granting James additional duties on tobacco and other imports in 1685. James met little opposition when he requested additional sources of revenue after Parliament had granted to him the supply given to Charles at the Restoration. Bishop Burnet claimed that the House of Commons "was more forward to give, than the king was to ask: to which the king thought fit to put a stop by a message, intimating that he desired no

125

more money that session." One would expect that Burnet exaggerated the largess of the summer session of James's first Parliament, but certainly there was comparatively little dissent to his request for additional revenue. Unlike Charles, James secured from Parliament an adequate supply to cover the normal expenses of government. To the revenues enjoyed by his brother, Parliament granted James new taxes which yielded about £400,000 per year: a duty on French linens, brandy, and silk, limited to five years, and impositions for eight years on wine and vinegar and on tobacco and sugar. In large measure, the rising of Monmouth accounted for Parliament's generosity. The bill providing for additional revenue and the bill to attaint Monmouth proceeded through Parliament together and received James's approval on June 16, 1685.[1]

Though willing to vote James revenue, Parliament was not of one voice about the specific means of raising the additional money. Particularly did controversy swirl around the proposal to place more taxes upon tobacco and sugar. The noted economist and head of the Commissioners of the Customs, Sir Dudley North, advocated new burdens upon tobacco and sugar as well as the duties on wines and vinegar, but in an effort to placate the merchant community, North rejected additional customs duties and called for an excise tax paid by the first wholesaler or retailer who purchased the commodity from the importer. In theory, no additional burden would fall upon the tobacco merchants or planters, and thus the scheme enabled James to raise the taxes on tobacco at the same time that the crown advocated reduction of the provincial tax burden on the Virginia settlers.[2]

North's proposal nonetheless provoked "noises and clamours, from all parts of the Town," that "the utter ruin of all the plantations" would follow and that all the domestic and foreign trade which depended on the colonial staples would "be confounded at one single stroke." James, however, rejected all substitute proposals and elected to push ahead with North's bill. Opponents of Sir Dudley's measure appeared in the House of Commons, but a combination of "private inter-est," the cordial relationship of James with his first Parlia-ment, his assurance that the imposition would be remitted if after a year's trial trade suffered, and the able Parliamentary leadership of North overcame the opposition to the additional duties.[3]

Initially the benefits of the additional duty to the Ex-chequer were meager. Indeed, at first, the imposition threat-ened to decrease the crown's income by forcing a dispropor-tionate amount of tobacco into the reexport trade, where it paid only a halfpenny in duties after drawbacks. The argu-ment, advanced during the debates over the duties, that lower taxes produced more revenue seemed vindicated. As late as September 1685 the Virginia merchants in London still re-fused to sell the normal amounts in the home market. Soon, however, the tobacco merchants began to trade again in the domestic market, and the revenues poured into the Exchequer. While the collection fell short of the anticipated income of £200,000 annually from the new taxes on tobacco and sugar alone, the receipts came much closer to the original estimates than was usual.[4]

James recognized that the extent of the discrepancy between estimated and actual revenue yields depended in large measure upon the efficient enforcement of the Navigation Acts and the quantity of tobacco and sugar production in the colonies, and moved to extract the greatest benefits from the taxes. Especially did the home government strive to maximize the revenue yield of tobacco. Fearful that any "encouragement to neglect the planting of tobacco" would diminish the tobacco duties, the Lords of Trade in August dropped from Effingham's new instructions the traditional clause requiring governors to promote the growth of new staples. Since Bacon's Rebellion that instruction had remained in the governors' orders in con-flict with the newer injunction not to allow any legislation which impaired the royal revenue in any manner. The dele-tion placed the crown's official approval on a course of action followed since 1676 and signified the crown's open recognition that it no longer valued the potential of Virginia for diversification.[5]

While requiring Effingham to oppose diversification schemes, the crown itself also acted positively in two areas to enhance the tobacco revenues. James's ministers and customs officials first urged that the governor push the effort to obtain from the assembly a law which would establish official "wharfes and keys" to facilitate control of commerce without promoting the concentration of population in port towns. Then in 1688 the crown sought a law from the legislature prohibiting the export of bulk tobacco.

The latter measure originated from the larger tobacco merchants of London. These merchants did not sulk in the coffee houses after James's first Parliament imposed the additional duty against their protests. Before a year lapsed they resurrected a proposal, first presented in the early 1670's, which tried to fuse their own desire for profits and the ever increasing interest of the crown in the tobacco revenue. Much fraud in the collection of the customs would be eliminated, they suggested, if London were the sole port of entry for tobacco. Further, the merchants argued that a crown-chartered company in London with the exclusive privilege of disposing of the imported tobacco would increase both the price and the royal revenue.[6]

When the proposal failed to win James's support, the prominent tobacco merchants secured the additional help of Virginia planters then in London and submitted another scheme tailored to the task of turning the king's need for tobacco revenue to their own advantage. In August 1687 the government received a petition for prohibiting the exportation of bulk tobacco from Virginia and Maryland. The large London merchants by and large engaged in legitimate trade. They sent large ships to the Chesapeake and secured the better grades of tobacco not in bulk but packed in hogsheads. Theirs was an orderly trade. As in the period just after the Restoration, the big London traders resented the irregular methods of the lesser merchants. The outports in the north-west of England and also in Ireland used smaller ships, which facilitated smuggling. Especially did bulk tobacco lend itself to clandestine trade. In bulk, the staple was easily handled and could be loaded and unloaded anywhere. Even at regular ports of entry, ship captains could misrepresent the amount of bulk tobacco in the ship's cargo, while customs officers could readily check the actual number of hogsheads against the bill of lading. Individual seamen brought in and "hawked" in the streets of the ports small parcels of bulk tobacco, which in the aggregate came to a considerable amount. Even women and children would come onto ships in port and buy small packages of bulk tobacco for vending. All of this bulk tobacco which did not pay customs "sold at underrates." The petitioners maintained that a curb on bulk exportation from the Chesapeake would end this illegal competition and increase the tobacco custom collections by a sixth.[7]

The argument was appealing to the crown. The Commissioners of the Customs offered no objection to the proposal, and the Lords of Trade recorded its approval in late October 1687. Soon after, the king ordered the proprietor of Maryland and the royal governor in Virginia to secure laws from their respective legislatures outlawing the exportation of bulk tobacco.[8]

On the surface the effort to maximize the fruits of the new imposition on tobacco by promoting official quays and prohibiting trade in bulk tobacco conflicted with the crown's concurrent campaign to reduce the role and energy of the assembly. The home government was now urging bold intervention of the legislature into the economy. The purpose, however, was fiscal reform rather than economic innovation. While the measures required special assembly sessions in which Effingham sought statutes with far reaching implications for the trade patterns of the provincial economy, the policies for improving the enforcement of the acts of trade aimed fundamentally at increment in the permanent provincial revenues and thus a decline in the necessity of frequent assemblies, as well as a rise in duties for the Exchequer and greater freedom from Parliament for James.

A sharp reversal in a moderately favorable trend in tobacco prices received by the Virginia planters accompanied the crown's exertions to reap the full benefits of the new imposition on tobacco. The years between the tobacco riot and the accession of James had witnessed an improvement in tobacco prices. The riot itself had eliminated much of the surplus tobacco which had built up since 1677. Violent storms in the late summer of 1683 destroyed about half of the crop and eliminated any surplus, and in the following year excessive rain ruined perhaps five-sixths of the tobacco. Spring floods in 1685 swept away many newly planted seedlings and again prevented a glut in the market. Merchants arriving late in the Chesapeake found that the planters had already sold their relatively small quantities of tobacco. A surplus of shipping was indeed a rare experience for Virginians in the last half of the seventeenth century, and some planters decided not to ship any tobacco to England on consignment since the market in Virginia was good.[9]

The improvement, however, was transitory. By 1686 William Fitzhugh at one point feared he would not sell his crop for one-tenth of what he received in the previous year. At length the large quantity which he had available in one location enabled him to sell his tobacco for just over 1d per pound, but doubtless smaller planters who could not offer the inducement of large cargoes to ship captains fared worse. In 1687 the planters received barely enough for their tobacco to cover the expenses of freight and customs, and by 1688 planters were complaining that the price had never been lower. In fact the price of tobacco did not fall to the disastrous levels which prevailed during the Second and Third Dutch Wars, but a significant decline did begin after 1685, until on the eve of the Glorious Revolution a surplus of eight thousand hogsheads of tobacco remained unsold.[10]

The relative importance of the extra imposition among the forces which caused the reversal in the tobacco prices in

Virginia is a moot point. Following the new duty on tobacco, the retail price of tobacco in England rose from 1s 8d per pound in 1684 for "best Virginia" to 2s 6d in 1687. The prices in the European market, on the other hand, dropped. Though the merchants imported a considerable quantity of sweet-scented tobacco—the type generally sold in the home market—they sold little to the domestic wholesalers. Rather the merchants chose to reexport a much larger quantity of their tobacco to the continent, and a glut in that market resulted. From 1678 to 1680 tobacco reexports from London amounted to 4,958,000 pounds or about 38% of the total imports of 13,127,000 pounds. Two years after the additional duty, the London merchants imported about 11,646,600 pounds of tobacco and reexported 5,156,670 pounds to the continent, or nearly 45%. The price of Virginia tobacco in the Amsterdam markets dropped from 0.29 guilders per pound in 1686 to 0.19 guilders in 1688.[11]

The new imposition alone, however, did not account for this adverse trend. The political uncertainty in England as James's reign approached its overthrow dampened trade. In Virginia after 1685 nature did not intervene with severe floods, rains, or droughts to cut the quantity of production, but mediocre weather did diminish the quality of tobacco. Increased production and a decline in price was also in part an inevitable consequence of the higher prices between 1682 and 1685.[12]

The burgesses did not admit that complex conditions shaped the tobacco market but instead singled out the new tax as a single cause for the return of bad times. Even before the price of tobacco began its decline, the lower house angrily predicted the depression and resurrected demands for diversification schemes to forestall consequences of the new burden on the colony's staple.

The crown's attempts to obtain provincial legislation which buttressed Parliament's new revenue grant opened the door for the burgesses. Effingham in early November 1685 convened the General Assembly, officially announced the passage of the new imposition, and suggested that Virginians should rejoice that their labor would contribute "soe plentifully . . . to the Glory of the Crown and the honor and safety of your nation." Put in the context of Monmouth's Rebellion, Effingham's remarks implied that the planters should rejoice to see the revenue from their staple bolstering James against his Whiggish enemies. The assembly, Effingham suggested, might contribute concretely to the success of the new tax program by agreeing to a port act along the lines envisioned by the Commissioners of the Customs and the crown. Led again by Beverley who had assumed his position as clerk, the lower house proposed instead an expanded version of the ill-fated cohabitation act of 1680. Interest in the plan had not died completely during the upturn in tobacco prices, for members of Beverley's faction had invested heavily in the paper ports and awaited an opportunity to revive the scheme.[13] The additional tax on tobacco and fears of trouble in the tobacco market provided the occasion.

The bill formulated by the lower house in 1685 had two major faults from the viewpoint of Effingham and his councillors. First, it called for the creation of more than double the number of towns provided for in the earlier act. The burgesses suggested the promotion of no less than forty-five towns. The governor and upper house wanted no more than two towns for each major river, but reluctantly compromised on one site for each county. The second deficiency went to the heart of the disagreement between crown and burgesses over the basic purpose of port legislation. The burgesses' draft bill contained no provision for new fees for new customs officials who were to assist in the enforcement of the Navigation Acts and provincial revenue laws. Instead the bill provided that the salaries of the collectors in each port would come out of the 10% fee which district customs collectors already received. Cognizant of the fact that the district collectors' fees were already insufficient, Effingham recognized that the arrangement would effectively prevent the ports from playing the role which the crown envisioned. Without an adequate customs service, the ports would not enhance "the security of his Majesties revenue." Nor would the burgesses' version bolster the prerogative by providing desirable political spoils for the governor's distribution.[14]

Since most councillors were also district collectors, they did not hesitate to endorse an amendment to the burgesses' draft which established adequate fees for the customs officers in the ports; but owing to the duplicity of Beverley and the laxness of Effingham and the council, the amendment subsequently became a point of bitter dispute involving not only the issue of the purpose of ports but the legislative role and powers of the governor. There was little space on the burgesses' draft for amendments, thus the governor and council put their change on a separate slip of paper and simply attached it to the original bill. The only other amendment which related to the number of ports was written on the actual draft. As clerk of the lower house Beverley received the paper from the council and detached the fee amendment. The burgesses then gave their consent to the bill. When Beverley's engrossed copy of the bill came again before the governor and council, they carelessly assumed that, since the burgesses had consented to the bill as amended, the addition regarding officers' fees was included. The council with the governor presiding agreed to the bill and the lower house immediately gave its final approval to the measure. Had the capable and meticulous provincial secretary of state been present the oversight might not have occurred, but Nicholas Spencer was ill with the gout during the crucial session. Effingham himself later pleaded ill health as an excuse for his own slipshod behavior.

Virginia governors traditionally signed bills in a formal ceremony at the end of the session. Reading over the engrossed copies of the acts before this occasion, Effingham finally noticed the omission. He promptly informed the burgesses of the oversight and demanded a correction before he signed the port bill. Whether or not most burgesses had known of their clerk's maneuver, they now defended his conduct, refused to restore the amendment and declared that the bill was already law since the governor's signature on the final copy of a bill had traditionally been only a mere formality after his consent as a participant in the deliberations of the upper chamber.

The constitutional conflict superimposed upon the disagreement over economic policy strained the relations between Effingham and the lower house beyond the breaking point. The burgesses held that the gravest issue was at stake. They maintained that the governor had no right to the double veto power implied in Effingham's claim to a negative voice after his approval of a measure while sitting with the upper house. Proving that a governor was as adept as representatives at drawing analogies between colonial assemblies and the English Parliament when it served his purposes, Effingham informed the burgesses that no bill passed by the Lords and Commons was law until approved by the king.[15]

The protagonists were deaf to the arguments of the other. The burgesses refused to vote the public levy until Effingham yielded and signed the port bill without the contested amendment. The governor tried desperately to find a solution to the stalemate, offering twice to withhold his veto until he received a ruling from the crown if only the lower house would pass the levy. When his pleas went unheeded, Effingham prorogued the assembly and reported the debacle to the crown.[16]

Understandably, James concluded that the affair only demonstrated anew the irresponsible character of the Virginia assembly. He personally ordered Beverley dismissed from all offices and ruled that in the future the governor would appoint the clerk of the lower house. As a special mark of displeasure, James also personally dissolved the offending assembly. Effingham's vindication was not complete, however, for the ruling upon the basic controversy of the governor's veto power did not sustain the position of a double negative. The crown ruled that the governor was a "distinct body" from the councillors and possessed neither a vote or veto in the upper house even though he might participate in their legislative deliberations.[17]

The port act itself which occasioned all the dissension received neither the approval nor a veto from the crown. The

Commissioners of the Customs rendered a negative opinion in the summer of 1687, but the privy council took no action owing to the mounting crisis that ended only in the flight of James.

The refusal to act was intolerable to the burgesses, especially since Maryland seemed to be succeeding where Virginians had failed. In 1683 the Maryland assembly, in imitation of the Old Dominion, passed its own town act which set aside some forty sites for development as ports. The measure restricted imports and exports to these locations after August 1685 and provided a number of incentives to the settlers to reside and build in the designated areas. The Maryland assembly passed similar acts in 1684, 1686, and 1688, and considerable effort went into the undertaking. In the end, little came of the endeavors, which the proprietor himself strongly favored for the same reason the crown had wanted ports—collection of duties. In the early 1690's the laws were not included in a general revision of Maryland's statutes. But in late 1688 the burgesses of Virginia, ever jealous that its sister colony might gain some advantage, fearfully imagined that the Maryland ports were "filled with warehouses" and growing rapidly into thriving commercial centers which would attract the scarce shipping in the Chesapeake Bay.[18]

The persistent agitation of the burgesses for new port legislation led to the bitter stalemate in the last session of the assembly prior to the Glorious Revolution, the meeting which witnessed the culmination of the conflict since 1676 between the crown and the lower house's concepts of the proper role of the provincial government in the economic life of the colony.

Upon instructions from home Effingham convened a new assembly for the purpose of passing a law prohibiting the export of bulk tobacco. The lower house which gathered in late April at Jamestown was the first since Bacon's Rebellion free of the influence of Beverley, who died in the spring of 1687 shortly after Effingham ejected him from all offices. The governor's opposition, however, did not lack leadership. Philip

Ludwell now stepped into Beverley's shoes and was well qualified to fill the role. Like Beverley, he was capable of ruthless actions to gain his ends. His ambition led him into fraudulent manipulations of the headright system, excessive even for a time when abuse of the land-grant processes was widespread. After importing forty indentured servants and securing an order for two thousand acres of land, he did not hesitate to append a zero to each figure and take possession of twenty thousand acres for four hundred headrights. Governor Effingham "in the hope of gaining him" appointed him a collector; but this was not enough to satisfy the ambitions of Ludwell, who had married Berkeley's widow and lived at Green Springs nursing resentment over the rise to power of Nicholas Spencer, who had succeeded his older brother Thomas Ludwell as secretary of state. Philip Ludwell could rest content only with a major colonial position, which he eventually secured when the Carolina proprietors in 1699 made him governor of Albemarle and later of both Carolinas. In North Carolina he tasted of his own medicine when a Captain Gibbs condemned him as "a Rascal, imposter, & Usurper" and threatened to resist his authority by force.[19] In 1688, however, it was Ludwell who was the thorn in the side of a governor.

As the 1688 session of the Virginia assembly approached, Effingham tried to curtail Ludwell's influence. He dismissed Ludwell from the council, and when the dissident then won election to the lower house denied him the seat on the grounds that a dismissed councillor was ineligible for election. The voters of James City County thumbed their noses at the governor and returned Ludwell's nineteen year old son-in-law in his stead. Ludwell, meanwhile, engaged in "cabals" with the burgesses, and his house in Jamestown adjacent to the building in which the lower house sat became the real headquarters of the lower house.[20]

Effingham played into Ludwell's hands by inflaming the burgesses with a haughty contempt for the right of representative government. He bluntly declared that the burgesses had no choice but to yield to James's demand for a prohibition of the export of bulk tobacco. Only the king's charity allowed the assembly a voice in the matter for James might have "only said *ffiat* let it be done & it should have been done so," Effingham announced, "yet he hath referr'd it to you Gentlemen to be your own Carvers & please yourselves in the method of a law, for the prohibition of it. . . . " Eight years earlier the threats of Culpeper had helped to produce a compliant assembly, but nearly a decade of political conflict with royal governors had reduced the burgesses' susceptibility to intimidation. Effingham only inflamed the representatives to greater defense of their rights by his warning that their claim to autonomy of action as representatives of the people would force James to exert the full prerogative powers and demonstrate "how far short the Subjects of Plantations are in point of privilege to the Inhabiting Subjects of *England*."[21]

Not only the measures from England which he championed and his condescending bearing toward the provincials, but his personal conduct in office embittered the relations between governor and burgesses and destroyed all chance of agreement by the end of his administration. Only two years before his appointment Effingham had inherited a peerage with a noble history but little wealth and, while the historian Robert Beverley exaggerated when he charged in 1705 that Effingham's sole motive was personal greed, the governor did in fact regard his colonial appointment as an opportunity to repair the fortunes of the Howard family. Immediately after arriving in Virginia, he carefully surveyed the possibilities of increasing the governor's income and reported to his wife that with careful management he could make £2,500 annually. When his estimate of the legitimate profits proved excessive, he yielded to temptation and indulged in extralegal procedures. The governor introduced the use of a new seal for various official documents; imposed, without the consent of the council as required by his commission, a fee of two hundred pounds of tobacco for its use; and required all teachers and lawyers to secure a license and pay fees. His conduct contrasted sharply with Berkeley's, whose expenditures of his own fortune in behalf of the colony had established a rapport with the assembly.[22]

So far did the relationship between governor and burgesses deteriorate by 1688 that the mere endorsement of a measure by the governor or his political supporters in the council was enough to kill it. Encouraged by Ludwell, the representatives "obstructed Everything that proceeded not from their owne braine. . . ." Even though the restriction of bulk tobacco offered an opportunity for combining the crown's concern for increasing the revenue with the burgesses' eagerness to reduce the quantity of tobacco on the market, the lower house refused to approve the bill and demanded instead that the upper house engage in a new attempt to formulate port legislation. Neither Effingham nor the council shared the burgesses' alarms over Maryland's imagined progress in developing ports, nor would they risk affronting the crown by participating in new deliberations on a port act until the king indicated his official judgment of the earlier law. The standoff with the lower house advocating a new port act and the upper chamber a curtailment of bulk tobacco exports could not be broken.[23]

Faced with an intransigent lower house, Effingham adjourned the assembly. The governor hoped that the burgesses' stand would prompt James to abandon the hope of achieving crown policy through the assembly in Virginia. Effingham counseled the home government that an arbitrary prohibition on the export of bulk tobacco by royal proclamation would impress upon the pretended advocates of the people's interest that "their priviledge is not so great as they fancy. . . ." His ambitions of governing a southern dominion similar to Andros's regime to the North were written between the lines of his argument that a royal restriction on bulk tobacco would have the salutary consequence of causing Virginians to "fear least they falle under the same method of Government with New England, & New York. . . ," an arrangement which he regarded as "much Easier both to the People and Governors."[24]

With Effingham's advice that representative government in Virginia had outlived its usefulness and the burgesses' veiled threat prior to their dissolution that civil disorders would result from the governor's failure to bend to their demands, the polarization of the colony's politics was complete. A decade and a half earlier governor, council, and burgesses were united in support of an economic policy of experimentation and a political arrangement characterized by both a direct dependence upon the crown and guarantees of the central role of the assembly in provincial government. By 1689 the colony's leadership was arrayed into contending camps. Fundamentally the dissension among the colony's leadership occurred because the crown stifled the burgesses' ambition to play a dynamic role in the economic development of the colony and threatened the political position of the lower house while at the same time demanding vigorous assembly action to exploit the full potential of the tobacco revenues.

Rumors of the Glorious Revolution reaching Virginia at the climax of the long developing division within the leadership of the province served as a catalyst which threatened to precipitate from the tension the violence predicted earlier by the House of Burgesses. Discontent at the time of Monmouth's Rebellion in 1685 indicated that some Virginians wanted "only an opportunity" to overthrow Effingham, and the early reaction in Virginia to rumors of James's overthrow was remarkably similar to the occurrences that ended in rebellion in New England, New York, and Maryland. When news of William's landing at Torbay arrived, "it was in the mouths of all the mobile that there was no king in England and so no Government here." Amid these rumors of uncertain conditions in England and growing restlessness in Virginia, Effingham at a session of the council on February 27, 1689, announced his intention "suddenly to take Voyage to England . . . ," and sailed with a fleet of tobacco ships some time after the middle of March.

Then during the closing days of March wild rumors of Catholic and Indian plots spread through both Maryland and

Virginia. Most of these stories began in frontier Stafford
County, Virginia, and were "Improved by some Evil Members who desire[d] to fish in disturbed Waters. . . ." Especially
did the Reverend John Waugh and George Mason, two adherents of the Beverley-Ludwell faction in Stafford County, attempt to manipulate the tales much as Coode and Leisler did
in Maryland and New York. Nicholas Spencer concluded later
that only the decisive action of the council under his leadership forestalled rebellion.[25]

Spencer was only partly correct in his explanation for
the lack of revolution in Virginia in 1689. By prompt and
effective action in suppressing rumors and riots and in pro-
claiming the news of William and Mary's accession, the
council did help to prevent the turmoil in certain frontier
counties from growing and spreading throughout the province,
but other factors were decisive, too. Unlike the Dominion
of New England, Virginia retained an institution—the assembly—which provided the disgruntled factions with a forum
to challenge and checkmate royal policy. Maryland's assembly,
too, could occasionally thwart the proprietor's designs, but the
country party of Coode could never hope to gain dominant
power in Maryland except by overthrowing the proprietor and
substituting the crown in its stead. Since some burgesses in
Virginia still tended to identify their grievances with the person
of the governor, they hoped to secure satisfaction simply by
securing Effingham's removal. Unfounded rumors that Effingham was to be removed from office may have made rebellion
seem unnecessary.[26] Moreover, during the crucial months of
1689 there was no one in Virginia to lead a revolt and nobody
to overthrow. The death of Beverley in 1687 and Ludwell's
leaving for England to present a petition of grievances against
the governor in the summer of 1688 deprived Effingham's opposition of a leader capable of assuming the role of a Leisler
or a Coode. Waugh and Mason could not hold a candle to
Beverley and Ludwell when it came to demagoguery. Moreover, Effingham's departure as discontent mounted toward a
potential rebellion removed the symbol of oppression.

Granting the influence of all these factors, it is also probable that Virginia escaped the upheavals which occurred in the other major colonies on the mainland owing to the fact that the crown's policy which antagonized Berkeley's self-proclaimed heirs and split provincial authority did not produce deep and widespread discontent among the small planters. Poll taxes were smaller during the 1680's when the lower house often withheld tax levies from the governor. Assembly sessions were less frequent and the cost of government lighter. The stalemate in government killed both the economic designs of the burgesses and the crown's schemes for reform of revenue collection. However much of the crown's new colonial posture alienated a portion of the planter elite, it produced lower taxes, infrequent assemblies, and no burdensome and impractical projects which had characterized the administration of Berkeley and contributed to rebellion a dozen years earlier.

7

PROVINCIAL MERCANTILISM

During the seventeenth century a basic continuity prevailed in Virginia leadership's expectations of their economy. None doubted the land's fecundity. Their understanding of the social function of a variegated economy remained constant as well. Economic variety seemed an essential basis for a stratified and stable society. An important change, however, also occurred in the rationale for diversification. Between the Restoration and Bacon's Rebellion the economic justification for the provincial government's designs was identical to the ideas which prompted England's colonial expansion at the beginning of the century and which underlay the program of the Virginia Company under the leadership of Sandys. A diversified economy was desirable because it would benefit England. This rationale was not altruistic, for the further assumption was that the prosperity of the mother country best guaranteed the welfare of Virginia. Virginia's elite accepted the belief that plantations served themselves by succoring England. Berkeley's immediate political heirs were unable to perceive the identity of interests between crown and colony, yet were incapable as well of formulating an alternative rationale for diversification which went much beyond immediate benefits to individuals.

In the decade and a half following the Glorious Revolution some Virginia leaders reasserted the view that the true interests of the mother country and the colony were similar. Significantly, a prominent spokesman for this position was a councillor whose office required commitment to the prerogative but whose birth in the colony engendered loyalty to Virginia. William Byrd II argued eloquently that deprivation of the colonists' rights as Englishmen might benefit the selfish purposes of some governors but not the king's interests. Similarly he held that some moderation of the crown's opposition toward diversification was compatible with its interest in the revenues derived from an expanding tobacco trade. Harsh restrictions on provincial economic experiments would only breed resentment and incline the planters to abandon the planting of tobacco altogether when faced with depression in the market. Limited diversification, general prosperity, and, consequently, an expansion of the tobacco trade, too, would result in the long run.[1] Byrd's view did not copy Berkeley's precisely though a basic similarity existed in their assumption of an identity of interests between Virginia and England. The governor had believed that what was good for England was good for Virginia; the councillor reversed the relationship: England's welfare depended on Virginia's.

Other members of the provincial leadership class on the other hand moved to the logical conclusion implied in the first Robert Beverley's lack of interest in the needs of England. His son and namesake discovered a fundamental conflict between the economic interest of England and the colony. Robert Beverley II's political frustration (he never attained the council) doubtless heightened his sensitivity to the exploitative aspect of his colony's connection with England and encouraged in him a tendency to see conspiracy. He had no doubt that English merchants plotted with the home government to keep Virginia always in a dependent position. Though he rejoiced at the province's potential ability to furnish her with a variety of raw materials, he deplored Virginians' dependence on the mother country for manufactured supplies.

He charged that his fellow colonists sheared sheep "only to cool them" and urged the development of clothing manufactures. "Nay they are such abominable Ill-husbands," he wrote, "that tho' their country be over-run with Wood, yet they have all their Wooden Ware from *England;* their Cabinets, chairs, Tables, Stools, Chests, Boxes, Cast-Wheels, and all other things, even so much as their Bowls, and Birchen Brooms, to the Eternal Reproach of their Laziness." Beverley recorded no sentiment even remotely implying the desirability of Virginia's eventual independence, but, without plumbing the full implications of his advice, he did advocate a high degree of economic self-sufficiency. For him Virginia's welfare was an end in itself. He espoused a provincial mercantilism which Berkeley would have deplored. An expression of identity to England and of partnership between colony and crown in 1660, by 1700 the diversification had become for some a symbol of a new loyalty. Some of the Virginia elite were coming to think of themselves as primarily Virginians, and Beverley's version of the old economic vision mirrored this fact.[2]

The alienation from the mother country and the concomitant interest in greater economic autonomy followed the emergence to political power of native-born Virginians. The arrival of the "new immigrants" during the English Civil War and Interregnum forestalled a natural transition to indigenous leadership earlier, but the decline in the last third of the century of settlement in Virginia of "Persons of good Character and Reputation" allowed the provincials to inherit the mantle of authority by default after the Glorious Revolution. In 1699 at least thirty of the forty-eight burgesses were second-generation colonists. Only nine can be positively identified as immigrants. In contrast, during the period between the Restoration and Bacon's Rebellion only fifteen persons can be identified as native Virginians out of a total of fifty-seven burgesses who sat in Berkeley's "long assembly." Many of the representatives in 1699 occupied places their fathers first held. George Mason and Rice Hooe, Stafford County's two burgesses, were both sons of fathers who earlier represented the same county. Half of the thirty were sons of immigrants who had sat in the House of Burgesses. Henrico's representatives were brothers whose father and grandfather both served that county in the same capacity. As if to symbolize the emergence of this Virginia-born generation of leaders, the 1699 session of the assembly convened at Jamestown, and then adjourned to Middle Plantation, the site soon chosen for the construction of a new capital, Williamsburg.[3]

The "natives" were more numerous in the highest ranks of government, too. In 1691 Peter Beverley, the son of Robert Beverley I, obtained the position of clerk of the lower house which his father enjoyed and abused during Culpeper's and Effingham's administrations. Speaker of the House in 1699 was Robert Carter, son of Colonel John Carter, who settled in Upper Norfolk County in the early 1640's. Robert Carter was just beginning a career which earned him the title "King Carter." William Byrd II was at the turn of the century the provincial agent in England and would soon return to fill the shoes of his father, who died in 1704. Dudley Digges, the son of the Interregnum governor, Edward Digges, obtained a council spot in 1698, and seven years later became auditor and surveyor general of Virginia. The four individuals appointed to the council in the last year of the seventeenth and the first year of the eighteenth century were all second-generation colonists who obtained prominence in the wake of the immigrant fathers' course.[4]

The native Virginia leadership after 1689 confronted a home government whose attitude toward colonial affairs differed markedly in some important respects from James II's. A more sympathetic, or at least tolerant, attitude toward colonial assemblies emerged. If crown officials scoffed at the idea that provincial assemblies were small parliaments, they nevertheless recognized the position of colonial legislatures in the scheme of empire. The closing decade of the seventeenth century witnessed also a change in the attitude of the

crown toward the economic development of the empire as a
whole. Especially after the creation of the Board of Trade in
1696, the king's ministers exhibited greater interest in economic experimentation and long-range development of the
empire's untapped potentials, which was comparable to the
spirit which had died in the bud shortly after the Restoration.
Virginia, however, was not a beneficiary of the broader concept of empire at the end of the century. The crown's projects
for economic innovation in the empire were directed at the
royal colonies in New England and New York and the proprietary provinces of the Carolinas. At the same time that
the Board of Trade pursued a vigorous campaign to promote
naval stores there, it hoped that the Chesapeake Bay settlers
would not "turn their thoughts to anything but the Culture
of Tobacco." William III agreed to relinquish the additional
excise duty on sugar which James secured in 1685, but the
revenue from tobacco was too large to forego, particularly
since the wars with France increased the revenue needs of the
government. Parliament constantly renewed the additional
imposition on tobacco, and in 1697, ignoring colonial protests, placed still another duty of one penny per pound on
tobacco not reexported from England. By 1705 the average
annual tax yield from tobacco was nearly £400,000.[5]

Following the Glorious Revolution, the crown, as before,
was apprehensive of any action which even remotely threatened to disrupt the tobacco trade. When Governor Francis
Nicholson suggested a plan to set up a trading company in
Virginia which would control the Indian trade in the west
and, consequently, combat French influence in the Missis-
sippi Valley, he received a sharp rebuke from the Board of
Trade, which feared the scheme might "interfere with or discourage the planting of tobacco, which is the maine thing to
be pursued in that colony." Sir Charles Hedges informed
Governor Edward Nott in 1705 that he should not permit
tobacco planters to divert their energies to the production of
naval stores "or any other undertaking." "Souls! Damn your
souls! Make Tobacco!" was the alleged response of Attorney

General Seymour to the Reverend James Blair's argument that the Old Dominion needed a college to educate ministers who could save the souls of the planters. If Seymour's remark was extreme—the crown did give considerable support to the College of William and Mary—it was only an exaggeration of Whitehall's continued tendency to gauge Virginia's value solely by the annual returns of the customhouse.[6]

The home government continued and expanded as well James II's policy of positive action to increase the income from the impositions on tobacco authorized by Parliament. William's privy council revived the idea of prohibiting the export of bulk tobacco from the colonies, and when the Virginia and Maryland assemblies again refused to cooperate, William's ministers sought to accomplish the same objective by securing from Parliament in 1698 a ban on its import into the British Isles. Perhaps the most radical action came on the eve of the penny increase in the duty on tobacco imported into England. The crown adopted a new land policy which had, among other objectives such as a decrease in the power of the large landed interest which dominated the council, the purpose of increasing the population and tobacco production of the colony. The recognition that a relationship existed between large undeveloped land holdings, sparse population, and unrealized tobacco revenue was not new in the late 1690's. Giles Bland at the time of Bacon's Rebellion had argued that the crown could redress a major grievance of the common planters and increase its revenue at the same time by forcing large holders to surrender their undeveloped land. The suggestion subsequently appeared in vague instructions to Culpeper and later governors to prevent land engrossment, but little was done. The newly organized and energetic Board of Trade made the first serious appraisal of land-grant practices in the colonies as a whole and Virginia in particular. The Board found persuasive the contention of Edward Randolph that "The Inhabitants & Planters have bin and at this time are discouraged & hinderd from planting Tobacco in that Colony, and Servants are not so willing to goe there as formerly because the Members of the Councill & others who make an Interest in the Government, have procured very large Tracts of land. . . ." Randolph urged a limitation of five hundred acres on future grants to one person, strict collection of quitrents, including arrears, and an impartial survey of present land claims. The measures would force the reversion of considerable land to the crown for redistribution to smaller planters, who would actually cultivate the plots. The end result would be the increase in the king's revenue as tobacco production expanded.[7]

From the view of the crown Virginia's economic position seemed at a critical stage after 1689. As early as 1692 Edward Randolph feared the desire of the planters to grow cotton and gloomily predicted tobacco cultivation would be abandoned in less than a decade. In the first decade of the new century the crown received frantic reports of several Virginia counties in which the planters had "laid down the growth of more Tobacco. . . . Instead whereof they grow Flax, Hemp, Cotton & work the same up for Cloathing."[8] Radical measures seemed necessary to crown servants if Virginia were to remain in its proper place in the empire. Francis Nicholson's alarm over the alleged movement to cotton and hemp cultivation led him to urge on the home government an act of Parliament forbidding the growth of these commodities and the manufacture of any clothing in the colonies. The fact that diversification schemes of Virginians, like Beverley's after 1689, expressed a spirit of provincial mercantilism only deepened the mother country's apprehension over economic innovation in the colony. The tension between crown and colony fed on itself. English opposition to diversification increased Virginians' disaffection toward the mother country and heightened their desire for greater economic independence, which in turn enlarged the home government's resolve to preserve Virginia's one-crop economy. In the view of some provincials the "inhuman Memorials" of crown servants like Nicholson threatened for Virginians "a Bondage worse than ever was known in Egypt or Algiers" and evidenced a design "to prey upon our poor Country, and render it needy and ruinous. . . ."[9] In the mind of the crown the interest of Virginians in diversification represented a desire for ending all dependence upon the mother country. The upshot of the vicious cycle was estrangement of some Virginia leaders from the mother country. The growth of loyalty to the particular welfare of the colony was greater perhaps at the close of the century than in any preceding generation or until the eve of the American Revolution.

Indeed, by the end of the century an attitude bordering on chauvinism possessed some. "Methinks we see already that happy time when we shall surpass the Asiaticans in civility, the Jews in Religion, the Greeks in Philosophy, the Egyptians in Geometry, the Phenicians in Arithmetick, and the Caldeans in Astrology, O Happy Virginia!" The student of the College of William and Mary who made this prediction in 1699 only caricatured the sentiments of his elders. Undoubtedly another scholar also communicated the climate of opinion of the colony when he argued the wisdom of providing for education in Virginia rather than depending upon England "or other forreigne parts." Sending Virginia youths to England was analogous to "turning of Creatures out of their own Element . . ." for the very air in the mother country was unnatural to one "born & bred" in the colony. Even after the expense and inconvenience of sending a son to England for schooling, the planter would have a debauched young man for his pains. The "Flesh Potts of Egypt" would corrupt the innocent Virginian and his "English humor" would make him dissatisfied with the virtuous environment of his native country.[10]

The allegiance to Virginia's particular welfare expressed itself more concretely in new diversification designs after 1689, especially schemes for town promotion. In their specific provisions the plans often were no more than elaborations upon earlier statutes, but the expectation of their ultimate consequences was quite different. The lower house, where the provincial mercantilism found its advocates, now openly de-

clared that "if an Act pass for the Erecting of Towns all
Manufactories will be Encouraged Thereby." Edward Randolph's observations convinced him that diversification and
town promotion represented nothing less than a repudiation
of English colonial mercantile doctrine and a bid for complete
economic independence. "The General Assembly are now
sitting," he reported in 1693. "Towns or no towns is the word.
I find one maine end of towns is to settle Manufactures &
to live without any dependence upon England. . . ."[11]

The burgesses' desire for progress toward economic autonomy had, however, one consequence not unlike Berkeley's
intense hope of transforming the colony overnight to accord
with the needs of England as he imagined them. Though opposite in content, both loyalties produced an impatience with
economic legislation which did not promise quick and dra-
matic results. Both identities impeded careful assessment and
measured action. Greater realism, then, did not follow in the
train of the new attachment to the colony's distinct economic
well-being. The new identity like the old served to reinforce
the persisting faith in the colony's potential for rapid development.

Added to these influences encouraging the burgesses'
advocation of grandiose economic measures after 1689 as
before was the growing tendency of the representatives to
provide in their legislation benefits for all counties. Apparent
under the leadership of the first Beverley, the trait culminated
after the Glorious Revolution. The burgesses "always appointed too many towns . . . for every Man desiring the Town
to be as near as is possible to his Door . . . they commonly
contriv'd a Town for every County. . . ."[12] The burgesses'
solicitude for the interests of both their county and their
colony caused a dogged opposition to the moderate port
measures acceptable to the crown.

The troubled state of affairs in the mainland British
provinces following the Glorious Revolution presented the
burgesses with an opportunity to secure legislation embodying

provincial mercantilism. In the early part of his administration the newly arrived lieutenant governor Francis Nicholson "Studied Popularity." In every way—from organizing "Olympick Games" for the entertainment of the planters to acquiescence in every desire of his first assembly—he sought to ingratiate himself with the colonists and avoid controversy. His actions reflected his exaggerated fears that Virginians might join the other colonists up and down the Atlantic coast who had risen in revolt in 1689. Serving as lieutenant governor in New York under Sir Edmund Andros's Dominion of New England, Nicholson had himself recently fled the wrath of the rebel, Jacob Leisler. He had no intention of going on his travels again.[13]

When the assembly met in April 1691, the lieutenant governor consequently offered no serious opposition to any of the schemes to improve the province. He ignored many of his royal instructions on the assumption that the king could undo whatever he had done to keep the peace in Virginia. Nicholson admitted that he sanctioned some of the laws "only to Please them att Present" and advised the Lords of Trade that the colonists "bee kept in hopes & have noe absolute Deniall, soe long as New England, Pennsylvania, Maryland & the two Carolinas are unsettled . . . for they may bee Fatall Examples by Encouraging the Mob" in Virginia. Not since the days of Berkeley had a chief executive worked so harmoniously with the assembly, and, though Nicholson's motives were quite different from Sir William's, the result was much the same. The legislature filled the statute book with projects designed to transform the economy and society of Virginia.[14]

From the standpoint of actual results, the significant accomplishment of Nicholson's first assembly was the groundwork laid for the establishment of the College of William and Mary. The legislature appointed a committee to draw up a charter, dispatched James Blair to England to secure royal approval and backing, and imposed new taxes for the support of the proposed college. No less important to leading Virginians at the time, however, was a new act to create port towns. As before, the lower house demanded and the council opposed the creation of a large number of ports. The former wanted twenty—the number specified in the 1680 law—and the latter no more than twelve. The compromise solution called for twenty towns, of which only fifteen were ports of entry, for all imports of merchandise and export of tobacco, and markets for the actual retail of all imported merchandise. The remaining five were to enjoy the retail market privileges only and were to secure their imports from, and send exports to, one of the ports of entry. In violation of his royal instructions, Nicholson sanctioned the large number of ports and also agreed that the law should go into effect in October 1692 before commercial facilities could possibly be provided. The session supplemented the town act with laws requiring all tithables to produce and process a pound of flax and hemp and authorizing the payment of private tobacco debts in these and other commodities.[15]

The stalemate in government which had characterized the years before 1689 had ended, but only briefly. Even before the end of his brief administration, the lieutenant governor "tack'd about, and was quite the Reverse of what he was in the first." The disappearance of the imagined danger of disorder in Virginia emboldened Nicholson to take a more independent position. While the 1691 legislature was in session, Leisler was hanged by the new royal governor for New York, Henry Sloughter. Lionel Copley received his commission as the first royal governor of Maryland in June 1691 and arrived in the colony in March 1692. Two months later Sir William Phips landed in Boston and reestablished royal government in Massachusetts under a new charter. Nicholson, who kept a watchful eye on the course of events in all of the rebellious colonies, decided that he could now reassert the crown policy in Virginia. In July 1692 he boasted to the Lords of Trade that he had energetically encouraged the planting of tobacco and discouraged diversification schemes and forecast that the king's tobacco revenue collection would set a new record owing to his diligent efforts.[16]

Nicholson discovered, however, that he had fanned hopes in Virginia which did not easily die. Following the enactment of the port law in the spring of 1691, the county governments surveyed and laid out the towns. Twelve of the twenty locations were sites designated as ports by the port act of 1680. The county courts had in most cases surveyed these locations and some individuals had already purchased lots and built warehouses. Efforts to develop the paper ports now increased. By the spring of 1692 "considerable progress" had been made and some leading planters began to invest heavily in efforts to develop the port sites.[17]

The preparations produced murmurs of discontent among some planters who were displeased with the return of energetic government resolved upon transforming the colony, and, in the process, disturbing their accustomed patterns of living. In King and Queen County especially "evill minded persons" obstructed the survey of the towns. Only explicit royal action, however, could annul the results of Nicholson's permissiveness during his first year in Virginia, and as usual the home government's dilatory consideration of colonial affairs aggravated rather than resolved the uncertain situation. Nicholson's successor, Sir Edmund Andros, took over the administration of Virginia in September 1692, less than a month before the scheduled implementation of the port act. With no instructions from London, Andros acted indecisively. He attempted neither enforcement of the act nor its suspension by calling a special assembly session. Instead, while pleading to the home government for explicit orders, he allowed implementation of the act to depend on each locale. Perhaps it was his recent overthrow and incarceration in Massachusetts which caused the governor's irresolution, but whatever the reason an uneven and uncertain execution of the statute resulted. Trading was confused. Many captains avoided Virginia and sailed instead to Maryland for cargoes, compounding the problem of a shipping scarcity owing to the war. Hostility to execution of the port act mounted during the late winter and early spring of 1693 as the planters tried to dispose of their tobacco.

Confronted with this crisis, the assembly which met belatedly in March reluctantly heeded Andros's tardy request and suspended operation of the law.[18]

In England the debate over the issue was a repeat of the conflict over whether the details of a port act should stress customs administration or "cohabitation." The larger merchants were conspicuously allied with the crown in opposition to the burgesses' version of port legislation. Michjah Perry, his brother Richard, and Thomas Lane, who together formed the largest firm engaged in the plantation tobacco trade at this time, led a merchant lobby which opposed tobacco smuggling as much as the king and hoped that the establishment of official wharves would reduce the competition from traders whose smaller operations made the risk of illegal trade acceptable. Perry, Lane, and Perry and their allies viewed port schemes in the same light as earlier proposals to ban the export of bulk tobacco and to regulate the sailing of tobacco ships. These large merchants wanted to regularize trade patterns in Virginia and their interest in more centralized commercial activity was part of an ongoing conflict with the smaller traders. The large merchants, however, had no wish to promote cohabitation and manufactures in Virginia. Like the crown they wanted "Towns on a Modest Account" and opposed acts which created an excessive number of ports, which limited commercial transactions to specific sites, or which granted special inducements for the settlement in towns.[19]

The Reverend James Blair and William Sherwood, both in England seeking support for the proposed college, urged the crown's approval of the port bill and the diversification statutes and for a time imagined they were close to success. The merchants' "Buzzing amongst the Committee," however, removed any chance that the Lords of Trade would recommend a reversal of James II's position. Both the crown's and the interest of the influential merchants dictated the decision to reject all diversification acts and any port statute which went beyond "Modest provisions" designed to regularize trade without stimulating urban growth.[20]

For the remainder of Andros's administration and throughout Nicholson's second appointment to Virginia, both the crown, supported by the large English merchants and most councillors, and the lower house attempted to force the other to agree to its variant of port legislation. For the remainder of Andros's government the burgesses refused to accept the modifications in the 1691 law recommended by the home government or to consider the proposal for the prohibition of bulk tobacco exports until their own port bill received the royal assent. Andros tried to gain compliance on the port legislation by approving a statute for the encouragement of linen but the representatives remained adamant. Between the departure of Andros and the arrival of Nicholson in December 1698 the council formulated a compromise measure which retained restrictions on the sale of tobacco outside town sites while permitting the retail of imports up and down the rivers; provided for public construction of storage facilities at the ports; and set the number of entrepôts at two for each river, except the James, which was to have three. The burgesses, however, refused even to debate the merits of an alternative to the 1691 act.[21]

The bitter personal and political quarrels between leading councillors and governors Andros and Nicholson from 1693 until Nicholson's recall in early 1705 increased the difficulty of reaching compromise upon port legislation. As the memory of the Glorious Revolution receded somewhat in their minds, both governors exhibited a "spirit of Government" which threatened the dominant political and social status coveted by leading members of the council. The Reverend James Blair was the most conspicuous spokesman for this councillor faction composed of the powerful Harrison, Ludwell, and Burwell families. Blair desired "to be the first minister" of the colony and reacted shrilly to any sign of independent action by the governors. Conflict was inevitable, first, owing to ill-defined division of the ecclesiastical powers of the governor and the office of commissary, or Bishop of London's representative in Virginia, a post held by Blair; second, because the increasingly detailed and specific instructions from London to the governors reduced the need of consultation with the councillors; and, third, because the crown's land policy specifically, and its posture toward Virginia in general, were hostile to an increase in the power of a councillor elite. Politics became a running feud between Blair's faction and the colonial governors, interrupted only by a brief honeymoon period after the removal of Andros.[22] The climate of political hostility was inhospitable for the growth of compromise on any issue, including diversification and particularly the port acts. A stalemate in government similar to Effingham's administration prevailed.

The state of the tobacco market at the turn of the century did not particularly strengthen any inclinations toward compromise which might have existed. The immediate economic need for economic reformation was less acute after the early 1690's. A convoy system worked out by the home government helped to solve the problems of scarce shipping and high costs for freight and insurance which had marked the opening years of King William's War. Tobacco became "a comodity soe vendable . . . that thousands . . . gott good estates by it." Particularly after the Peace of Ryswick, the planters enjoyed a good market for their tobacco. The end of hostilities between France and England and the prospect of securing new tobacco outlets in Muscovy and France drove the trade "to the greatest height, that it ever was. . . ." English merchants enthusiastically dispatched ships and goods to Chesapeake Bay. The crop was not large, and the planters enjoyed a sellers' market.[23]

The market remained good for a few years even after the outbreak of war again in 1701. Indeed, initially hostilities actually increased demand, for the London agents of the French tobacco purchasers, fearing that trade with England would soon be prohibited, expanded their purchases of tobacco. As late as 1704 tobacco sold in Virginia for about twopence per pound.[24]

The stalemate between council, governor, and burgesses over diversification and ports then came to an abrupt end when the arrival of a compliant lieutenant governor coincided with a downturn in tobacco prices. By 1705 it was clear that the earlier hopes of new opportunities in Russia were premature. New competition rather than new markets had in fact appeared in the early years of the new century. The amount of cheap grades of tobacco produced in Holland increased from ten to twenty-seven million pounds between 1700 and 1706. Combined with the general effect on trade of the War of the Spanish Succession, these factors forced prices of tobacco down in Virginia in some cases to a farthing per pound. Under these circumstances Lieutenant Governor Edward Nott arrived. In London seeking Nicholson's dismissal, Blair had correctly predicted two months before his appointment that Nott would be all that the Virginia planter elite desired. What seemed in Blair's view an objective understanding and a "very calm healing temper" was in reality Nott's inclination to defer to the provincial leadership.[25]

The town act which resulted from the combination of a weak governor and a depressed economy was the final attempt at wholesale promotion of numerous ports and the last major effort at government-induced diversification until the closing years of the colonial period. On the eve of Nott's departure for Virginia, the larger merchants had urged the crown to seek again the assembly's approval of carefully limited port legislation. The crown determined to make a new effort, and at his first assembly, which convened in late 1705, the lieutenant governor dutifully urged the lower house to comply. The burgesses accepted instead a bill drafted under the guidance of Robert Beverley II. The measure aimed at promoting artisan and craftsmen centers. Included among the privileges of town residents were exemptions from all poll taxes for fifteen years and three-fourths of any future duties levied on the trade of the colony. The bill also relieved inhabitants

from military duty outside the port in time of peace and provided that even in war a resident could refuse to march more
than fifty miles from his town.[26]

The burgesses hoped as well to encourage urban growth
by guaranteeing town inhabitants a voice in their local government and representation in the assembly. The lower house's
bill outlined a two-stage evolution in the government of the
ports. When the population reached thirty families exclusive
of "ordinary keepers," the measure authorized inhabitants
over twenty-one to elect for life eight "benchers" to form a
governing council. After sixty families settled in a port, the
people might choose fifteen "brethern assistants," with the
power to make local laws and levy taxes, and elect a burgess
to the provincial legislature. The council with difficulty persuaded the burgesses to reduce somewhat the number of
ports designated in the act, then recommended Nott's approval
of the measure as the best that could be expected.[27]

With the lieutenant governor's acceptance of the council's advice, the fifteen-year struggle between the assembly
and governor for another port act ended, but agreement between burgesses, council, and lieutenant governor in Virginia had come under the same conditions as in 1691—
acquiescence in the provincial mercantilism espoused by the
lower house—and thus Nott's compliance did not resolve
the basic conflict. The surrender to the lower chamber's
measure only insured a veto by the home government. The
queen's advisers had no difficulty recognizing the intent of
Beverley's measure, and though their action was dilatory it
was never in doubt. In 1709 the town act, together with
similar measures passed by the Maryland legislature, received
the royal disallowance. "The whole act," declared the home
government, "is designed to Encourage by great Priviledges
the settling in Townships, and such settlements will encourage
their going on with the Wollen and other manufactures there.
. . . The Establishing of Towns and Incorporating of the
Planters as intended thereby, will put them upon further
Improvements of the . . . manufactures, And take them off

from the Planting of Tobacco which would be of Very Ill consequence, not only in respect to the Exports of our Woolen and other Goods and Consequently to the Dependence that Colony ought to have on this Kingdom, but likewise in respect to the Importation of Tobacco hither for the home and foreign Consumption, Besides a further Prejudice in relation to our shipping and navigation."[28]

The mutual intransigence of the crown, the merchants, and the burgesses prevented the implementation of any port legislation, and undoubtedly the inflexibility on both sides was inevitable. Compromise required more than greater flexibility toward the number of ports, the restrictions on commerce at the entrepôts, or the privileges granted to inhabitants, for these points were only the concrete expressions of a much deeper conflict involving the basic understanding of the crown about Virginia's role in the empire and the fundamental identities of Virginians. A meaningful concession on the specific provisions of the act required either a reversal of the alienation toward England experienced by Virginia leaders for whom Beverley spoke or an end to the growing fears of the crown that diversification in Virginia would end "the Dependence that Colony ought to have on this Kingdom. . . ."

The struggle over diversification by port legislation in the years following the Glorious Revolution, however, was not without significant consequences, even though the full implementation of no statute occurred. The protracted conflict was an important part of the condition which at the end of the century encouraged a further development of the new political relationship between leaders and freemen anticipated by the maneuvers of the first Robert Beverley. Together with other political issues, the dissension over port legislation increased the split in the colony's leadership which opened following Bacon's Rebellion. Both advocates and opponents of provincial mercantilism were tempted to strengthen their hand with popular support. Following his brief acquiescence in diversification schemes to keep the peace in Virginia after the Glorious Revolution, Nicholson, for example, went directly to the common planters and encouraged their hostility toward many of the measures he had originally sanctioned.[29]

The advocates of provincial mercantilism were especially inclined to practice a new politics, for their native birth and identity to Virginia reduced the differences in sentiment and outlook between them and the common planters and made political familiarity more palatable. In anticipation of the assembly session which drew up the last port act, the leading supporters of radical port legislation in Middlesex County, thus, "made it their Business" to send political allies "about the County to all meetings, Horse races, & feasts, & to Peoples houses both day & night" seeking signatures on petitions. "Some they would have forced to sign their paper, others when they were drunk they persuaded to sign it, they put the hands of other without their orders." The proceedings appeared to some "more like ye beginnings of ye Plant cutting year than a just Grievance. . . ."[30] Aiming at greater economic autonomy, the advocates of provincial mercantilism helped foster instead the evolution of political practices away from the aloof paternalism of Berkeley's era to the more popular style which prevailed at the beginning of the eighteenth century.

A rough analogy exists between the appearance of a closer relationship between leadership and the people at the end of the century and the creation of the Virginia assembly by the Virginia Company in 1619. In both instances, the political innovation was in part a means of enlarging support for diversification designs by increasing the participants involved in the deliberative process. The Virginia Company reasoned that the settlers would support the various economic schemes pushed by Sandys if they had a voice through representative government in determining or at least sanctioning those designs.[31] The same basic logic undergirded the efforts of provincial leaders to involve the common planters in the agitation for legislation for ports.

Undoubtedly the demise of the style of leadership personified by Berkeley would have occurred even if the clash over diversification had not encouraged the new political techniques. The emergence of a familiar relationship between leadership and constituents was a product of numerous and complex factors.[32] In large measure, however, the political transition issued from the condition of divided and factious leadership, and that dissension existed in part owing to the deep division over the question of diversification, issues closely related to it such as land policy, and, ultimately, the question of Virginia's proper place in the empire. The agitation for diversification at the turn of the century, then, was closely tied to the general drift in political relationships in colonial Virginia from a style of prescription, rooted in the assumption that the citizenry was incapable of knowing the common good, toward tactics of persuasion, which implicitly rested on the conviction that the ordinary planters were subject to manipulation and that individual self-interest and the general welfare were not incompatible.

The campaign for the port act of 1705 ended the period of comprehensive public programs to secure immediate and thorough economic diversification by government intervention into the economy. In the second decade of the century Robert Beverley literally labored in his vineyards to prove that the province could produce wine. Lacking public subsidy, he resorted to a wager of one thousand guineas that he could within two years make seven hundred gallons from one vintage. The most energetic experimenter was William Byrd II. Like Beverley, Byrd hoped Virginia could produce the "cheerer of Gods & Men." He invested as well in mines, silk, and potash, and devised a plan for canals linking Virginia and North Carolina, but especially in the two decades after 1710 Byrd's chief design was hemp production. A naval store product, hemp symbolized Byrd's conviction that economic innovation in Virginia squared with England's interest.[33]

The assembly for the remainder of the colonial period after the failure of the 1705 port scheme passed specific acts regulating or promoting specific aspects of the economy, but no drastic scheme aiming at a total revolution in the Virginia economy occurred. In the 1720's legislation was passed to reduce the quantity of tobacco produced. In 1730 the tobacco inspection act, anticipated by the crown-annulled bill which Spotswood wrung from a reluctant assembly in 1713, established numerous warehouses to which all planters brought their tobacco for scrutiny by public inspectors who possessed the power to destroy inferior grades. The assembly subsequently extended the idea of prohibiting the export of inferior tobacco to other commodities. By the end of the colonial period some form of inspection system existed for flour, corn, wheat, bread, beef, pork, pitch, tar, turpentine, shingles, and staves. These measures, however, differed fundamentally from the economic legislation of the previous century. In the seventeenth century, tobacco controls were a means of fostering new forms of economic activity, but the eighteenth-century legislation did not have this as its central purpose. Governor Hugh Drysdale, in support of a measure aimed at reducing tobacco production, argued that the act was necessary to strengthen the market and discourage the planters from "falling on other manufactures prejudiciall to the trade of Great Britain." The author of the 1730 act, Governor Gooch, aimed also at discouraging economic pursuits which were undesirable from the standpoint of British colonial mercantilism. Assuming that Virginians were an indolent people who would abandon economic habits only out of necessity, he concluded that a system which bolstered the price of tobacco would keep the planters growing that staple.[34]

Inspection systems for other exports came after the commodities became a significant part of the colony's trade. The intent of the inspection statutes was not to instigate new economic activity but to encourage more rapid and regular growth of established commerce. On the whole, provincial government in the eighteenth-century colonial period sought to strengthen the existing economic patterns rather than transform the economic structure. Cultivation in contrast to inno-

vation became the chief characteristic of government intervention.

In part the demise of grandiose schemes for comprehensive economic revolution resulted because in the eighteenth
century Virginia experienced a gradual trend toward diversification. The need for drastic measures declined. In 1710
the colony exported nearly a quarter of a million bushels of
corn and wheat, 6,500 barrels of pitch and tar, and in addition significant quantities of pork, beef, furs, and forest
products. Although tobacco accounted for the overwhelming
share of the value of exports in 1710, perhaps two-thirds of
the total shipping tonnage clearing from the province's ports
carried no tobacco. In the eighteenth century trade with the
West Indies initiated earlier reached significant proportions.
By one estimate Virginians bartered in 1730 ten to twenty
thousand bushels of wheat and double that amount of corn
for rum, sugar, salt, molasses, and wine produced in the
islands. Significant exports of these products to Madeira also
existed by the start of the fourth decade of the century. The
value of lumber exports to the West Indies, such as staves,
shingles, clapboard, and plank was £1,000. Pork exports
amounted to £3,750, and beef exports had also made a
small beginning. By the 1730's important supplementary cargoes to England had also emerged. Only a rare ship failed
to add to its cargo a quantity of staves and plank. For example, ships clearing the Rappahannock River for Great
Britain in the year ending April 25, 1731, carried over
100,000 staves, as well as 265 tons of iron, 2,400 feet of
plank, and small amounts of miscellaneous products.[35]

By the start of the second quarter of the eighteenth
century, the province seemed to Virginians "altered wonder-
fully, and far more advanced and improved in all respects.
. . ."[36] The economic diversification moreover continued and
at a more rapid pace. According to estimates by colonial
governors Gooch and Dinwiddie, corn and wheat represented
4% of the total value of tobacco in 1742. By 1755 the per-
centage for these grains was eight. In 1742 Virginians export-

ed 3.9 bushels of corn and wheat for every hogshead of
tobacco; by 1755 they shipped 5.8 bushels. In 1742 tobacco
accounted for 80% of the total value of exports. Thirteen
years later the tobacco share was only 60%.[37] These developments in the colonial economy reduced the impetus for the
sort of drastic government intervention aimed at stimulating
economic innovation which had characterized the period
from 1650 to 1705.

The decreased need for economic revolution, however,
was not a sufficient cause for the demise of comprehensive
public economic designs. The end of radical designs comparable to Berkeley's and the two Beverleys' resulted also
from the increased ability of ordinary planters to influence
the actions of the burgesses. The more persuasive familiar
style of leadership adapted to generate popular support for
economic experimentation by the government contained the
seed of destruction for those comprehensive economic
schemes. Though initially resorted to by factions of a divided
leadership seeking tacit and passive support for their ideas,
the new political techniques fostered a relationship between
leaders and constituents in which decisive influence could be
exercised by constituents on leaders as well. At the time of
Bacon's Rebellion the common planters had apparently desired only the right to know and approve the rationale of
public policies formulated by leaders. By the administration
of Alexander Spotswood constituencies were in the habit of
selecting representatives whose inclinations were previously
known and who were sensitive to the will of the ruled. In
Spotswood's opinion, the "meaner sort of People" had come
to control elections and selected only "their most familiar
Companions," who "for fear of not being chosen again,"
avoided any action that might "be disrelished out of the
House by ye Comon People."[38] A democracy in which leaders
faithfully sought and reflected the wishes of the voters did
not, of course, exist as Spotswood's descriptions of the power
of the common planters seem at times to suggest, but a significant increase in the influence exercised on leadership by

the people had occurred. In its increasingly familiar relationship with the voters, leadership came to defer often to the views of the people. Undertaken as a means of shaping the sentiments of the common planters, the new political relationship led in fact to frequent acquiescence in the popular will.

Opposition to expensive, grandiose, energetic government designs to stimulate economic innovation was one outlook of the common planters which their leadership in the House of Burgesses came to mirror. In 1711 the representatives resolved "That there is no occasion at this time to bring in a bill to encourage Woollen Cotten, Fflax, and Hemp Manufactorys." The action not only implied repudiation of provincial mercantilism but foreshadowed an indifference toward the crown's rejection of the last town act.[39] The new arrangement of political power which accorded a larger role to the common planters brought in its train a decline in agitation for government action to achieve the traditional vision. By the second decade of the eighteenth century the "Axiom" of Berkeley's assembly "that never any Community of people had good done to them, but against their wills" had given way and leadership often accepted a new function. The burgesses, Spotswood reported, always "resolved not to depart from that general Maxim of recommending themselves to the people by opposing everything that required expense. . . ."[40] The rising political influence of the common planter marked the demise of the half-century effort to transform the Virginia economy first by government prescription and then increasingly by persuasion and consent.

EPILOGUE

Englishmen who founded Virginia did not view the land as an untouched wilderness. It was easier to imagine that rapid success in the new world was probable if one regarded nature in America as predesigned or arranged by God to yield to the labors of man. In the second half of the seventeenth century, Virginia's provincial leadership continued to adhere to a belief in the peculiar fecundity of the land. If the environment were not only capable of but actually predisposed to the development of a highly diverse economy, the economic failure of Virginia lay obviously with man not the land.

The persistent depression in the tobacco market encouraged Virginia leadership to retain the belief that the colony was capable of infinite "improvements" if only the planters could be made to cooperate with the predisposition of the land toward diversification. The attractiveness of diversification was its promise to solve the economic ills of the colony, but important too as a consideration was the social and political orderliness leaders imagined would follow from economic transformation and prosperity. The experience of the provincial leadership confirmed in them the notion held widely by the seventeenth-century English upper classes generally that a careful structuring of the social and political order was necessary to arrest the insubordinate proclivities of ordinary men toward their proper rulers. Always implicit in the thinking of articulate Virginia leaders was the belief that great economic diversification was necessary to provide a proper base for a hierarchical social and political structure. A one-crop, homogeneous, agrarian economy seemed incapable of providing the variety of vocations and stations necessary for the traditional seventeenth-century concept of a healthy, orderly community.

The connection between diversification, social order and morality was most explicit when Virginia leaders discoursed on the role of town growth in fostering economic innovations. Promotion of "cohabitation" rested on the assumption that "if Towns and Ports can be brought to bear, the chief Obstruction to the Improvement of that Country will be removed." Particularly would towns facilitate *"good Discipline* and *careful tending* under faithful Teachers and Magistrates. . . ."[1]

Diversification, town growth, and greater social stability were thus closely connected in the mind of the Virginia provincial elite in the last half of the seventeenth century. Viewed broadly, leadership's conception consisted of two basic parts which in the historian's perspective appear incompatible: dynamic economic and demographic change and growth, on the one hand, and, on the other, political and social stability and a deferential society. In a rough way Virginia's leadership in the second half of the seventeenth century resembles Alexander Hamilton, who also imagined that drastic economic innovation was not only compatible with but actually a prerequisite for the establishment of social and political orderliness. In this very general sense, Virginia leaders in the six decades following 1650 are early examples of that conservative tradition in American history which has endorsed quite radical economic alterations as the preconditions for the growth or preservation of traditional, hierarchical social and political relationships.

In pursuit of economic diversification and the social stability it promised, Virginia leaders were hardly less per-

sistent than their New England counterparts who struggled
to prevent moral and spiritual declension in their societies. To
be sure, the goal of Virginia's rulers was perhaps not so coherent or as elaborately articulated as the Puritan vision of
godly, cohesive communities. Contrasted to John Winthrop or
Increase Mather, William Berkeley's or Robert Beverley II's
goals were less full-blown philosophies than clusters of ideas
which reinforced each other in ways the Virginians did not
always make explicit. The leaders in the Old Dominion no less
than their new world Calvinist counterparts, however, were
committed to preconceived goals for their province, and the
failure of Virginia's elite as compared to the greater success
of New England's rulers may have resulted not so much from
a lesser attachment of the former to its goal as from the goal's
more unrealistic character and the greater impediments to
even its partial realization.

The barriers were of several types. There were first the
environmental impediments which historians have traditionally
stressed in their explanations of the emergence of a one-crop
economy. Commercial entrepôts were unnecessary owing to
the extensive system of navigable rivers reaching far into the
country. Secondly, Virginia leadership faced growing opposition from the crown toward economic experimentation in the
Chesapeake colonies and the hesitancy of merchants to provide
credits for diversification. Thirdly, diversification efforts occurred during a period of frequent war. The three Dutch Wars,
King William's War, and Queen Anne's War were all crowded
into the six decades of diversification effort after the mid-
seventeenth century. The wars may have helped to sustain
interest in diversification by disrupting the tobacco market
and driving prices down, but the hostilities also siphoned off
governmental energies and resources which otherwise might
have been focused on economic reform.

These three kinds of barriers were formidable enough by
themselves, but Virginia's leaders were also handicapped by
their own ideas and attitudes. There were also, then, mental or
internal impediments. Chief among these was the undoubted

belief in the fecundity of Virginia's land. That emphasis gave birth to the hope of economic diversification, but it was so intense that it prevented a realistic assessment of the province's potential and hindered the growth of an awareness that economic reform in a labor- and capital-scarce economy demanded efficient marshaling of effort and resources in a limited number of economic spheres. Similarly, intense loyalty to England in Berkeley's era helped to sustain interest in diversification but also diverted attention from the more realistic opportunities for economic reform which did not benefit England directly. An opposite identity—provincial chauvinism—later functioned in a similar fashion, directing leadership's interests toward premature development of domestic manufactures and sustaining a tendency to seek too rapid economic change. The relative weights of the external and internal factors cannot, of course, be measured but the latter were certainly not inconsequential.

The goal of thorough economic reform required for even its partial realization a strong inclination among the common planters to follow the commands of the provincial leadership. The provincial leaders possessed, however, few of the attributes of a ruling class which engender awe and respect in the people. The leaders were men of new wealth whose style of life did not set them distinctly apart from the lesser planters. Moreover, the rulers sought to govern within a context lacking strong supporting social and religious institutions. Public policy demands were issued to a citizenry ill-prepared to obey implicitly the will of authority. Institutions, like the church, which sought to fit men for a hierarchical social environment were especially weak in Virginia, even though the thwarted individual economic expectations doubtless rendered the common planters needful of training which inculcated deferential attitudes.

The combination of rulers with large goals but small capacity to command contributed first to the instability which erupted in Bacon's Rebellion in 1676 and then helped to foster at the century's end a new approach to the people by some of the leaders. The shift in the political style between Berkeley and his chief supporters to the Beverleys may be easily exaggerated. Yet in the decades following Bacon's Rebellion, the key techniques which political leaders in the eighteenth-century colonial period employed regularly in their relationship with the common planters first appeared. For the first time in the conflict over tobacco control in the early 1680's, the lower house ordered its journals read publicly in the counties to the citizens in order to stimulate support for its position. The organization of petition drives by assembly leaders seeking to strengthen their hand also occurred and was especially notable and well organized by the time of the agitation for the last port act. Elections by the beginning of the eighteenth century are described as events where candidates treat and flatter the electorate. The lower house also increasingly designed the details of its diversification legislation to appeal to the immediate interests of a wider spectrum of the population in all counties.

Between the Interregnum and the early eighteenth century, the changing groups of provincial leadership retained the belief that government action in the economy could effect a thorough alteration in the economy and social structure of Virginia. No leader imagined that ordinary planters would labor properly without strong guidance by government, but, parallel with the persistence of the assumption that the role of political leadership was to employ the power of government to reshape the economy, was a change in the techniques some provincial leaders were willing to use to attain their goals. Berkeley's generation sought mere compliance and did not imagine that the mass of planters was capable of comprehending the elite's grand conception of a colony with a highly diversified economy serving as the most valuable of Charles II's plantations. While there is no explicit evidence that the Virginia leaders at the century's end entertained a higher opinion of the ordinary Virginian's capacity to comprehend the true interest of the colony, those rulers were more inclined to obtain the people's positive subscription to diversification schemes. Especially did the two Robert Beverleys resort to new tactics of leadership which aimed at stimulating public support for diversification schemes. The evolution of the leadership's style involved the beginnings of the transformation in the technique of government, a change from the leadership style of prescription to the methods of persuasion.

In the end, the consequences of the prolonged struggle to achieve a diversified economy were thoroughly incongruous with the initial motives behind the effort. Designed as a solution to the economic ills of the tobacco economy, the various diversification schemes often only disrupted the economy still more. Begun as economic plans to fit Virginia to the economic needs of the mother country, diversification became an expression of some Virginia leaders' misgivings about excessive dependence upon England. Originating as an economic design aimed at providing the groundwork for a deferential social order, the pursuit of diversification became one of the causes for the emergence of political practices which found leaders appealing to the people and eventually deferring to the will of their constituents.

NOTES

Notes to Chapter 1

1. Bernard Bailyn, "Politics and Social Structure in Virginia," in James Morton Smith, ed., *Seventeenth-century America: Essays in Colonial History* (Chapel Hill, 1959), 94-95; *EVB,* I, 49, et passim; *VMHB,* II (1894-1895), 383-385; Philip A. Bruce, *Social Life of Virginia in the Seventeenth Century* (Richmond, 1907), 53; Edmund Jennings Lee, *Lee of Virginia, 1642-1892* (Philadelphia, 1895), 83-85; Henry Norwood, *A Voyage to Virginia . . .* , in Force, *Tracts,* I, No. XI, 34.

2. *Randolph Papers,* VII, 486-492; Colonel Quary's Memorial, Massachusetts Historical Society, *Collections,* 3d Ser., VII (Boston, 1838), 232-234.

3. William Bullock, *Virginia Impartially Examined . . .* (London, 1649), 1; John Hammond, *Leah and Rachael, or the Two Fruitful Sisters, Virginia and Maryland . . .* , in Clayton Hall, ed., *Narratives of Early Maryland, 1633-1684* (New York, 1910), 277-308.

4. E. P. Thompson, "Time, Work-Discipline, and Industrial Capitalism," *Past and Present,* No. 38 (1967), 56-97.

5. Edmund Berkeley and Dorothy Smith Berkeley, eds., *The Reverend John Clayton: A Parson with a Scientific Mind, His Scientific Writings and Other Related Papers* (Charlottesville, 1970), 64; Bullock, *Virginia Impartially Examined;* Hugh Jones, *Present State of Virginia,* ed., Richard L. Morton (Chapel Hill, 1956), 77.

172

6. William S. Powell, ed., *Ye Countie of Albemarle in Carolina* (Raleigh, 1958), 3; T[homas] M[athews], "The Beginning, Progress, and Conclusion of Bacon's Rebellion, 1675-1676," in Force, *Tracts,* I, No. 8, pp. 25-26; William Fitzhugh to William Haywood, Jan. 20, 1687, Davis, *Fitzhugh,* 202-203.

7. Philip A. Bruce, *Economic History of Virginia in the Seventeenth Century* (New York, 1896), I, 629.

8. Bullock, *Virginia Impartially Examined,* 11-12, 36; *A Description of the Province of New Albion and A Direction for Adventurers with small Stock to Get Two for One, and Good Land Freely* (London, 1648), in Force, *Tracts,* II, No. 7, p. 32; Melvin Herndon, *Tobacco in Colonial Virginia: "The Sovereign Remedy"* (Williamsburg, 1957), 46-48.

9. William Byrd to Mr. Grendon, June 21, 1684, *Virginia Historical Register and Literary Companion,* I (1848), 117.

10. H. R. McIlwaine, ed., *Minutes of the Council and General Court of Colonial Virginia, 1622-1632, 1670-1676, With Notes and Excerpts from Original Council and General Court Records Into 1683, Now Lost* (Richmond, 1924), 214, 294; Richard B. Morris, *Government and Labor in Early America* (New York, 1946); J. C. Ballagh, *White Servitude in the Colony of Virginia* (Baltimore, 1895), 85-97; Thomas J. Wertenbaker, *The Planters of Colonial Virginia* (Princeton, 1922), 98.

11. Hening, *Statutes,* II, 298; Susie Ames, *Studies of the Virginia Eastern Shore in the Seventeenth Century* (Richmond, 1911), 37-42; William Fitzhugh to Nicholas Hayward, Jan. 30, 1687, Davis, *Fitzhugh,* 202; [William Sherwood], Virginia's Deploured Condition , . . . , *Massachusetts Historical Society, Collections,* 4th Ser., IX (Boston, 1871), 164.

12. Polly Cary Mason, ed., *Records of Colonial Gloucester County, Virginia* (Newport News, 1946-1948), I, 1-83.

13. The estimates on the proportion of landholders derive from calculations made from data on the militia strength in the counties of Virginia in the late seventeenth and early eighteenth century, and on the number of landholders listed in the 1705 quitrent roll, a census of landholders prepared to facilitate more effective collection of quitrents by crown officials. See Evarts B. Greene and Virginia D. Harrington, *American Population Before the Federal Census of 1790* (New York, 1932), 148-149, and Robert Beverley, *History and Present State of Virginia,* ed., Louis B. Wright (Chapel Hill, 1947), 253. The estimates on the distribution of landed wealth derive from Lorenz curve analysis of the quitrent rolls conveniently printed in Wertenbaker, *The Planters,* 183-247.

14. Philip A. Bruce, *Institutional History of Virginia in the Seventeenth Century* (New York and London, 1910), I, 194-207; George M. Brydon, *Virginia's Mother Church and the Political Conditions Under Which It Grew* (Richmond, 1947-1952), I, passim.

15. William S. Perry, ed., *Historical Collections Relating to the American Colonial Church* (Hartford, 1870), I, 11; *VMHB*, I (1893-1894), 242-243, II (1894-1895), 1-15; *Historical Statistics of the United States, Colonial Times to 1957* (Washington, 1960), 756.

16. William Meade, *Old Churches, Ministers, and Families of Virginia* (Philadelphia, 1861), I, 231, 356-360, 385, et passim.

17. Perry, ed., *Historical Collections*, I, 15; Bruce, *Institutional History of Virginia*, I, 131 ff.

18. For contrasting treatments of the Blair-Nicholson controversies see Richard L. Morton, *Colonial Virginia* (Chapel Hill, 1960), I, Ch. 23, and Stephen S. Webb, "The Strange Career of Francis Nicholson," *WMQ*, 3d Ser., XXIII (1966), 513-548.

19. Beverley, *History*, 261.

20. Fitzhugh to Nicholas Hayward, Jan. 30, 1686, Davis, *Fitzhugh*, 203; G. F. Wells, *Parish Education in Colonial Virginia* (New York, 1923), 23 et passim.

21. Governor Nicholson to the Board of Trade, March 1703, CO 5/1313.

22. Louis B. Wright and Marion Tinling, eds., *The Secret Diary of William Byrd of Westover, 1709-1712* (Richmond, 1941), 190, 222, 304, 553.

23. Morgan P. Robinson, "Virginia Counties: Those Resulting from Virginia Legislation," *Bulletin of the Virginia State Library*, IX (1916), 91-93 and maps 3-8; Meyer Jacobstein, *The Tobacco Industry in the United States*, Columbia University, *Studies in History, Economics and Public Law*, XXVI, No. 3 (New York, 1907), 23; Robert A. Brock, "A Succinct Account of Tobacco in Virginia," *Tenth Census of the United States, 1880*, III (Washington, 1883), 224; Jacob M. Price, "The Economic Growth of the Chesapeake and the European Market, 1697-1775," *Journal of Economic History*, XXIV (1964), 497; Representation of the Lords of Trade on the North American Continent, 1721, Additional MSS. 23615, fol. 44, British Museum.

24. John Smith, *Advertisement for the Unexperienced Planters of New England, or any where, Or the Path-way to erect a Plantation* (London, 1631), in Edward Arber and A. S. Bradley, eds., *Travels and Works of Captain John Smith, President of*

Virginia and Admiral of New England, 1580-1631 (Edinburgh, 1910), II, 929; Smith, "The Proceedings of the English Colonie in Virginia Since their First beginning from England in the year of our Lord 1606 till this Present 1612," ibid., I, 89, 173; William Berkeley, *A Discourse and View of Virginia* (London, 1662), 1; Henry Hartwell, James Blair, and Edward Chilton, *The Present State of Virginia and the College,* ed., Hunter Dickson Farish (Williamsburg, 1940), 3-4; Beverley, *History,* 118-119, 156; Thomas Ludwell to Lord Arlington, Feb. 12, 1677, CO 1/21: 37.

25. Thomas Harriot, *Narrative of the First English Plantation of Virginia* (London, 1903), 13-20; Berkeley, *Discourse,* 1; Beverley, *History,* 117-156.

26. E. G. R. Taylor, ed., *The Original Writings and Correspondence of the Two Richard Hakluyts* (London, 1935), II, 323; Robert Johnson, *Nova Britannie, Offering Most Excellent Fruits by Planting in Virginia, Exciting all Such as be Well Affected to Further the Same* (London, 1609), reprinted in *American Colonial Tracts Monthly,* I (1897), No. 6, p. 10; Edwin C. Rozwenc, "Captain John Smith's Image of America," *WMQ,* 3d Ser., XVI (1959), 32-33; Treasurer and Council for Virginia to the Governor and Council in Virginia, Aug. 1, 1622, in Susan M. Kingsbury, ed., *The Records of the Virginia Company of London* (Washington, 1906-1935), III, 669-670; George Sandys to Samuel Wrote, March 28, 1623, quoted in Richard Beale Davis, *George Sandys, Poet Adventurer: A Study in Anglo-American Culture in the Seventeenth Century* (New York, 1955), 139.

27. Hartwell, Blair, and Chilton, *Present State of Virginia,* 10-13; John Clayton, "Account of Several Observables in Virginia," Royal Society of London, *Philosophical Transactions,* XVII (London, 1694), 791-792.

28. Observations by Master George Percy, 1607, in Lyon G. Tyler, ed., *Narratives of Early Virginia, 1606-1625* (New York, 1907), 7, 16.

29. John Smith, *A Map of Virginia . . .* (Oxford, 1612), in Arber and Bradley, eds., *Works of John Smith,* I, 48, 63.

30. John Spencer Bassett, ed., *The Writings of "Colonel Wm. Byrd of Westover in Virginia Esqr."* (New York, 1901), 392.

31. Beverley, *History,* 319; Berkeley, *Discourse,* 5-6; Hartwell, Blair and Chilton, *Present State of Virginia,* 4; Anthony Langston, "On Towns and Corporations, and on the Manufacture of Iron," *WMQ,* 2d Ser., I (1921), 101.

32. Conyers Read, "Mercantilism: The Old English Pattern of a Controlled Economy," in Conyers Read, ed., *The Constitution Reconsidered,* 2d ed. rev. (New York, 1968), 71-72.

33. Berkeley, *Discourse,* 4, 7.

34. Disadvantages by Priviledged Places, 1679, Coventry Papers, LXXVIII, fol. 444. Philip Ludwell to Coventry, June 16, 1679, ibid., fol. 386; Proposals for Virginia, 1676, ibid., LXXVIII, fol. 258.

35. George Milner, Proposals in order to the Improvement of the Country of Albemarle in the Province of Carolina in point of Townes, Trade, and Coyne, n.d. Egerton MSS. 2395, foll. 661-665, British Museum.

36. [Roger Green], *Virginia's Cure: or an advisive Narrative Concerning Virginia, Discovering the True Ground of that Churches Unhappiness,* in Force, *Tracts,* III, No. 15, pp. 10-11.

Notes to Chapter 2

1. William G. Stanard and Mary Newton Stanard, compilers, *The Colonial Virginia Register: A List of Governors, Councillors and Other Officials . . .* (Albany, 1902), 37, 51, 72; *JHB, 1619-1658/9,* xxiv; *EVB,* passim. Two helpful guides to biographical data on individual burgesses are Earl G. Swem, compiler, *Virginia Historical Index* (Roanoke, 1934-1936), and Robert A. Stewart, *Index to Printed Virginia Genealogies, Including Key and Bibliography* (Richmond, 1930).

2. Thomas Renalls to his sister, April 1658, *WMQ,* 1st Ser., VII (1898-1900), 112; Nicholas Hayward to Mr. Dodman and Daniel Lisson, Feb. 17, 1656, ibid., XV (1906-1907), 178; William Moule to Francis Moule, Sept. 18, 1653, ibid., XIV (1905-1906), 102.

3. Hening, *Statutes,* I, 130, 141-142, 152, 165, 203-207, 209-213.

4. Ibid., I, 488, 399, 479, 587-589; Robert H. Palgrave, ed., *The Dictionary of Political Economy* (New York, 1891-1899), III, 477; John Thirsk, *English Peasant Farming* (London, 1957), 112-117; Dalby Thomas, *An Historical Account of the Rise and Growth of the West-India Colonies,* reprinted in *The Harleian Miscellany,* IX (London, 1810), 424.

5. Hening, *Statutes,* 126, 163, 191, 206, 214, 245, 246, 412-414.

6. Ibid., 469-470, 420.

7. Lyon G. Tyler, "Pedigree of a Representative Virginia Planter," *WMQ,* 1st Ser., I (1892), 80-89, 140-141; Virginia Historical Society, *Collections,* XI (1892), 107-109; Samuel

Hartlib, *The Reformed Virginia Silk-Worm* . . . (London, 1655), in Force, *Tracts*, III, No. 13, pp. 27-28.

8. *JHB, 1619-1658/59*, 105; John D. Burk, *History of Virginia from its First Settlement to the Commencement of the Revolution* (Petersburg, 1804-1816), II, 116-117; Queries concerning his Highness' Interest in the West Indies, Egerton MSS 2395, fol. 86, British Museum; Overture of Thomas Povey, Additional MSS 11411, foll. 11-12; Charles M. Andrews, *British Committees, Commissions, and Councils of Trade and Plantations* (Baltimore, 1908), 52-53 et passim.

9. Committee for Managing Affairs of Jamaica and other Affairs in the West Indies to the Lord Protector, Egerton MSS 2395, fol. 147; *JHB, 1619-1658/59*, 115, 128-130.

10. Harold Hartley, *The Royal Society: Its Origins and Founders* (London, 1960).

11. Charles II to Virginia, Feb. 20, 1662, Egerton MSS 2543, fol. 22; Letter and queries from Mr. Povey, March 4, 1661, Egerton MSS 2395, foll. 296-297.

12. Andrews, *British Committees,* 67-68; *Shaftesbury Papers and Other Records Relating to Carolina* . . . , South Carolina Historical Society, *Collections* (Charleston, 1897), 14, 317.

13. Stock, *Proceedings and Debates,* I, 282; Andrews, *British Committees,* 62; E. B. O'Callaghan and Berthold Fernow, eds., *Documents Relative to the Colonial History of the State of New York* (Albany, 1856-1887), III, 30; Charles M. Andrews, *The Colonial Period of American History* (New Haven, 1934-1938), IV, 57-58.

14. Instructions for the Council Appointed for forraigne Plantations, 1660, CO 1/14: 113; Instructions to the Council of Trade, Egerton MSS 2395, foll. 268-269.

15. Frederick T. Jane, *Heresies of Sea Power* (London, 1906), 151; Shaw, *Cal. Treasury Bks.,* vol. *1660-1667,* I, Introduction. On the crown's fiscal position at the time of the Restoration, see also G. N. Clark, *The Later Stuarts, 1660-1717* (Oxford, England, 1955), 5-8.

16. Council for Foreign Plantations to Virginia, Feb. 18, 1661, and Instructions for the Council for Foreign Plantations, 1660, CO 1/14:113, 151.

17. Council for Foreign Plantations to Virginia, Feb. 18, 1661, CO 1/14: 155.

18. Minutes of the Council for Foreign Plantations, Aug. 5, 1661, CO 1/14: 160; Petition of planters and merchants of Virginia to the King, May 26, CO 1/16: 160.

19. Minutes of the Council for Foreign Plantations, May 26 and June 13, 1662, CO 1/16: 167.

20. Andrews, *British Committees,* 75; Letter from Mr. Povey, March 4, 1661, Egerton MSS 2395, fol. 296; *Shaftesbury Papers,* 14.

21. Instructions to Berkeley, Sept. 14, 1662, Coventry Papers, LXXVI, foll. 63-65.

22. Petition of Berkeley, Henry Chicheley, Edward Digges, and other planters of Virginia to the King, Aug. 1662, CO 1/16: 220; Petition of Planters and Merchants of Virginia to the King, May 26, 1662, CO 1/16: 160; Petition of Merchants, Traders, and Planters trading to Virginia and Maryland, Jan. 8, 1663, CO 1/17: 1; Humble Remonstrance of John Bland, *VMHB,* I (1893-1894), 143-145, 155; Petition of Merchants, Planters, Shipwrights, etc., to the King, June 13, 1662, CO 1/16: 165; The Reasons mentioned in the Petition of Merchants, planters, Shipwrights, etc . . . , CO 1/16: 166; Instructions to Berkeley, Sept. 14, 1662, Coventry Papers, LXXVI, foll. 63-65.

23. George Alsop, *A Character of the Province of Maryland* (London, 1666), in Hall, ed., *Narratives of Early Maryland,* 363; Bruce, *Economic History of Virginia,* II, 368; Petition of Berkeley to the Council for Foreign Plantations, 1662, CO 1/16: 183-184; Hening, *Statutes,* II, 221-222, 228, 232-234.

24. W. L. Grant and James Munro, eds., *Acts of the Privy Council of England, Colonial Series* (London, 1908-1912), I, 27, 592; Charles H. Firth and R. S. Rait, eds., *Acts and Ordinances of the Interregnum, 1642-1660* (London, 1911), II, 870; Petition to the Council of the Lord Protector, March 24, 1655, CO 1/12: 101; Petition of Samuel Mathews to the Lord Protector, March 1655, CO 1/12: 95. A detailed description of the efforts to curtail tobacco growing in England appears in Charles M. MacInnes, *The Early English Tobacco Trade* (London, 1926), Chs. III-IV.

25. [John Worlidge], *Systema Agriculturae: The Mystery of Husbandry Discovered* . . . (London, 1681), 166; *The Diary of Samuel Pepys, M.A., F.R.S., Clerk of the Acts and Secretary to the Admiralty,* ed., Henry B. Wheatley (London, 1928), VII, 117-118.

26. Humble Remonstrance of John Bland, *VMHB,* I (1893-1894), 152; Proposals Concerning building Towns in Virginia, Egerton MSS 2395, fol. 666.

27. [Green], *Virginia's Cure,* in Force, *Tracts,* III, No. 15, pp. 5-7, 18.

28. Instructions to Berkeley, Sept. 14, 1662, Coventry Papers, LXXVI, fol. 64.

29. Humble Remonstrance of John Bland, *VMHB,* I (1893-

1894), 152-154; Berkeley, *Discourse*, 8; Instructions to Berkeley, Sept. 14, 1662, Coventry Papers, LXXVI, fol. 65.

30. Anthony Langston, "On Towns and Corporations, and on Manufacture of Iron," *WMQ*, 2d Ser., I (1921), 101-102; Berkeley to Clarendon, July 30, 1666, Clarendon MSS 84, foll. 230-231, Bodleian Library; Berkeley, *Discourse*, 7-8; Petition of Berkeley to the Council for Foreign Plantations, 1662, CO 1/16: 183-194.

31. Minutes of the Council of Foreign Plantations, July 21, and Aug. 4 and 11, 1662, CO 1/14: 164-166; Instructions to Berkeley, Sept. 14, 1662, Coventry Papers, LXXVI, fol. 65.

32. Wesley Frank Craven, *The Colonies in Transition, 1660-1713* (New York, 1968), 32-33, 39-40.

Notes to Chapter 3

1. Herndon, *Tobacco in Colonial Virginia*, 46-48; Bruce, *Economic History of Virginia*, I, 394; *Historical Statistics of U.S.*, 756; W. Stitt Robinson, Jr., *"Mother Earth": Land Grants in Virginia, 1607-1699* (Williamsburg, 1957), 43-44.

2. Jerome E. Brooks, *Tobacco, Its History Illustrated by the Books, Manuscripts, and Engravings in the Library of George Arents, Jr., Together with an Introductory Essay* (New York, 1937-1943), I, 107n.

3. Berkeley letter, March 30, 1663, Egerton MSS 2395, fol. 362.

4. Hening, *Statutes*, II, 119; *JHB, 1659/60-1693*, 12, 23.

5. Lee, *Lee of Virginia*, 83-85; *EVB*, I, 122, 128; *WMQ*, 1st Ser., XIX (1909-1910), 208-209; Burk, *History of Virginia*, II, Appendix xxxiii.

6. The Lord Baltimore's Answer to the Representation delivered to his Majesty in Council the 6th October 1667 from the Governor and Council of the Colony of Virginia, CO 1/21: 269-270; Articles of Agreement at a Conference held at Mr. Allerton's by Commissioners of Virginia and Maryland, CO 1/17: 230.

7. Hening, *Statutes*, II, 191; Michael G. Kammen, "The Causes of the Maryland Revolution of 1689," *Maryland Historical Magazine*, LV (1960), 292-313; *Mary. Arch.*, I, 484-485; V, 16.

8. Hening, *Statutes*, II, 210; Remonstrance of the Governor, Council, and Burgesses of Virginia to the King, received Aug. 3, 1664, CO 1/18: 202. Chicheley was a member of the new generation of political leaders. In the English Civil War he

fought with the King. After the King's execution, Sir Henry was arrested, charged with complicity in a Royalist plot, and detained for a brief time in the Tower of London. He then went to Virginia, after giving security to Cromwell's government not to promote the king's interest in the colony. Soon after his arrival in Virginia he married the wealthy widow of a prominent planter. In 1656 he became a burgess. Later he served as lieutenant governor of the colony and was acting governor after the death of Herbert Jeffreys in 1676 and again during the frequent absences of Lord Culpeper in the early 1680's. Bruce, *Social Life of Virginia,* 61; *VMHB,* III (1895-1896), 39.

9. *VMHB,* XXX (1922), 328, XI (1903-1904), 359; Minutes of the Council for Foreign Plantations, Aug. 4, 1662, CO 1/14: 164; Alfred Beaven, *The Aldermen of the City of London* (London, 1908-1913), I, 50; Theophilus Jones, *A History of the County of Boucknock* (London, 1805), II, 670.

10. Answer of the Lord Baltimore to . . . certain proposals for lessening the quantity of tobacco, Nov. 19, 1664, CO 1/18: 318-319; see also A Representation of the Necessity of Lessening the Quantity of Tobacco, Nov. 19, 1664, CO 1/18: 313.

11. Answer of the Lord Baltimore to . . . certain proposals . . . , Nov. 19, 1664, CO 1/18: 318-319.

12. A Representation of the Necessity of Lessening the Quantity of Tobacco, Nov. 19, 1664, CO 1/18: 313; Remonstrance of the Governor, Council, and Burgesses of Virginia to the King, received Aug. 3, 1664, CO 1/18: 202.

13. Shaw, *Cal. Treasury Bks.,* I, xxxii, II, vii-viii; David Ogg, *England in the Reign of Charles II* (Oxford, 1934), II, 283.

14. Order in Council, Nov. 25, 1664, CO 1/18: 323; Petition of Sir William Berkeley to the King, June 1669, CO 1/24: 123; Thomas Ludwell to Arlington, April 10, 1665, CO 1/19: 75.

15. Herndon, *Tobacco in Colonial Virginia,* 46-48; Thomas Ludwell to Arlington, Feb. 12, 1667, CO 1/21: 37; Berkeley to Arlington, July 13, 1666, CO 1/30: 199-200; Edward Hickman, Samuell Calle, and John Mannington to John Alexander, Sept. 18, 1663, *WMQ,* 1st Ser., VIII (1899-1900), 262-263.

16. Virginia governor and council to the King, June 24, 1667, CO 1/21: 118-121.

17. *CRNC,* I, 183-187; *Mary. Arch.,* II, 49, 143-144.

18. Hening, *Statutes,* II, 224-226; Virginia governor and council to the King, June 24, 1667, CO 1/21: 118-121.

19. Agreement between Virginia, Maryland, and North Carolina, July 12, 1666, CO 1/21: 193.

20. *JHB, 1659/60-1693*, 37; William P. Palmer, et al., eds., *Calendar of Virginia State Papers and Other Manuscripts, 1652-1781* (Richmond, 1875-1893), I, 7; *VMHB,* XVIII (1910), 2-3n; Drummond letter dated Sept. 3, 1666, Jefferson Library MSS, Virginia, Foreign Business and Inquisitions, Library of Congress; Names and Short Characters of those that have been executed for Rebellion, CO 5/1571: 54. On the Indian raid see Lawrence E. Lee, *Indian Wars in North Carolina, 1663-1763* (Raleigh, 1963), 14-16.

21. *JHB, 1659/60-1693*, 35; Virginia governor and council to the King, June 24, 1667, CO 1/21: 118-121; Hening, *Statutes,* II, 229-232; Commission to Thomas Ludwell and others, Nov. 8, 1666, CO 1/20: 295; Further articles of agreement between the Virginia and Maryland commissioners appointed to negotiate a cessation, Dec. 11, 1666, CO 1/20: 338. Rumors of the London fire and the subsequent disruption of trade gave added impetus to putting a cessation into effect. Berkeley to Richard Nicholls, Jan. 22, 1667, Blathwayt Papers, Huntington Library; Thomas Ludwell to Clarendon, Feb. 12, 1667, New York Historical Society, *Collections for 1869* (New York, 1870), 160.

22. Virginia governor and council to the King, June 24, 1667, CO 1/21: 118-121; Thomas Ludwell to Arlington, June 18, 1666, CO 1/20: 219; Berkeley and others to Arlington, June 13, 1666, ibid., 199-200; Philip Ludwell letter dated Sept. 17, 1666, VMHB, V (1897–1898), 58; Berkeley to Nicholls, July 30, 1666, Blathwayt Papers, Huntington Library.

23. *Mary. Arch.,* III, 558-561.

24. Andrews, *British Committees,* 78-85; Lord Baltimore's Instrument for voiding the cessation, Nov. 24, 1666, CO 1/20: 319; *Mary. Arch.,* III, 561-562.

25. Thomas Ludwell to Lord Berkeley, Nov. 7, 1667, CO 1/21: 282-283; Berkeley letter dated Dec. 11, 1667, CO 1/21: 286.

26. Virginia governor and council to the King, June 24, 1667, CO 1/21: 118-121; Lord Baltimore's Answer . . . to the Representation delivered to the Council, Oct. 6, 1667 from the Governor and Council of Virginia, Oct. 16, 1667, CO 1/21: 269-270; Order in Council, Oct. 30, 1667, CO 1/21: 281.

27. Lord Baltimore's Answer . . . CO 1/21: 269-270.

28. *Mary. Arch.,* II, 143-144.

29. Hening, *Statutes,* II, 226-227, 233-234.

30. Order in Council, Oct. 30, 1667, CO 1/21: 281.

Notes to Chapter 4

1. An answer to a Declaration of the Present State of Virginia, May 1623, Kingsbury, ed., *Recs. of Va. Company,* IV, 145.

2. Berkeley to Arlington, June 13, 1670, CO 1/25: 80-81; Copy of a letter supposed to be Bacon's, Coventry Papers, LXXVII, fol. 442-443; Unsigned paper probably written by Giles Bland, CO 1/21: 58; *JHB, 1659/60-1693,* 46; Proclamation of Berkeley, CO 1/36: 137.

3. *JHB, 1659/60-1693,* 28, 43; Thomas Ludwell to Lord Berkeley, Nov. 7, 1667, CO 1/21: 282-283; Thomas Ludwell letter dated Sept. 17, 1666, *VMHB,* XXI (1913), 40.

4. Manning C. Voorhis, "Crown Versus Council in the Virginia Land Policy," *WMQ,* 3d Ser., III (1946), 502; Voorhis, The Land Grant Policy of Colonial Virginia, 1607-1774, Ph.D. dissertation, University of Virginia, 1940, Ch. II; Fairfax Harrison, *Virginia Land Grants: A Study of Conveyance in Relation to Colonial Politics* (Richmond, 1925); Wesley Frank Craven, *The Southern Colonies in the Seventeenth Century 1607-1689* (Baton Rouge, 1949), 269-289, 293-294, 302-309.

5. Morgan Godwyn, *The Negro's and Indian's Advocate, Suing for their Admission to the Church* . . . (London, 1680) reprinted in Brydon, *Virginia's Mother Church,* I, 511-512. For previous studies of Berkeley's role in the economic planning undertaken after the Restoration by the provincial government see Harold Lee Hitchens, "Sir William Berkeley, Virginia Economist," *WMQ,* 2d Ser., XVIII (1938), 158-173, and especially Sister Joan de Lourdes Leonard, "Operation Checkmate: The Birth and Death of a Virginia Blueprint for Progress, 1660-1676," ibid., 3d Ser., XXIV (1967), 44-74.

6. Arber and Bradley, eds., *Works of John Smith,* II, 928; Berkeley to the King, July 22, 1668, CO 1/23: 42; Governor, Council, and Burgesses to the King, July 22, 1668, CO 1/23: 41; Thomas Ludwell letter of June 7, 1669, CO 1/24: 118; Berkeley's Petition to the King, June 1669, CO 1/24: 123; Berkeley letter of June 20, 1671, CO 1/26: 196. For a description of efforts to produce silk in Virginia, see Charles E. Hatch, Jr., "Mulberry Trees and Silkworms: Sericulture in Early Virginia," *VMHB,* LXV (1957), 3-61.

7. Clarence W. Alvord and Lee Bidgood, *The First Explorations of the Trans-Allegheny by the Virginians* (Cleveland, 1912), 47-51, 166-167.

8. Lyman Carrier, "The Veracity of John Lederer," *WMQ,* 2d Ser., XIX (1939), 441-443.

9. Berkeley to Arlington, May 27, 1669, CO 1/24: 116; Thomas Ludwell to Arlington, June 27, 1669, CO 1/25: 85; Berkeley to Arlington, June 13, 1669, CO 1/25: 80-81; Alvord and Bidgood, *First Explorations,* 69, 179, 184, 192, 206-209.

10. Berkeley letter of March 30, 1663, Egerton MSS 2395, fol. 362; Samuel H. Younge, *The Site of Old "James Towne," 1607-1789* (Richmond, 1907), 43-45; *Narratives of the Indian and Civil War in Virginia in the Years 1675 and 1676,* Force, *Tracts,* I, No. 11, pp. 24-25; Hening, *Statutes,* II, 172-176.

11. Fairfax Harrison, "The Proprietors of the Northern Neck," *VMHB,* XXXIII (1925), 113-153, 223-267, XXXIV (1926), 19-64.

12. Hening, *Statutes,* II, 313-314; Thomas Ludwell to Coventry, Nov. 21, 1676, Coventry Papers, LXXVII, fol. 299; Thomas Ludwell to Arlington, June 26, 1671, CO 1/26: 213; Fairfax Harrison, *Landmarks of Old Prince William* (Richmond, 1924), II, 42-43.

13. Berkeley to Danby, Feb. 1, 1675, *VMHB,* XXXII (1924), 191-192.

14. Governor and Council to the King, March 28, 1663, Egerton MSS 2395, fol. 360; Thomas Ludwell to Arlington, June 26, 1671, CO 1/26: 231; Burk, *History of Virginia,* II, appendix, xxi-xxiv, lii-liii; Memorial presented to Coventry, April 15, 1676, Coventry Papers, LXXVII, fol. 74; Notes Explanatory of some of the heads annexed to the petition of the Virginia agents, Coventry Papers, LXXVII, foll. 44-45; Hening, *Statutes,* II, 313-314; Thomas Ludwell to Coventry, Nov. 21, 1676, Coventry Papers, LXXVII, fol. 299.

15. Hening, *Statutes,* II, 85, 120-125, 179, 185, 306-307, 514; Bruce, *Economic History of Virginia,* II, 411-412; *JHB, 1659/60-1693,* 20-22.

16. Ibid., 20; Hening, *Statutes,* II, 121-122, 174-175, 178, 272-273.

17. Ibid., 123, 172-176.

18. *JHB, 1659/60-1693,* 20, 49; Reverend Moray to Sir Robert Moray, Feb. 1, 1665, *WMQ,* 2d Ser., II (1922), 157-158; Hening, *Statutes,* II, 199; "Notes from Surry County Records in the Seventeenth Century," *WMQ,* 2d Ser., XIX (1929), 531-532; "York County Levy," ibid., 1st Ser., XXVI (1917-1918), 32.

19. Berkeley letters dated April 18 and March 30, 1662, Egerton MSS 2395, foll. 362, 365; Petition of Berkeley to the King, June 1669, CO 1/24: 123; Berkeley letter of June 21, 1669, CO 1/24: 121; Thomas Ludwell letter of June 7, 1669,

CO 1/24: 118; Berkeley letter of June 20, 1671, CO 1/26: 192.

20. Reverend Moray to Sir Robert Moray, June 12, 1665, *WMQ*, 2d Ser., II (1922), 158-161; Berkeley to Secretary Bennet, March 30, 1663, CO 1/17: 43; Berkeley letters of March 30 and April 18, Egerton MSS 2395, foll. 362, 365.

21. Answer of William Gooch to the Queries of the Board of Trade, July 23, 1730, CO 5/1322: 119; Andrew Burnaby, *Travels Through the Middle Settlements in North America in the Years 1759 and 1760* (Ithaca, 1960), 15.

22. Richard S. Dunn, "The Barbadoes Census of 1680: Profile of the Richest Colony in English America," *WMQ*, 3d Ser., XXVI (1969), 4; Andrews, *Colonial Period*, II, 253.

23. "Captain Thomas Yong's Voyage to Virginia and Delaware Bay and River in 1634," Mass. Hist. Soc., *Collections*, 4th Ser., IX (Boston, 1871), 110-111; "A Brief Journal of a Voyage in the Barque Virginia," *Northern Neck of Virginia Historical Magazine*, VI (1965), 488; A Representation of the Necessity of Lessening the Quantity of Tobacco, Nov. 1664, CO 1/18:313.

24. Bullock, *Virginia Impartially Examined*, 9; William Byrd to Sadlier and Thomas, Nov. 10, 1686, *VMHB*, XXV (1917), 133; Byrd to John Thomas, Feb. 12, 1687, ibid., 251; Records of Lower Norfolk County, vol. 1656-1660, 133, Virginia State Library, Richmond; Records of Rappahannock County, vol. 1663-1668, 85, Va. St. Lib.

25. Berkeley, *Discourse*, 11; Virginia council to the King, Oct. 11, 1673, CO 1/30: 179.

26. Bruce, *Economic History of Virginia*, II, 141-142; Hening, *Statutes*, II, 85, 179.

27. Thomas Ludwell to Lord Berkeley, June 24, 1667, CO 1/21: 116-117; Thomas Ludwell to Arlington, Feb. 12, 1667, CO 1/21: 37.

28. Henry Chicheley letter of July 16, 1673, CO 1/30: 113.

29. Vincent Ponko, Jr., *The Privy Council and the Spirit of Elizabethan Economic Management, 1558-1603*, American Philosophical Society, *Transactions*, new ser., LVIII, Part 4 (Philadelphia, 1968), 58 et passim.

30. William Sherwood letter of June 1, 1676, CO 1/37: 1; Beverley, *History*, 74.

31. Wilcomb E. Washburn, *The Governor and the Rebel: A History of Bacon's Rebellion in Virginia* (Chapel Hill, 1957), 162-166.

32. Craven, *Southern Colonies*, 375-379.

33. Edward D. Neill, *Virginia Carolorum: The Colony Under the Rule of Charles the First and Second* (Albany, 1886), 295; *JHB, 1659/60-1693,* 23; Alvord and Bidgood, *First Explorations,* 66-67, 136-137, 150-152.

34. Bacon's Manifesto, CO 1/37: 178-179; Declaration of the People, CO 1/37: 41.

35. Isle of Wight County Grievances, CO 1/39: 223-227; Exact Repertory of the General and Personall Grievances presented to us (His Majesty's Commissioners) by the People of Virginia, CO 5/1371: 299, 317; Surry County Grievances, CO 1/39: 207-208; Rappahannock County Grievances, CO 1/39: 197-198; York County Grievances, CO 1/39: 242; Commissioners' comments on the Lancaster County grievances, CO 1/39: 218.

36. Commissioners to the Lords of Trade, Dec. 1677, CO 1/41: 278-279; Edward Hill in answer to diverse false scandalous articles drawn up against him, CO 1/40: 73; *VMHB,* III (1896), 250-251; Personal Grievances of Divers Inhabitants . . . Proved before his Majesty's Commissioners, CO 5/1371: 339-340; A List of the Names of those Worthy Persons whose Service and Sufferings by . . . Bacon . . . render them most deserving of his Majesty's Royal Remark, CO 5/1371: 354; The Humble Remonstrance and Address of the Inhabitants of Charles City County, 1677, CO 1/41: 148-151.

37. *JHB, 1659/60-1693,* 73; Berkeley, *Discourse,* 7.

38. Surry County, Isle of Wight County and Rappahannock County Grievances, CO 1/39: 207-208, 223-227, 197.

39. Berkeley, *Discourse,* 7.

Notes to Chapter 5

1. Hist. MSS Comm., Twelfth Report, Appendix, Part VII, *Manuscripts of S. H. Le Fleming* (London, 1890), 129; Thomas Ludwell to Coventry, Oct. 13, 1676, and Proposals for the Better Accomodating his Majesty's Affairs in Virginia . . . , Coventry Papers, LXXVII, foll. 254, 295; *Randolph Papers,* II, 267; Michael G. Hall, *Edward Randolph and the American Colonies, 1676-1703* (Chapel Hill, 1960), 29-30; Coventry to the Earl of Essex, Oct. 2, 1676, Coventry Papers, LXXIV, foll. 47-48. The most comprehensive account of the impact of Bacon's Rebellion on England is Wilcomb E. Washburn's *The Effect of Bacon's Rebellion on Government*

in *England and Virginia,* United States National Museum *Bulletin,* No. 225 (Washington, 1962), 137-151.

2. Ibid., 147; Shaw, *Cal. Treasury Bks.,* V, pt. I, xiv, xxxiv-xxxvi; Edwards Pike, ed., *Selections from the Correspondence of Arthur, Earl of Essex, 1676-1677,* Camden Society Publications, 3d Ser., XXIV (London, 1913); Arthur Bryant, ed., *The Letters, Speeches, and Declarations of King Charles II* (London, 1935), 289.

3. Arlington to Secretary Williamson, Oct. 2, 1676, F. H. Blackburne, ed., *Calendar of State Papers, Domestic Series, Reign of Charles II,* XVIII (London, 1909), 348; The Present state of the soldiers designed for Virginia, Nov. 1, 1676, CO 1/38: 58; An account from Mr. Pepys on the Distribution on ship board of the forces designed for Virginia, CO 1/38: 78-80; An estimate of the charge of transporting one thousand men . . . to Virginia, Oct. 1676, CO 1/37: 233; Establishment for officers and soldiers to be sent for our service to Virginia, Oct. 1676, CO 1/37: 231; Memorial of all the estimates made and given this office of Ordnance for his Majesty's Service . . . , Nov. 6, 1676, CO 1/38: 76; Additional establishment for forces designed for Virginia, CO 1/38: 63; Secretary Williamson's Notes concerning the expedition to Virginia, CO 1/38: 297-312; Stock, *Proceedings and Debates,* I, 412; Ogg, *England in Reign of Charles II,* II, 539.

4. Philip Ludwell to Berkeley, June 12, 1676, Allerton to Thomas Ludwell, Aug. 4, 1676, Berkeley letter of June 3, 1676, and Copy of a letter supposed to be Bacon's, Coventry Papers, LXXVII, foll. 117-118, 160, 103, 442-443.

5. Giles Bland to Williamson, April 28, 1676, *VMHB,* XX (1912), 352-356. On Bland's English background and connections, see Washburn, *Governor and Rebel,* 105, 169.

6. Robert Southwell to Ormond, Nov. 13, 1677, Hist. MSS Comm., *Ormond,* new ser., V, 386.

7. Hall, *Randolph,* 4, 45-46; Philip S. Haffenden, "The Crown and Colonial Charters, 1675-1688," *WMQ,* 3d Ser., XV (1958), 297-311, 452-466. Gertrude Ann Jacobsen, *William Blathwayt: A Late Seventeenth Century Administrator* (New Haven, 1932), 150 ff; Andrews, *Colonial Period,* IV, Ch. VI.

8. Instructions to the Commissioners, 1676, Coventry Papers, LXXVII, fol. 285; Hening, *Statutes,* II, 424.

9. Berry and Moryson to Secretary of State, Feb. 12, 1677, A particular account how wee your Majesty's Commissioners have observed and comply'd with our instructions, Commissioners to the General Assembly, Feb. 27, 1677, and Berkeley's Proclamation, CO 5/1371: 29, 365-366, 107-113, 272-286; Commissioners to Thomas Watkins, March 27,

1677, Moryson to Mr. Cooke, May 28, 1678, and Jeffreys to Coventry, Coventry Papers, LXXVII, foll. 19, 245, 44; Hening, *Statutes*, II, 366-386.

10. *JHB, 1659/60-1693*, 73-74, 87, 89-91; Grievances of James City County, CO 1/39: 194-195; Thomas Ludwell and Francis Moryson to the King, June 18, 1676, Coventry Papers, LXXVI, foll. 128-129; An Exact Repertory of the General and Personal Grievances presented us (his Majesty's Commissioners) by the People of Virginia, CO 5/1371: 296-297; Giles Bland, State of Virginia, *VMHB*, XX (1912), 354-356.

11. Commissioners to Secretary Williamson, April 13, 1677, CO 5/1371: 53; Moryson to Blackwith, Oct. 25, 1678, CO 1/42: 352; Jeffreys to the Burgesses, Oct. 23, 1677, and Burgesses to Jeffreys, Oct. 23, 1677, Coventry Papers, LXXVIII, foll. 123-124; Thomas Jefferson Wertenbaker, *Virginia Under the Stuarts* (Princeton, 1914), 213-214.

12. Order in Council, Oct. 30, 1678, CO 1/42: 356.

13. Hening, *Statutes*, II, 462; Berkeley to Coventry, Feb. 9, 1677, Coventry Papers, LXXVII, fol. 382; Thomas Ludwell to Coventry, July 16, 1677, Coventry Papers, LXXVIII, fol. 76; Thomas Ludwell to Williamson, July 16, 1677, CO 1/41: 35-36. For a detailed discussion of the crown's decision regarding pardons to rebels and the right of Berkeley's supporters to sue for damages suffered in the rebellion, see Washburn, *Governor and Rebel*, 145-152.

14. Instructions to Culpeper, Dec. 6, 1679, CO 1/47: 265-266. A similar policy for Jamaica in 1678 provided a precedent. Archibald P. Thornton, *West-India Policy Under the Restoration* (Oxford, 1956), 173-175.

15. Hening, *Statutes*, I, 176, 192, 218, 247, 301, II, 130, 176-177, 413, 466-469; Culpeper's Speech to the Burgesses, June 24, 1680, *VMHB*, XIV (1906-1907), 368-369; *JHB, 1659/60-1693*, 130-131.

16. Ibid., 148; *EJC*, I, 2-5; Instructions to Culpeper with an account of his lordships compliance therewith, CO 1/18: 35-71.

17. Lawrence H. Leder, *Robert Livingston, 1654-1728, and the Politics of Colonial New York* (Chapel Hill, 1961), 57-210.

18. Jack P. Greene, *The Quest for Power, The Lower Houses of Assembly in the Southern Royal Colonies, 1689-1776* (Chapel Hill, 1963), 127; *JHB, 1659/60-1693*, passim.

19. Philip Ludwell to Thomas Ludwell, June 13, 1676, Coventry Papers, LXXVII, fol. 121; Nicholas Spencer to Secretary Coventry, July 9, 1680, CO 1/45: 189-190.

20. Ibid.; [William Sherwood], Virginia's Deploured Condition,

Mass. Hist. Soc., *Collections,* 4th Ser., IX (Boston, 1871), 163-165; Philip Ludwell to Coventry, June 16, 1679, Coventry Papers, LXXVIII, fol. 386; Proposals for Virginia, Coventry Papers, LXXVIII, fol. 258.

21. Commissioners to the Lords of Trade, Dec. 1677, CO 1/41: 278-279; Morton, *Colonial Virginia,* I, 274; Washburn, *Governor and Rebel,* 86; Some Observations upon the insolent carriage and behavior of Robert Beverley, ca. 1678, Coventry Papers, LXXVIII, fol. 321; A List of . . . worthy persons . . ., CO 5/1371: 354; Sarah Drummond to Francis Moryson, July 8, 1678, CO 5/1371: 540-541. For depositions regarding Beverley's conduct during Bacon's Rebellion see CO 1/41: 295-300.

22. *EVB,* I, 46-47, 126, 128; Stanard and Stanard, compilers, *Colonial Va. Register,* 15-17, 35, 38. On Chicheley's lack of leadership, see Culpeper to the Earl of Dartmouth, March 18, 1683, Hist. MSS Comm., Eleventh Rpt., Appendix Pt. V, *Manuscripts of the Earl of Dartmouth* (London, 1887), 80-81.

23. *JHB, 1659/60-1693,* 137; Hening, *Statutes,* II, 471-478; Humble Address of the Council and Burgesses to the King, CO 1/47: 83; William Fitzhugh to Francis Partis, July 1, 1680, Davis, *Fitzhugh,* 82; Spencer to Coventry, July 9, 1680, CO 1/45: 189.

24. *JHB, 1659/60-1693,* 122-131, 148; *VMHB,* XIV (1906-1907), 368-369; *EJC,* I, 14; Henry Chicheley to Coventry, May 20, 1679, *CSPA, 1677-1680,* 360-361.

25. *JHB, 1659/60-1693,* 129-134, 136, 138, 144-145; Journal of the Lords of Trade, Sept. 17, 1681, *VMHB,* XXV (1917), 368; Spencer to Coventry, July 9, 1680, CO 1/45: 189-190.

26. Culpeper to his sister, Sept. 20 and Oct. 5, 1680, *Va. Hist. Register,* III (1850), 191-193; Culpeper letter of July 8, 1680, CO 1/45: 88; Spencer to Coventry, July 9, 1680, CO 1/45: 189.

27. Culpeper, The Present State of Virginia, CO 1/47: 260-262; Culpeper's Proposals for Virginia, Oct. 18, 1681, CO 1/47: 130; Order in Council, Oct. 14, 1680, *VMHB,* XXV (1917), 268; Blathwayt to Chicheley, Oct. 30, 1680, Blathwayt Papers, Colonial Williamsburg, XIII; Privy Council to Culpeper, Oct. 14, 1680, *VMHB,* XXV (1917), 265-267; Report of the Commissioners of the Customs touching a cessation of planting, Jan. 10, 1681, CO 1/46: 165.

28. Henry Guy to the Commissioners of the Customs, July 12, 1681, CO 1/46: 60; Philip Ludwell to Culpeper, July 25, 1681, CO 1/47: 80-83; Keith Feiling, *A History of the Tory Party, 1640-1714* (Oxford, 1924), 175; Report of the Commissioners of the Customs, Dec. 12, 1681, CO 1/47: 252-

253; Journal of the Lords of Trade, Dec. 13, 1681, and Dec. 15, 1681, Order in Council, Dec. 21, 1681, Culpeper to Chicheley, Dec. 23, 1681, *VMHB*, XXVI (1919), 45-46, 135, 175.

29. *EJC*, I, 19; An Account of the Government of Virginia by the Council, May 4, 1683, CO 1/51: 316-318; McIlwaine, ed., *Minutes of the Council and General Court*, 521; Middlesex County Court Order Book, 1680-1684, foll. 60-64, Va. St. Library.

30. Ibid., *VMHB*, VIII (1900-1901), 188-189.

31. Culpeper's report on Virginia, 1683, *VMHB*, III (1895-1896), 229-230; Spencer to Secretary Jenkins, May 8, 1683, CO 1/48: 230-231; Hening, *Statutes*, III, 561.

32. *EJC*, I, 10-12; Order in Council, Nov. 22, 1681, *VMHB*, XXV (1917), 374; Philip Calvert to Henry Meese, Dec. 29, 1681, *Mary. Arch.*, XX, pp. xii-xiv; Lord Baltimore to Blathwayt, March 26, 1682, CO 1/48: 185; Culpeper's Reasons for Continuing the Small Forces . . . in Virginia, Oct. 25, 1681, *VMHB*, XXV (1920), 369.

33. *JHB, 1659/60-1693*, 160-167; *LJC*, I, 15-16; Spencer to Secretary Jenkins, May 8, 1682, and Chicheley to Jenkins, May 18, 1682, CO 1/48: 228, 230-231.

34. Spencer to Blathwayt, May 29, 1682, Blathwayt Papers, Colonial Williamsburg, XVI; Cecil Baltimore to Jenkins, May 18, 1682, *Mary. Arch.*, V, 357-358; Chicheley to the King, May 8, 1682, Blathwayt Papers, Huntington Library; Affidavit of Spencer, Col. Bacon, and Philip Ludwell, Sept. 20, 1683, ibid.; Spencer to Jenkins, May 8, May 30, and June 7, 1682, CO 1/48: 230-231, 261, 313; *EJC*, I, 17-20.

35. Spencer to Jenkins, May 8, 1682, CO 1/48: 231; W. H. Whiting, "Notes on Major Henry Whiting," *WMQ*, 2d Ser., X (1930), 47-51; *EJC*, I, 14, 41; William Fitzhugh to John Cooper, June 5, 1682, Davis, *Fitzhugh*, 126; Fitzhugh to Beverley, Jan. 1, 1683, ibid., 132; *VMHB*, XIX (1911), 149.

36. Spencer to Jenkins, May 30, 1682, Chicheley to Jenkins, May 30, 1682, and Charles Scarburgh to Jenkins, June 16, 1682, CO 1/48: 261, 275, 336; Culpeper's Report on Virginia, *VMHB*, III (1895-1896), 275-276.

37. Baltimore to Jenkins, May 18, 1682, CO 1/48: 240; Report of the Lords of Trade to the King, June 24, 1682, and Order in Council, June 14, 1682, *VMHB*, XXVII (1923), 123-127.

38. *LJC*, I, 20-23; Hening, *Statutes*, II, 493-497, 503-507; Culpeper's Report on Virginia, *VMHB*, III (1895-1896), 228-229.

39. Ibid., 230-231; Spencer to Blathwayt, May 9, 1683, Blath-

wayt Papers, Colonial Williamsburg, XVI; Chicheley to Jenkins, Aug. 10, 1682, CO 1/49: 100; William Byrd to Thomas Gover, May 20, 1684, *Va. Hist. Register*, I (1848), 115; *EJC*, I, 55.

40. Ibid., 32-33, 46; Fitzhugh to Culpeper, Jan. 8, 1683, Davis, *Fitzhugh*, 134-135; Culpeper's Report on Virginia, *VMHB*, III (1895-1896), 324.

41. For an interpretation stressing the continuity between Berkeley and Beverley see Washburn, *Governor and Rebel*, 150-152.

Notes to Chapter 6

1. Stock, *Proceedings and Debates*, I, 370-379; *Bishop Burnet's History of the Reign of King James II* (London, 1852), 43; John Viscount Lonsdale, *Memoir of the Reign of James II* (London, 1857), 451; Shaw, *Cal. Treasury Bks.*, IV, Introduction; Ogg, *England in the Reigns of James II and William III* (Oxford, 1955), 144.

2. Ibid., 143-144; Thomas B. Macaulay, *History of England from the Accession of James the Second* (New York, 1866), II, 108-110; Dalby Thomas, *An Historical Account of the Rise and Growth of the West-India Colonies* . . . (London, 1690), reprinted in *Harleian Miscellany*, IX (London, 1810), 403-404; Roger North, *Lives of the Right Hon. Francis North . . ., The Hon. Sir Dudley North . . ., and The Hon. and Rev. Dr. John North*, new edition (London, 1726), III, 161-164; Stock, *Proceedings and Debates*, I, 423-424.

3. North, *Lives of the Norths*, III, 161-164; Patrick McGrath, ed., *Records Relating to the Society of Merchants Venturers of the City of Bristol in the Seventeenth Century*, Bristol Record Society, Publications, XVII (Bristol, 1952), 252-253; *History and Proceedings of the House of Commons from the Restoration to the Present Time* (London, 1742-1744), II, 174; MacInnes, *Early English Tobacco Trade*, 169-170; The Virginia Trade Stated, CO 1/41: 310; Thomas Bruce, Earl of Ailesbury, *Memoirs* (Westminster, 1890), I, 105-107.

4. *Randolph Papers*, IV, 27, 42; Shaw, *Cal. Treasury Bks.*, VIII, Pt. I, xxv-liv; Hist. MSS Comm., Sixteenth Report, *Manuscripts of the Earl of Egmont*, I, Pt. II (London, 1905), 155.

5. Circular letter from the King to the Plantations, June 26, 1685, and Journal of the Lords of Trade, Aug. 18, 1685, *CSPA, 1685-1688*, 59, 76; Instructions to Lord Howard of Effingham, Aug. 30, 1685, *VMHB*, XIX (1911), 341.

6. Draft of Tobacco Bill, 1686, Harleian Manuscripts 1238, foll. 37-62, British Museum.

7. Godolphin to John Pory, Sept. 23, 1692, CO 5/1306: 131; Petition of Merchants, Owners, and Planters of Virginia and Maryland to the King, Aug. 1687, CO 1/63: 74; Some reasons why bulke tobacco from Virginia and Maryland ought to be prohibited being exported . . . , CO 1/63: 76-77; Thomas H. Wynne, ed., *History of the Dividing Line and Other Notes, from the Papers of William Byrd of Westover in Virginia, Esquire* (Richmond, 1866), II, 140-159.

8. Commissioners of the Customs to the Lords of Trade, Oct. 11, 1687, CO 1/63: 239; Journal of the Lords of Trade, Oct. 25, 1687, and Orders in Council, Oct. 28 and Nov. 4, 1687, *CSPA, 1685-1688,* 459-460, 464.

9. William Fitzhugh to John Cooper, March 19, 1683 and May 18, 1685, Davis, *Fitzhugh,* 139-140, 166; Spencer to the Lords of Trade, May 29, 1683, CO 1/51: 340; Spencer to Sunderland, July 21, 1684, CO 1/55: 30; Spencer to Blathwayt, Aug. 14, 1683, Blathwayt Papers, Colonial Williamsburg, XVI; Effingham to Blathwayt, Aug. 28, 1684, ibid., XIV; William Byrd to Mr. North, Dec. 29, 1684, and Byrd letter of March 29, 1685, *VMHB,* XXIV (1916), 232, 351; Byrd to his father, June 5, 1685, *Va. Hist. Register,* II (1848), 81; Effingham to his wife, March 1684, Effingham Papers, IV, fol. 16, Library of Congress.

10. Byrd to Perry and Lane, July 8, 1686, and Byrd letter of Jan. 1689, *VMHB,* XXV (1917), 131-132, 359; Spencer to Blathwayt, March 29, 1687 and March 1, 1689, Blathwayt Papers, Colonial Williamsburg, XVI; *EJC,* I, 133-134; William Fitzhugh to John Cooper, April 18, 1687 and May 10, 1688; Davis, *Fitzhugh,* 220-221, 239-240.

11. James Edwin T. Rogers, *History of Agriculture and Prices in England* (Oxford, 1886-1902), V, 467-469, VI, 440, 444-446, 606, 673; Robert Southwell to John Pory, Nov. 28, 1689, CO 5/1305; An Account of all the Tobacco from Dec. 25, 1688 to Dec. 25, 1689 . . . , CO 5/1305: 241; Jacob M. Price, *The Tobacco Adventure to Russia: Enterprise, Politics, and Diplomacy in the Quest for a Northern Market for English Colonial Tobacco,* American Philosophical Society, *Transactions,* new ser., LI (Philadelphia, 1961), 5, 103; *Randolph Papers,* IV, 27.

12. William Byrd to Perry and Lane, March 29, 1685, *Va. Hist. Register,* II (1849), 78; Byrd to Perry and Lane, Dec. 11, 1688, *VMHB,* XXV (1917), 353; Spencer to the Lords of Trade, May 29, 1683, CO 1/51: 340.

13. *LJC,* I, 72-73; *EJC,* I, 55; Byrd to Thomas Gover, May 20,

1684, *Va. Hist. Register,* I (1848), 115; Effingham to Blathwayt, June 6, 1681, Blathwayt Papers, Colonial Williamsburg, XIV; Hening, *Statutes,* III, 58-60.

14. *LJC,* I, 95-96; Effingham to the Lords of Trade, Feb. 10, 1686, CO 1/59: 87-89; *JHB, 1659/60-1693,* 503-505.

15. Copy of the Fair Engrossed Bill for Ports . . . , CO 1/58: 327-330; Effingham to the Lords of Trade, Feb. 10, 1686, CO 1/59: 87-89; Effingham's Answer to Ludwell's Second Petition and Paper of Particulars, Oct. 1689, CO 5/1305: 19; Spencer to the Lords of Trade, March 1686, CO 1/59: 153-154; *LJC,* I, 100-101.

16. Ibid.

17. James II to Effingham, Aug. 1, 1686, *VMHB,* XIX (1911), 8-9; *JHB, 1659/60-1693,* 272-273.

18. *Mary. Arch.,* VII, 609-619, XIII, 111-120, 132-139, 218-220, XVII, 219-220, 358, 403, 406, 409; *JHB, 1659/60-1693,* 312.

19. Thomas Jefferson Wertenbaker, *Patrician and Plebeians in Virginia* (Charlottesville, 1910), 97-98; Effingham's Answer . . . , CO 5/1305: 19; Effingham to Sunderland, Feb. 22, 1687, CO 1/67: 245-246; Captain Gibbs' . . . Declaration, June 2, 1680, *CRNC,* I, 363-364.

20. *EJC,* I, 88; William Byrd to Warham Horsmanden, April 16, 1688, *VMHB,* XXV (1917), 259; Edward M. Greenfield, "Some New Aspects of the Life of Daniel Parke," ibid., LIV (1946), 308; Effingham to Blathwayt, May 23, 1688, Blathwayt Papers, Colonial Williamsburg, XIV.

21. *JHB, 1659/60-1693,* 291, 309-310.

22. Beverley, *History,* 95-97; Granville Leverson-Gouver, "Howards of Effingham," Surry Archeological Society, *Collections,* IX (1883), 406-407, 431; Effingham to his wife, Feb. 23, 1684, and Nov. 22, 1683, Effingham Papers, IV, 14, 10; Effingham's Answer . . . , May 23, 1689, CO 5/1305: 11; Effingham's Answer to Mr. Ludwell's Second Petition . . . , ibid., 19; Col. Ludwell's Petition, Nov. 1689, ibid., 21.

23. *JHB, 1659/60-1693,* 307, 310, 311-317, 322-323; *EJC,* I, 96; Spencer to Blathwayt, May 17, 1688, Blathwayt Papers, Colonial Williamsburg, XVI; Spencer to Sunderland, May 17, 1688, CO 1/64: 321-323; Effingham to Blathwayt, Jan. 18 and May 23, 1688, Blathwayt Papers, Colonial Williamsburg.

24. Effingham to Blathwayt, May 23, 1688 and March 30, 1685, Blathwayt Papers, Colonial Williamsburg, XIV; Spencer to Sunderland, May 17, 1688, CO 1/64: 321-323; *EJC,* I, 96.

25. *JHB, 1659/60-1693,* 316-318, 310; Effingham to Blathwayt, May 13, 1685, and Spencer to Blathwayt, April 27, 1689,

Blathwayt Papers, Colonial Williamsburg, XIV, XVIII; Effingham to the Lords of Trade, Feb. 10, 1686, CO 1/59: 87-89;
EJC, I, 75, 101-107; Spencer to the Lords of Trade, April 29,
1689, CO 5/1305: 7; *Mary. Arch.*, VIII, 83-84, 88-89, 92-
93; William Byrd to Thomas Methwould, March 5, 1689,
VMHB, XXV (1917), 364; Some Questions proposed to us
[by] their Majesty's Council of Virginia . . . , July 7, 1692,
VMHB, XX (1912), 123-125; Beverley, *History*, 97.

26. Effingham to Blathwayt, Aug. 26, 1687, Blathwayt Papers,
Colonial Williamsburg, XIV.

Notes to Chapter 7

1. Louis B. Wright, ed., "William Byrd's Opposition to Governor Francis Nicholson," *Journal of Southern History*, XI
(1945), 71-72.

2. Robert Beverley to David Gwyn, Feb. 12, 1704, CO 5/1314:
35; Beverley, *History*, 295.

3. Ibid., 287; Louis B. Wright, ed., *An Essay Upon the Government of the English Plantations on the Continent of America
(1701): An Anonymous Virginian's Proposals for Liberty
Under the British Crown* (San Marino, 1945), 30. For lists of
burgesses and biographical data see *JHB, 1659/60-1693*, and
1695-1702, passim; Stanard and Stanard, compilers. *Colonial
Va. Register; EVB*, I, 213-214.

4. Louis Morton, *Robert Carter of Nomini Hall: A Virginia
Tobacco Planter of the Eighteenth Century*, 2d ed. (Williams-
burg, 1945), Ch. 1; W. G. Stanard, "Major Robert Beverley
and His Descendants," *VMHB*, II (1896-1897), 169-170;
EVB, I, 146-147; John Spencer Bassett, ed., *The Writings of
Colonel Byrd* xl ff.

5. Quoted in Paul R. Kelbaugh, "Tobacco Trade in Maryland,
1700-1725," *Maryland Historical Magazine*, XXVI (1931),
19; Stock, *Proceedings and Debates*, II, 31, 37, 42, 75, 78-82,
144-145, 149, 151-152, 159-162, 164, 182, 190, 196, 199-
201, 209-210, 499, 457-459; Humble Representation of the
Council of Virginia, in *History of Dividing Line and Other
Tracts*, II, 206-210.

6. Hedges to the Governor of Virginia, April 20, 1705, William
P. Palmer, et al., eds., *Calendar of Virginia State Papers . . .*
(Richmond, 1875-1893), I, 89-90; Board of Trade to Nichol-
son, Jan. 4, 1700, *VMHB*, XXI (1914), 40-41; Charles
Campbell, *Introduction to the History of the Colony and
Ancient Dominion of Virginia* (Richmond, 1847), 101.

7. Pickering, ed., *Statutes at Large,* 10 Wm. III, c. 10; State of Virginia, 1676, *VMHB,* XX (1912), 356; Instructions to Culpeper with an account of his Lordships compliance thereto, Sept. 23, 1683, CO 1/48: 47-48; *Randolph Papers,* VII, 486-492.

8. Ibid., VII, 431; Unsigned notes, ca. 1700, Rawlinson MSS 271; Arthur Bagley, A Short State of the Virginia Trade, Egerton MSS 291; Curtis Nettels, "The Menace of Colonial Manufactures, 1690-1720," *New England Quarterly,* IV (1931), 230-269, offers a general discussion of English fears.

9. Wright, ed., "Byrd's Opposition to Nicholson," *Jour. Southern Hist.,* XI (1945), 68-79; Beverley to David Gwyn, Feb. 12, 1704, CO 5/1314: 35.

10. Speeches of Students of the College of William and Mary, Delivered May 1, 1699, *WMQ,* 2d Ser., X (1930), 325-329, 336.

11. *JHB, 1702-1712,* 165; *Randolph Papers,* VII, 435.

12. Hartwell, Blair, and Chilton, *Present State of Virginia,* 5, 12-13; Mr. Clayton's Second Letter Concerning his Further Observations on Virginia, in Edmund Halley, ed., *Miscelanea Curiosa . . . ,* 2d ed. (London, 1708), III, 295-296; [Mungo Inglis], The Several Sources of the Odium and Discouragement Which the College of William and Mary . . . lyes Under, 1704, *VMHB,* VII (1899-1900), 391.

13. Beverley, *History,* 97-98; *EJC,* I, 243-244.

14. Nicholson to the Lords of Trade, June 10, 1691, CO 1/1306: 41; Nicholson to Blathwayt, June 10, 1691, Blathwayt Papers, Colonial Williamsburg, XV; *LJC,* I, 172.

15. Ibid., I, 138-144; *JHB, 1659/60-1693,* 351; Hening, *Statutes,* II, 507, III, 50-69; Nicholson to the Lords of Trade, June 10, 1691, CO 5/1306: 41.

16. Beverley, *History,* 100; Nicholson to the Lords of Trade, July 16, 1692, and to Nottingham, Nov. 13, 1691, CO 5/ 1306: 119, 64.

17. Hening, *Statutes,* III, 58-60; *EJC,* I, 212-213; Memorial from the General Assembly of Virginia, April 30, 1692, Blathwayt Papers, Colonial Williamsburg, XV; Petition of John Mercer, *VMHB,* V (1897-1898), 278-279.

18. *JHB, 1659/60-1693,* 386, 423, 436; Hening, *Statutes,* III, 108-109; Andros to Blathwayt, Nov. 3, 1692, and Jan. 16, 1693, Blathwayt Papers, Colonial Williamsburg, III; Andros to the Lords of Trade, Nov. 3, 1692, CO 5/1306: 134; William Byrd letter of June 4, 1691, and Byrd to Mr. Harper, June 9, 1691, *VMHB,* XXVIII (1920), 14, 21.

19. Stock, *Proceedings and Debates,* III, 460; Memorial to the

Honorable Commissioners of their Majesty's Customs . . . , *History of the Dividing Line and Other Tracts,* II, 162-165. On Perry see Elizabeth Donnan, "Eighteenth Century English Merchants: Micajah Perry," *Jour. of Economic and Business History,* IV (1931-1932), 70-98.

20. Letter initialed J. M., June 3, 1693, Blathwayt Papers, Colonial Williamsburg, XV; Blathwayt to Nicholson, Jan. 5 and Feb. 18, 1692, ibid.; Report of the Commissioners of the Customs upon certain laws past in the Assembly of Virginia, March 15, 1692, CO 5/1306: 93.

21. *Randolph Papers,* VII, 435, 448, 452; *JHB, 1659/60-1693,* 456-457, 480-482, *1695-1702,* 149, 152, 255; Andros to Blathwayt, Jan. 5, 1694, Blathwayt Papers, Colonial Williamsburg, III; Hening, *Statutes,* III, 171-172; *EJC,* I, 385, 394-396.

22. Louis B. Wright, ed., "William Byrd's Defense of Sir Edmund Andros," *WMQ,* 3d Ser., II (1945), 62; Memorandum of the Virginia Clergy, 1704, ibid., 2d Ser., XIX (1939), 369-370; Craven, *Colonies in Transition,* 268-274. The harmony of Nicholson's first year after his replacement of Andros allowed the only significant attempt at economic intervention in the decade and a half after the 1691 port legislation. In 1699 the assembly resolved to construct a new capital at Middle Plantation. Many Virginia leaders assumed that Williamsburg would fulfill the hopes earlier entertained for Jamestown. Its geographic location and the presence of "two brave Creeks" connecting the site to the James and York rivers seemed to guarantee that Williamsburg would soon become "such a Town as may equal if not outdo Boston, New York, Philadelphia, Charleston, and Annapolis . . ." Speeches of Students of the College of William and Mary, *WMQ,* 2d Ser., X (1930), 329-333.

23. William Byrd to Blathwayt, Oct. 30, 1680, Blathwayt Papers, Colonial Williamsburg, XIII; Byrd to Perry and Lane, July 19, 1690, *VMHB,* XXV (1918), 133; William Fitzhugh to Nicholas Haywood, May 20, 1691, Davis, *Fitzhugh,* 290-292; Michael G. Kammen, ed., "Maryland in 1699," *Jour. Southern Hist.,* XXIX (1963), 370; Arthur Bagley, A Short State of the Virginia Trade, Egerton MSS 921; Nicholson to the Board of Trade, Feb. 14, 1699, CO 5/1310.

24. Bagley, A Short State of the Virginia Trade; "Journey of Francis Louis Michel," *VMHB,* XXIV (1916), 31; Robert Bristow Letterbook, fol. 26a, Va. St. Library.

25. Lewis C. Grey, *History of Agriculture in the Southern United States* (New York, 1941), I, 268-269.

26. *JHB, 1702-1712,* 130, 190, 212.

27. Hening, *Statutes,* III, 404-419; *EJC,* III, 111.

28. *Journals of the Commissioners for Trade and Plantations* (London, 1920-1938), I, 297, 306, II, 26, 92-93, 95, 112-113; Reasons for Repealing the Acts passed in Virginia and Maryland relating to ports and towns, 1709, Palmer, et al., eds., *Cal. Va. State Papers,* I, 157-158.

29. Nicholson to the Lords of Trade, July 16, 1692, CO 5/1306: 119; Beverley, *History,* 100.

30. Petition of Certain Justices of Middlesex County, April 2, 1705, *VMHB,* VIII (1900-1901), 128-133.

31. Wesley Frank Craven, *Dissolution of the Virginia Company: The Failure of a Colonial Experiment* (New York, 1932).

32. John C. Rainbolt, "The Alteration in the Relationship between Leadership and Constituents in Virginia, 1660-1720," *WMQ,* 3d Ser., XXVII (1970), 411-434.

33. Jacques Fontaine, *Memoirs of a Huguenot Family* (New York, 1953), 26-27, 265, 282; William Byrd to Mr. Warren, July 15, 1728, and July 1729, *VMHB,* XXXVI (1928), 39-40, 116-117; Byrd to Mr. Collenson, July 18, 1735, ibid., 353-355; Byrd to Col. Bladen, July 1728, ibid., 115-116; Byrd to Sir Hans Sloane, May 31, 1737, Sloane MSS 4055, foll. 112-113, British Museum; The Humble Memorial of William Byrd Esqr. concerning the propagation of hemp, and other naval stores . . . , CO 323/7: 150-151; Byrd to [Mr. Tenserfe], ca. June 1729, Byrd Papers, 1728-1729, Colonial Williamsburg; Byrd to Archibald Campbell, ca. May 1729, ibid.; F. Hall, *The Importance of the British Plantations . . .* (London, 1731), 75-76.

34. *VMHB,* XX (1912), 158-167, 177-178; Hening, *Statutes,* IV, 247-271, V, 164-168, 350-355, VI, 60-64, 146-147, 233-235, VII, 570-575, VIII, 143-145, 351-352, 511-514; Governor Drysdale to the Board of Trade, June 29, 1723, CO 5/1319: 27; Governor Gooch to the Board of Trade, Oct. 5, 1732, CO 5/1323: 127; Governor Gooch to Sir Thomas Gooch, June 28, 1729, Jan. 7, 1730, April 9, 1730, May 28, 1730, and Aug. 5, 1735, Gooch MSS, Benacre Hall, Suffolk, England (microfilm, Colonial Williamsburg).

35. *JHB, 1702-1712,* 325; Account of the 2s per Hhgs., Port Duties, and Head Money Arising in York River District, May 24, 1704 to April 16, 1705, *VMHB,* XXVI (1918), 53; Governor Gooch to the Board of Trade, July 23, 1730, CO 5/1322: 119; CO 5/1443: 33, 53, 62, 73, 89, 101, 108; CO 5/1442: 45, 48-49, 50-51, 53, 57-58; CO 5/1443: 5-6, 8-10, 12-14, 16, 19-20, 23, 25-26, 28-29, 32.

36. Jones, *Present State of Virginia,* 45-46.

37. Gooch to the Board of Trade, Aug. 11, 1742, CO 5/1325: v, 32; Report from Governor Dinwiddie on the Present State of Virginia, Jan. 1755, in Robert A. Brock, ed., *The Official Records of Robert Dinwiddie, Lieutenant-Governor of Virginia, 1751-1758* (Richmond, 1883-1884), I, 386.

38. Spotswood to Secretary Stanhope, July 15, 1715 and to the Board of Trade, Oct. 24, 1715, Robert A. Brock, ed., *The Official Letters of Alexander Spotswood, Lieutenant-Governor of the Colony of Virginia, 1710-1722* ... (Richmond, 1882), II, 124, 134-135.

39. *JHB, 1702-1712,* 305, 250, 260, *1712-1726,* 13, 16, 50, 85-86, 137-138, 146, 182, 188, 329, 388.

40. Spotswood to the Secretary of State, Feb. 8, 1712, in Brock, ed., *Letters of Spotswood,* I, 144.

Note to Epilogue

1. Hartwell, Blair, and Chilton, *Present State of Virginia,* 3-4, 10-13; [Green], *Virginia's Cure,* Force, *Tracts,* III, No. 15, pp. 10-11.

BIBLIOGRAPHY

Abbreviations of Commonly Cited Works

CO	Colonial Office Group in British Public Record Office.
CRNC	William A. Saunders, *Colonial Records of North Carolina.*
CSPA	W. Noel Sainsbury, et al., eds. *Calendar of State Papers, America and West Indies.*
Davis, *Fitzhugh*	Richard Beale Davis, ed. *William Fitzhugh and His Chesapeake World, 1676-1701.*
EJC	H. R. McIlwaine, W. L. Hall and Benjamin Hillman, eds. *Executive Journals of the Council of Colonial Virginia.*
EVB	Lyon G. Tyler, ed. *Encyclopedia of Virginia Biography.*
Force, *Tracts*	Peter Force, ed. *Tracts and Other Papers Relating Principally to the Origin, Settlement, and Progress of the Colonies in North America.*
Hening, *Statutes*	William W. Hening, ed. *Statutes at Large: Being a Collection of all the Laws of Virginia.*
JHB	John Pendleton Kennedy and H. R.

	McIlwaine, eds. *Journals of the House of Burgesses of Virginia.*
LJC	H. R. McIlwaine, ed. *Legislative Journals of the Council of Virginia.*
Mary. Arch.	William H. Brown, et al., eds. *Maryland Archives.*
Randolph Papers	Robert N. Toppan and Alfred T. S. Goodrick, eds. *Edward Randolph, Including His Letters and Official Papers.*
Shaw, *Cal. Treasury Bks.*	William A. Shaw, et al., eds. *Calendar of Treasury Books.*
Stock, *Proceedings and Debates*	Leo F. Stock, ed. *Proceedings and Debates of the British Parliaments Respecting North America.*
VMHB	*Virginia Magazine of History and Biography.*
WMQ	*William and Mary Quarterly.*

Primary Sources

Manuscripts

Additional Manuscripts 25120, British Museum, Official Letters from Henry Coventry, Secretary of State, to the Residents in Portugal and the Governors of the Plantations, 1674-1679 (Library of Congress transcripts)

Additional Manuscripts 23615, British Museum, Representation of the Lords Commissioners for Trade and Plantations on the North American Continent, 1721 (Library of Congress transcripts).

Additional Manuscripts 23218, British Museum: Two Letters of Governor William Berkeley (Library of Congress transcripts).

Bagley, Arthur. A Short State of the Virginia Trade. Egerton Manuscripts 921, vol. I, British Museum (microfilm at the University of Virginia Library).

Blathwayt Papers of Colonial Williamsburg.

Blathwayt Papers, Huntington Library.

Coventry Papers, vols. LXXVI-LXXVIII of Bath Manuscripts, Longleat, England (microfilm at Library of Congress).

Effingham, Papers of Baron Howard of. Library of Congress.

Egerton Manuscripts 2395. British Museum (Library of Congress transcripts and microfilm at the University of Virginia Library).

Middlesex County, Virginia Records, vol. 1680-1694. Virginia State Library. Richmond.

Public Record Office, Colonial Office Group 1/1-69 (microfilm at the University of Virginia Library and at Colonial Williamsburg).

Public Record Office, Colonial Office Group 5/1305-1306, 1354, 1358, 1371 (microfilm at the University of Virginia Library and Colonial Williamsburg).

Printed

Alsop, George. *A Character of the Province of Maryland.* London, 1666. Reprinted in Clayton C. Hall, ed. *Narratives of Early Maryland, 1633-1684.* New York, 1910.

Andrews, Charles M., ed. *Narratives of the Insurrections, 1675-1690.* New York, 1915.

Arber, Edward, and A. S. Bradley, eds. *Travels and Works of John Smith, President of Virginia, and Admiral of New England, 1580-1631.* 2 vols. Edinburgh, 1910.

Bassett, John Spencer, ed. *The Writings of "Colonel Wm. Byrd of Westover in Virginia, Esqr."* New York, 1901.

Berkeley, Edmund, and Dorothy S. Berkeley, eds. "Another Account of Virginia: By the Reverend John Clayton," *VMHB,* LXXVI (1968), 415-436.

————, eds. *The Reverend John Clayton: A Parson With a Scientific Mind. His Scientific Writings and Other Related Papers.* Charlottesville, 1965.

Berkeley, William. *A Discourse and View of Virginia.* London, 1662.

Beverley, Robert. *History and Present State of Virginia.* Ed., Louis B. Wright. Chapel Hill, 1947.

Bishop Burnet's History of the Reign of King James II. London, 1852.

Boyd, William K., ed. *William Byrd's History of the Dividing Line Betwixt Virginia and North Carolina.* Raleigh, 1929.

Brock, Robert A., ed. *The Official Letters of Alexander Spotswood, Lieutenant Governor of the Colony of Virginia, 1710-1722.* 2 vols. Richmond, 1882.

————, ed. *The Official Records of Robert Dinwiddie, Lieutenant-Governor of Virginia, 1751-1758.* 2 vols. Richmond, 1883-1884.

Brown, William H., et al., eds. *Maryland Archives.* 69 vols. Baltimore, 1883-1962.

Bruce, Thomas, Second Earl of Ailesbury. *Memoirs.* 2 vols., London, 1890.

Bryant, Arthur, ed. *The Letters, Speeches, and Declarations of King Charles II*. London, 1935.

Bullock, William. *Virginia Impartially Examined, and Left to Publick View.* . . . London, 1649.

"Captain Thomas Yong's Voyage to Virginia and Delaware Bay and River in 1634," Massachusetts Historical Society, *Collections*, 4th Ser., IX. Boston, 1871.

Child, Josiah. *A Discourse About Trade*. London, 1698.

Clayton, John, "Account of Several Observables in Virginia," Royal Society of London, *Philosophical Transactions*, XVII. London, 1694.

Colonel Quarry's Memorial to the Lords Commissioners of Trade and Plantations, 1703, Mass. Hist. Soc., *Collections*. 3d Ser., VII. Boston, 1838.

Daniell, F. H. Blackburne, ed. *Calendar of State Papers, Domestic Series, Reign of Charles II*. XVIII. London, 1909.

Davis, Richard Beale, ed. "A Sermon Preached at James City in Virginia, April 23, 1686," *WMQ*, 3d Ser., XVII (1960), 371-394.

————, ed. *William Fitzhugh and His Chesapeake World, 1676-1701*. Chapel Hill, 1963.

Firth, Charles H., and R. S. Rait, eds. *Acts and Ordinances of the Interregnum, 1642-1660*. 3 vols. London, 1911.

Force, Peter, ed. *Tracts and Other Papers Relating Principally to the Origin, Settlement, and Progress of the Colonies in North America from the Discovery of the Country to the Year 1776*. 4 vols. Washington, 1836-1846.

Grant, W. L., and James Munro, eds. *Acts of the Privy Council of England, Colonial Series*. 6 vols. London, 1908-1912.

[Green, Roger]. *Virginia's Cure, or an advisive Narrative Concerning Virginia: Discovering the True Ground of that Churches Unhappiness*. Reprinted in Force, ed., *Tracts*, III. No. 15.

Hall, Clayton G., ed. *Narratives of Early Maryland, 1633-1684*. New York, 1910.

Hammond, John. *Leah and Rachael, or the Two Fruitful Sisters, Virginia and Maryland: Their Present Condition, Impartially stated and Related*. London, 1656. Reprinted in Force, ed. *Tracts*, III. No. 14.

Hartlib, Samuel. *Reformed Virginia Silk Worm: Or a Rare and New Discovery of a Speedy Way, and Easie Means, Found Out by a Young Lady in England . . . For the Feeding of Silk-worms in the Woods*. London, 1655. Reprinted in Force, ed. *Tracts*, III. No. 13.

Hartwell, Henry, James Blair, and Edward Chilton. *The Present*

State of Virginia and the College. Ed., Hunter D. Farish. Williamsburg, 1950.

Hening, William W., ed. *Statutes at Large: Being a Collection of all the Laws of Virginia from the First Session of the Legislature in the Year 1619*. 13 vols. Richmond and Philadelphia, 1809-1823.

"The Humble Remonstrance of John Bland . . .," *VMHB*, I (1894-1895), 142-155.

Jones, Hugh. *Present State of Virginia*. Ed., Richard L. Morton. Chapel Hill, 1956.

Journals of the Commissioners for Trade and Plantations. London, 1920-1939.

Kammen, Michael G., ed. "Maryland in 1699: A Letter from the Reverend Hugh Jones," *Jour. of Southern History*, XXIX (1963), 362-372.

Kennedy, John Pendleton, and H. R. McIlwaine, eds. *Journals of the House of Burgesses of Virginia*. 13 vols. Richmond, 1905-1915.

Kingsbury, Susan M., ed. *The Records of the Virginia Company of London*. 4 vols. Washington, 1906-1935.

Langston, Anthony. "On Towns and Corporations, and on Manufacture of Iron." *WMQ*, 2d Ser., I (1921), 100-106.

Lonsdale, John, Lord Viscount. *Memoir of the Reign of James II*. London, 1857.

McIlwaine, H. R., ed. *Legislative Journals of the Council of Colonial Virginia*. 3 vols. Richmond, 1918-1919.

————, ed. *Minutes of the Council and General Court of Colonial Virginia, 1622-1632, 1670-1676*. . . . Richmond, 1924.

McIlwaine, H. R., W. L. Hall, and Benjamin Hillman, eds. *Executive Journals of the Council of Colonial Virginia*. 6 vols. Richmond, 1925-1966.

Makemie, Francis. *A Plain & Friendly Perswasive to the Inhabitants of Virginia and Maryland for Promoting Towns & Cohabitation*. London, 1705. Reprinted in *VMHB*, IV (1896-1897), 252-271.

Mason, Polly Cary, compiler. *Records of Colonial Gloucester County, Virginia*. 2 vols. Newport News, 1946-1948.

[Mathews, Thomas]. The Beginning, Progress, and Conclusion of Bacon's Rebellion, 1675-1676. Force, ed. *Tracts*, I. No. 8.

Palmer, William P., et al., eds. *Calendar of Virginia State Papers and Manuscripts Preserved in the Capital at Richmond, 1652-1781*. 11 vols. Richmond, 1875-1893.

A Perfect Description of Virginia: Being a full and true Relation of the Present State of the Plantation. . . . London, 1649. Force, ed. *Tracts*, II. No. 8.

Perry, William S., ed. *Historical Collections Relating to the American Colonial Church.* Vol. I. *Virginia.* Hartford, 1870.

Powell, William S., ed. *Ye Countie of Albemarle in Carolina.* Raleigh, 1958.

Sainsbury, W. Noel, et al., eds. *Calendar of State Papers, American and West Indies.* 43 vols. London, 1860-1962.

Saunders, William L., ed. *Colonial Records of North Carolina.* 10 vols. Raleigh, 1886-1890.

Shaw, William A., et al., eds. *Calendar of Treasury Books.* 32 vols. London, 1904-1958.

[Sherwood, William]. Virginias Deploured Condition; Or an Impartiall Narrative of the Murders committed by the Indians there, and of the Sufferings of his Majesty's Loyall Subjects under the Rebellious Outrages of Nathaniell Bacon Junior.... Mass. Hist. Soc., *Collections.* 4th Ser., IX (Boston, 1871), 162-176.

Stock, Leo F., ed. *Proceedings and Debates of the British Parliaments Respecting North America.* 5 vols. Washington, 1924-1941.

Taylor, E. G. R., ed. *The Original Writings and Correspondence of the Two Richard Hakluyts.* 2 vols. London, 1935.

Toppan, Robert N., and Alfred T. S. Goodrick, eds. *Edward Randolph, Including his Letters and Official Papers.* 7 vols. Boston, 1898-1909.

Tyler, Lyon G., ed. *Narratives of Early Virginia, 1606-1625.* New York, 1907.

Washburn, Wilcomb E., ed. "Sir William Berkeley's 'A History of our Miseries,'" *WMQ,* 3d Ser., XIV (1957), 403-413.

Williams, Edward. *Virginia: More Especially the South Part thereof, Richly and truly valued.* London, 1650. Force, ed. *Tracts,* III. No. 11.

Wright, Louis B., ed. *An Essay Upon the Government of the English Plantations on the Continent of America (1701): An Anonymous Virginian's Proposals for Liberty Under the British Crown.* San Marino, 1945.

————, ed. "William Byrd I and the Slave Trade," *Huntington Library Quarterly,* VIII (1945), 379-387.

————, ed. "William Byrd's Defence of Sir Edmund Andros," *WMQ,* 3d Ser., II (1945), 47-62.

————, ed. "William Byrd's Opposition to Governor Francis Nicholson," *Jour. of Southern History,* X (1945), 68-79.

————, and Marion Tinling, eds. *The Secret Diary of William Byrd of Westover, 1709-1712.* Richmond, 1941.

Wynne, Thomas H., ed. *History of the Dividing Line and Other*

Notes from the Papers of William Byrd of Westover in Virginia, Esquire. 2 vols. Richmond, 1866.

Secondary Sources

Alvord, Clarence W., and Lee Bidgood. *The First Explorations of the Trans-Allegheny Region by Virginians, 1650-1674.* Cleveland, 1912.

Andrews, Charles M. *British Committees, Commissions, and Councils of Trade and Plantations.* Baltimore, 1908.

_____. *The Colonial Period of American History.* 4 vols. New Haven, 1934-1938.

Bailyn, Bernard, "Politics and Social Structure in Virginia," James Morton Smith, ed. *Seventeenth-century America: Essays in Colonial History.* Chapel Hill, 1959.

Ballagh, J. C. *White Servitude in the Colony of Virginia.* Baltimore, 1895.

Brock, Robert A., "A Succinct Account of Tobacco in Virginia," *Tenth Census of the United States, 1880.* Vol. III. Washington, 1883.

Brooks, Jerome E. *Tobacco, Its History Illustrated by the Books, Manuscripts, and Engravings in the Library of George Arents, Jr., Together with an Introductory Essay.* 4 vols. New York, 1937-1943.

Bruce, Kathleen. *Virginia Iron Manufacture in the Slave Era.* New York, 1931.

Bruce, Philip A. *Economic History of Virginia in the Seventeenth Century.* 2 vols. New York, 1896.

_____. *Institutional History of Virginia in the Seventeenth Century.* 2 vols. New York and London, 1910.

_____. *Social Life of Virginia in the Seventeenth Century.* Richmond, 1907.

Brydon, George M. *Virginia's Mother Church and the Political Conditions Under Which It Grew.* 2 vols. Richmond, 1947-1952.

Burk, John D. *History of Virginia, From Its First Settlement to the Commencement of the Revolution.* 4 vols. Petersburg, 1804-1816.

Campbell, Charles. *History of the Colony and Ancient Dominion of Virginia.* Philadelphia, 1860.

Carrier, Lyman, "The Veracity of John Lederer," *WMQ,* 2d Ser., XIX (1939), 435-445.

Coulter, Calvin S. *The Virginia Merchant.* Ph.D. dissertation. Princeton University, 1944.

Crane, Verner W. *The Southern Frontier, 1670-1732.* Durham, 1928.

Craven, Avery O. *Soil Exhaustion as a Factor in the Agricultural History of Virginia and Maryland, 1606-1860.* Urbana, 1926.

Craven, Wesley Frank. *The Colonies in Transition, 1660-1713.* New York, 1968.

————. *Dissolution of the Virginia Company: The Failure of a Colonial Experiment.* New York, 1932.

————. *The Southern Colonies in the Seventeenth Century, 1607-1689.* Baton Rouge, 1949.

Dobson, Leonidas. *Alexander Spotswood.* Philadelphia, 1932.

Evans, Cerinda. *Some Notes on Shipbuilding and Shipping in Colonial Virginia.* Williamsburg, 1957.

Flippin, Percy S. *The Financial Administration of the Colony of Virginia.* Baltimore, 1915.

Greene, Evarts, and Virginia D. Harrington. *American Population before the Federal Census of 1790.* New York, 1932.

Greene, Jack P. *The Quest for Power: The Lower Houses of Assembly in the Southern Royal Colonies, 1689-1776.* Chapel Hill, 1963.

Grey, Lewis C. *History of Agriculture in the Southern United States.* 2 vols. New York, 1941.

————. "The Market Surplus Problem of Colonial Tobacco," *WMQ,* 2d Ser., VII, 232-245; VIII, 1-12.

Haffenden, Philip S., "The Crown and the Colonial Charters, 1675-1688," *WMQ,* 3d Ser., XV (1958), 297-311, 452-466.

Hall, Michael G. *Edward Randolph and the American Colonies, 1676-1703.* Chapel Hill, 1960.

Harrison, Fairfax. *Landmarks of Old Prince William.* 2 vols. Richmond, 1924.

————. "Parson Waugh's Tumult," *VMIIB,* XXX (1922), 31-37.

————. "The Proprietors of the Northern Neck: Chapters of Culpeper Genealogy," *VMHB,* XXXIII (1925), 113-153, 223-267, 333-358, XXXIV (1926), 19-64.

————. "Robert Beverley, the Historian of Virginia," *VMHB,* XXXVI (1928), 333-344.

————. *Virginia Land Grants: A Study of Conveyance in Relation to Colonial Politics.* Richmond, 1925.

Hatch, Charles E. "Glassmaking in Virginia," *WMQ,* 2d. Ser., XXI (1941), 119-138, 227-238.

————. "Mulberry Trees and Silkworms: Sericulture in Early Virginia," *VMHB,* LXV (1957), 3-61.

Hemphill, John M. Virginia and the English Commercial System, 1689-1733, Ph.D. dissertation. Princeton University, 1964.

Herndon, Melvin. "Hemp in Colonial Virginia," *Agricultural History,* XXXVII (1963), 86-93.

―――. *Tobacco in Colonial Virginia: "The Sovereign Remedy."* Williamsburg, 1957.

Hitchens, Harold Lee, "Sir William Berkeley, Virginian Economist," *WMQ,* 2d Ser., XVIII (1938), 158-173.

Jones, Howard Mumford, "The Literature of Virginia in the Seventeenth Century," *Memoirs of the American Academy of Arts and Science,* XIX, Pt. 2. Boston, 1946.

Kammen, Michael G. "The Causes of the Maryland Revolution of 1689," *Maryland Historical Magazine,* LV (1960), 293-333.

Laing, Wesley Newton. Cattle in Early Virginia. Ph.D. dissertation. University of Virginia, 1952.

Lee, Edmund Jennings. *Lee of Virginia, 1642-1892.* Philadelphia, 1895.

Leonard, Sister Joan de Lourdes. "Operation Checkmate: The Birth and Death of a Virginia Blueprint for Progress, 1660-1676," *WMQ,* 3d Ser., XXIV (1967), 44-74.

Lord, Eleanor L. *Industrial Experiments in the British Colonies of North America.* Baltimore, 1898.

MacInnes, Charles M. *The Early English Tobacco Trade.* London, 1926.

Menk, Patricia N. The Origins and Growth of Party Politics in Virginia, 1660-1705. Ph.D. dissertation. University of Virginia, 1945.

Middleton, Arthur P. "The Chesapeake Convoy System, 1662-1763," *WMQ,* 3d Ser., III (1946), 182-207.

―――. *Tobacco Coast. A Maritime History of Chesapeake Bay in the Colonial Era.* Newport News, 1953.

Morton, Richard L. *Colonial Virginia.* 2 vols. Chapel Hill, 1960.

Mudridge, Donald H. "The Papers of Howard, Baron of Effingham." Library of Congress, *Quarterly Jour. of Current Acquisitions,* X (1953), 63-74.

Nettels, Curtis P. "The Menace of Colonial Manufacturing, 1690-1720," *New England Quarterly,* IV (1931), 230-269.

Pearson, John C. "The Fish and Fisheries of Colonial Virginia," *WMQ,* 2d Ser., XXII (1942), 213-220, 353-360, XXIII (1943), 1-7, 130-135, 278-284, 435-439; 3d Ser., I (1944), 179-183.

Ponko, Vincent. *The Privy Council and the Spirit of Elizabethan Management, 1588-1603.* American Philosophical Society, *Transactions,* new ser., LVIII. Part. 4. Philadelphia, 1968.

Price, Jacob M. "The Beginning of Tobacco Manufacture in Virginia," *VMHB,* LXIV (1956), 1-29.

_____. "The Economic Growth of the Chesapeake and the European Market, 1697-1775," *Jour. of Economic History,* XXIV (1964), 496-511.

_____. *The Tobacco Adventure to Russia: Enterprise, Politics, and Diplomacy in the Quest for a Northern Market for English Colonial Tobacco, 1676-1772.* American Philosophical Society, *Transactions,* new ser., LI. Philadelphia, 1961.

_____. The Tobacco Trade and the Treasury, 1685-1733. Ph.D. dissertation. Harvard University, 1954.

Rainbolt, John C. "The Absence of Towns in Seventeenth-Century Virginia," *Jour. of Southern History.,* XXV (1969), 343-60.

_____. "The Alteration in the Relationship between Leadership and Constituents in Virginia, 1660-1720," *WMQ,* 3d Ser., XXVII (1970), 411-34.

_____. "A New Look at Stuart 'Tyranny': The Crown's Attack on the Virginia Assembly, 1676-1689," *VMHB,* LXXV (1967), 387-406.

Reps, John W. *Tidewater Towns: City Planning in Colonial Virginia and Maryland.* Williamsburg, 1972.

Riley, Edward M. "The Town Acts of Colonial Virginia," *Jour. of Southern History,* XVI (1950), 306-323.

Ripley, William Z. *The Financial History of Virginia, 1609-1776.* New York, 1893.

Rive, Alfred. "Consumption of Tobacco Since 1600," *Economic History,* I (1929), 57-75.

Robinson, Morgan P. "Virginia Counties: Those Resulting from Virginia Legislation," *Bulletin of the Virginia State Library,* I (1916), 1-283.

Robinson, W. Stitt, Jr. *Mother Earth: Land Grants in Virginia, 1607-1699.* Williamsburg, 1957.

Saloutos, Theodore, "Efforts at Crop Control in Seventeenth Century America," *Jour. of Southern History,* XII (1946), 45-66.

Stanard, William G., and Mary B. Stanard, compilers. *Colonial Virginia Register: A List of Governors, Councillors and other Officials.* . . . Albany, 1902.

Thompson, Robert P. The Merchant in Virginia, 1700-1775. Ph.D. dissertation. University of Wisconsin, 1955.

Tyler, Lyon G., ed. *Encyclopedia of Virginia Biography.* 5 vols. New York, 1915.

_____. "Virginia Under the Commonwealth," *WMQ,* 1st Ser., I (1892), 1-16.

Voorhis, Manning C. "Crown Versus Council in the Virginia Land Policy," *WMQ,* 3d Ser., III (1946), 499-514.

————. The Land Grant Policy of Colonial Virginia, 1607-1774. Ph.D. dissertation. University of Virginia, 1940.

Washburn, Wilcomb E. Bacon's Rebellion, 1676-1677. Ph.D. dissertation. Harvard University, 1955.

————. *The Effects of Bacon's Rebellion on Government in England and Virginia.* Smithsonian Institution, *United States National Museum Bulletin.* No. 225 (1963).

————. *The Governor and the Rebel: A History of Bacon's Rebellion in Virginia.* Chapel Hill, 1957.

————. "Governor Berkeley and King Philip's War," *New England Quarterly,* XXX (1957), 363-377.

Webb, Stephen S. "The Strange Career of Francis Nicholson," *WMQ,* 3d Ser., XXIII (1966), 513-548.

Wertenbaker, Thomas J. *Bacon's Rebellion, 1676.* Williamsburg, 1957.

————. *Patrician and Plebeian in Virginia.* Charlottesville, 1910.

————. *The Planters of Colonial Virginia.* Princeton, 1922.

————. *The Torchbearer of the Revolution: The Story of Bacon's Rebellion and Its Leader.* Princeton, 1940.

————. *Virginia Under the Stuarts.* Princeton, 1914.

Williams, David A. Political Alignments in Colonial Virginia, 1698-1750. Ph.D. dissertation. Northwestern University, 1959.

Wright, Louis B. *The Dream of Prosperity in Colonial America.* New York, 1965.

————. *The First Gentlemen of Virginia: Intellectual Qualities of the Early Colonial Ruling Class.* San Marino, 1940.

————. "Richard Lee I, A Belated Elizabethan in Virginia," *Huntington Library Quarterly,* II (1938-1939), 1-35.

Wyckoff, Vertrees J. *Tobacco Regulation in Colonial Maryland.* Baltimore, 1936.

INDEX

Agricultural reform, 85
Albemarle, 14, 57, 65; and
    cessation, 64; and limitation
    of tobacco production, 55;
    Philip Ludwell as governor,
    136. *See also* Carolina
Albemarle, Duke of, 42
Allerton, Isaac, 57
Andros, Sir Edmund, 21;
    governor of the Dominion
    of New England, 138;
    governor of New York, 151;
    governor of Virginia, 153,
    155, 156
Anglican Church. *See* church,
    established
Apprentices, 22
Aristocracy, Virginia. *See*
    leadership
Arlington, Lord, 80, 115
Arthur, Gabriel, 78
Assembly, Virginia, 98, 110,
    151; Berkeley's misison to
    England, 43; Berkeley,
    support for, 74, 75; crown's
    attitude toward, 104; and
    customs duties, 51;
    economic policies of, 83;

embargo, 53; leadership of,
    140; payment of tobacco
    debt, 48; promotion of port
    towns, 78; stint, 53, 60, 64;
    town law (1691), 154
Autonomy: economic, 150;
    provincial, 61, 100

Bacon, Nathaniel: in the council,
    112; criticism of Berkeley,
    74; influence of, 93-97;
    plantation expenses, 15;
    political style of, 117;
    rumors about, 101; view of
    the assembly, 102-103
Bacon's Rebellion, 66, 105;
    alleged causes, 34, 103, 104;
    causes, 97-98, 169; disputes
    left unsettled by, 108; effect
    on home government, 101;
    expense of troops sent to
    quell it, 115; impact of, in
    Virginia, 91-94, 101, 170
Baltimore, Lord, 60-62, 68, 70;
    Bacon's Rebellion, attitude
    toward, 120; port acts, 135;
    stint, policies toward, 45, 57,
    68, 69, 71-72; and town

209